Frederick William Robertson

Sermons Preached at Brighton

Frederick William Robertson

Sermons Preached at Brighton

ISBN/EAN: 9783337163570

Printed in Europe, USA, Canada, Australia, Japan

Cover: Foto ©Lupo / pixelio.de

More available books at **www.hansebooks.com**

SERMONS

PREACHED AT BRIGHTON.

BY THE LATE

REV. FREDERICK W. ROBERTSON.

THE INCUMBENT OF TRINITY CHAPEL.

THIRD SERIES.

NEW EDITION

HENRY S. KING & CO.
65 CORNHILL & 12 PATERNOSTER ROW, LONDON.
1875.

TO

THE CONGREGATION

WORSHIPPING IN

TRINITY CHAPEL, BRIGHTON,

From August 15, 1847, to August 15, 1853,

THESE

RECOLLECTIONS OF SERMONS

PREACHED BY THEIR LATE PASTOR,

ARE DEDICATED.

CONTENTS.

SERMON I.
Preached April 28, 1850.
THE TONGUE.

ST. JAMES iii. 5, 6.—"Even so the tongue is a little member, and boasteth great things. Behold, how great a matter a little fire kindleth! And the tongue is a fire, a world of iniquity: so is the tongue among our members, that it defileth the whole body, and setteth on fire the course of nature; and it is set on fire of hell." . . . . Page 1

SERMON II.
Preached May 5, 1850.
THE VICTORY OF FAITH.

JOHN v. 4, 5.—"For whatsoever is born of God overcometh the world: and this is the victory that overcometh the world, even our faith. Who is he that overcometh the world, but he that believeth that Jesus is the Son of God?" 15

SERMON III.
Preached Whitsunday, May 19, 1850.
THE DISPENSATION OF THE SPIRIT.

CORINTHIANS xii. 4.—"Now there are diversities of gifts, but the same Spirit." 29

CONTENTS.

SERMON IV.
Preached May 26, 1850.
THE TRINITY.

1 THESS. v. 23.—"And the very God of peace sanctify you wholly; and I pray God your whole spirit and soul and body be preserved blameless unto the coming of our Lord Jesus Christ." . . . . Page 43

SERMON V.
Preached June 2, 1850.
ABSOLUTION.

LUKE v. 21.—"And the Scribes and the Pharisees began to reason saying, Who is this which speaketh blasphemies? Who can forgive sins, but God alone?" 61

SERMON VI.
Preached June 9, 1850.
THE ILLUSIVENESS OF LIFE.

HEBREWS xi. 8—10.—"By faith Abraham, when he was called to go out into a place which he should after receive for an inheritance, obeyed; and he went out, not knowing whither he went. By faith he sojourned in the land of promise, as in a strange country, dwelling in tabernacles with Isaac and Jacob, the heirs with him of the same promise: for he looked for a city which hath foundations, whose builder and maker is God." 77

SERMON VII.
Preached June 23, 1850.
THE SACRIFICE OF CHRIST.

2 COR. v. 14, 15.—"For the love of Christ constraineth us; because we thus judge, that if one died for all, then were all dead: and that he died for all, that they which live should not henceforth live unto themselves, but unto him which died for them, and rose again." 90

CONTENTS.

SERMON VIII.

Preached June 30, 1850.

THE POWER OF SORROW.

2 COR. vii. 9, 10.—"Now I rejoice, not that ye were made sorry, but that ye sorrowed to repentance: for ye were made sorry after a godly manner, that ye might receive damage by us in nothing. For godly sorrow worketh repentance to salvation not to be repented of: but the sorrow of the world worketh death." . . . . Page 104

SERMON IX.

Preached August 4, 1850.

SENSUAL AND SPIRITUAL EXCITEMENT.

EPHESIANS v. 17, 18.—"Wherefore be ye not unwise, but understanding what the will of the Lord is. And be not drunk with wine, wherein is excess; but be filled with the Spirit." 112

SERMON X.

Preached August 11, 1850.

PURITY.

TITUS i. 15.—"Unto the pure all things are pure: but unto them that are defiled and unbelieving is nothing pure; but even their mind and conscience is defiled." 122

SERMON XI.

Preached February 9, 1851.

UNITY AND PEACE.

COL. iii. 15.—"And let the peace of God rule in your hearts, to the which also ye are called in one body; and be ye thankful." . 130

SERMON XII.
Preached January 4, 1852.
THE CHRISTIAN AIM AND MOTIVE.
MATT. v. 48.—" Be ye therefore perfect, even as your Father which is in heaven is perfect." . . . . Page 143

SERMON XIII.
Preached January 4, 1852.
CHRISTIAN CASUISTRY.
1 COR. vii. 18—24.—" Is any man called being circumcised? let him not become uncircumcised. Is any called in uncircumcision? let him not be circumcised. Circumcision is nothing, and uncircumcision is nothing, but the keeping of the commandments of God. Let every man abide in the same calling wherein he was called. Art thou called being a servant? care not for it: but if thou mayest be made free use it rather. For he that is called in the Lord, being a servant, is the Lord's freeman; likewise also he that is called being free, is Christ's servant. Ye are bought with a price; be not ye the servants of men. Brethren, let every man wherein he is called therein abide with God." 156

SERMON XIV.
Preached January 11, 1852.
MARRIAGE AND CELIBACY.
1 COR. vii. 29—31.—" But this I say, brethren, the time is short: it remaineth that both they that have wives be as though they had none; and they that weep as though they wept not; and they that rejoice as though they rejoiced not; and they that buy, as though they possessed not; and they that use this world as not abusing it: for the fashion of this world passeth away." 169

SERMON XV.
Preached January 11, 1852.
THE CHRISTIAN CHURCH A FAMILY.
EPH. iii. 14, 15.—" Our Lord Jesus Christ, of whom the whole family in Heaven and earth is named." 181

SERMON XVI.

Preached January 25, 1852.

THE LAW OF CHRISTIAN CONSCIENCE.

I COR. viii. 7—13.—" Howbeit there is not in every man that knowledge : for some, with conscience of the idol, unto this hour, eat it as a thing offered unto an idol; and their conscience being weak is defiled. But meat commendeth us not to God : for neither if we eat are we the better ; neither if we eat not are we the worse. But take heed lest by any means this liberty of yours become a stumbling-block to them that are weak. For if any man see thee which hast knowledge, sit at meat in the idol's temple, shall not the conscience of him which is weak be emboldened to eat those things which are offered to idols ; and through thy knowledge shall the weak brother perish for whom Christ died ? But when ye sin so against the brethren and wound their weak conscience ye sin against Christ. Wherefore if meat make my brother to offend I will eat no flesh while the world standeth, lest I make my brother to offend." . . . . Page 196

SERMON XVII.

Preached May 16, 1852.

VICTORY OVER DEATH.

I COR. xv. 56, 57.—"The sting of death is sin, and the strength of sin is the law. But thanks be to God which giveth us the victory through our Lord Jesus Christ." 212

SERMON XVIII.

Preached June 20, 1852.

MAN'S GREATNESS AND GOD'S GREATNESS.

ISAIAH lvii. 15. — "For thus saith the High and Lofty One that inhabiteth Eternity, whose Name is Holy. I dwell in the high and holy place—with him also that is of a contrite and humble spirit." 230

SERMON XIX.

Preached June 27, 1852.

THE LAWFUL AND UNLAWFUL USE OF LAW.

(A FRAGMENT.)

1 TIM. i. 8.—" But we know that the law is good, if a man use it lawfully." . . . . Page 246

SERMON XX.

Preached February 21, 1853.

THE PRODIGAL AND HIS BROTHER.

LUKE xv. 31, 32.—"And he said unto him, Son, thou art ever with me, and all that I have is thine. It was meet that we should make merry, and be glad: for this thy brother was dead, and is alive again; was lost, and is found." 253

SERMON XXI.

Preached May 15, 1853.

JOHN'S REBUKE OF HEROD.

LUKE iii. 19, 20.—"But Herod the tetrarch, being reproved by him for Herodias, his brother Philip's wife, and for all the evils which Herod had done, added yet this above all, that he shut up John in prison. 270

SERMONS.

I.

Preached April 28, 1850.

THE TONGUE.

"Even so the tongue is a little member, and boasteth great things. Behold, how great a matter a little fire kindleth! And the tongue is a fire, a world of iniquity: so is the tongue among our members, that it defileth the whole body, and setteth on fire the course of nature; and it is set on fire of hell."—St. James iii. 5-6.

IN the development of Christian Truth a peculiar office was assigned to the Apostle James.

It was given to St. Paul to proclaim Christianity as the spiritual law of liberty, and to exhibit Faith as the most active principle within the breast of man. It was St. John's to say that the deepest quality in the bosom of Deity is Love; and to assert that the life of God in Man is Love. It was the office of St. James to assert the necessity of Moral Rectitude; his very name marked him out peculiarly for this office: he was emphatically called, "the Just:" integrity was his peculiar characteristic. A man singularly honest, earnest, real. Accordingly, if you read through his whole epistle, you will find it is, from first to last, one continued vindication of the first principles of morality against the *semblances* of religion.

He protested against the censoriousness which was found connected with peculiar claims of religious feelings. "If any man among you seem to be religious and bridleth not his tongue, but deceiveth his own heart, this man's religion is vain." He protested against that spirit which had crept into the Christian Brotherhood, truckling to the rich, and despising the poor. "If ye have respect of persons ye commit sin, and are convinced of the law as transgressors." He protested against that sentimental fatalism which induced men to throw the blame of their own passions upon God. "Let no man say, when he is tempted, I am tempted of God; for God cannot tempt to evil; neither tempteth He any man." He protested against that unreal religion of excitement which diluted the earnestness of real religion in the enjoyment of listening. "Be ye doers of the word, and not hearers only; deceiving your own souls." He protested against that trust in the correctness of theological doctrine which neglected the cultivation of character. "What doth it profit, if a man *say* that he hath faith, and have not works? Can faith save him?"

Read St. James's epistle through, this is the mind breathing through it all:—all this *talk* about religion, and spirituality—words, words, words—nay, let us have *realities*.

It is well known that Luther complained of this epistle, that it did not contain the Gospel; for men who are hampered by a system will say—even of an inspired Apostle—that he does not teach the Gospel if their own favourite doctrine be not the central subject of his discourse; but St. James's reply seems spontaneously to suggest itself to us. The Gospel! how can we speak of the Gospel, when the first principles of *morality* are forgotten? when Christians are excusing themselves, and slandering one another? How can the superstructure of Love and Faith be built, when the very foundations of human character—Justice, Mercy, Truth—have not been laid?

    1st. The license of the tongue.
    2nd. The guilt of that license.

The first license given to the tongue is slander. I am not of course, speaking now of that species of slander against which the law of libel provides a remedy, but of that of which the Gospel alone takes cognisance; for the worst injuries which man can do to man, are precisely those which are too delicate for *law* to deal with. We consider therefore not the calumny which is reckoned such by the moralities of an earthly court, but that which is found guilty by the spiritualities of the courts of heaven—that is, the mind of God.

Now observe, this slander is compared in the text to poison—" the tongue is an unruly evil, full of deadly poison." The deadliest poisons are those for which no test is known: there are poisons so destructive that a single drop insinuated into the veins produces death in three seconds, and yet no chemical science can separate that virus from the contaminated blood, and show the metallic particles of poison glittering palpably, and say, "Behold, it is there!"

In the drop of venom which distils from the sting of the smallest insect, or the spikes of the nettle-leaf, there is concentrated the quintessence of a poison so subtle that the microscope cannot distinguish it, and yet so virulent that it can inflame the blood, irritate the whole constitution, and convert day and night into restless misery.

In St. James's day, as now, it would appear that there were idle men and idle women, who went about from house to house, dropping slander as they went, and yet you could not take up that slander and detect the falsehood there. You could not evaporate the truth in the slow process of the crucible, and then show the residuum of falsehood glittering and visible. You could not fasten upon any word or sentence, and say that it was calumny; for in order to constitute slander it is not necessary that the word spoken should be false—half truths are often more calumnious than whole falsehoods. It is not even necessary that a word should be distinctly uttered; a dropped lip, an arched eyebrow, a shrugged shoulder, a significant look, an incredulous expression of countenance, nay, even an emphatic silence, may do the work: and when the light and trifling thing which has done the mischief has fluttered off, the venom is left behind, to work and rankle, to inflame hearts, to fever human existence, and to poison human society at the fountain springs of life. Very emphatically was it said by one whose whole being had smarted under such affliction, " Adder's poison is under their lips."

The second license given to the tongue is in the way of persecution: " therewith curse we men which are made after the similitude of God." "We!"—men who bear the name of Christ—curse our brethren! Christians persecuted Christians. Thus even in St. James's age that spirit had begun, the monstrous fact of Christian persecution; from that day it has continued, through long centuries, up to the present time. The Church of Christ assumed the office of denunciation, and except in the first council, whose object was not to strain, but to relax the bonds of brotherhood, not a council has met for eighteen centuries which has not guarded each profession of belief by the too customary formula, "If any man maintain otherwise than this, let him be accursed."

Myriad, countless curses have echoed through those long ages; the Church has forgotten her Master's spirit and called down fire from heaven. A fearful thought to consider this as the spectacle on which the eye of God has rested. He looks down upon the creatures He has made, and hears everywhere the language of religious imprecations:—and after all, who is proved right by curses?

The Church of Rome hurls her thunders against Protestants of every denomination: the Calvinist scarcely recognises the Arminian as a Christian: he who considers himself as the true Anglican, excludes from the Church of Christ all but the adherents of his own orthodoxy; every minister and congregation has its small circle, beyond which all are heretics: nay even among that sect which is most lax as to the dogmatic forms of truth, we find the Unitarian of the old school denouncing the spiritualism of the new and rising school.

This is the state of things to which we are arrived. Sisters of Charity refuse to permit an act of charity to be done by a Samaritan; ministers of the Gospel fling the thunderbolts of the Lord; ignorant hearers catch and exaggerate the spirit,—boys, girls, and women shudder as one goes by, perhaps more holy than themselves, who adores the same God, believes in the same Redeemer, struggles in the same life-battle, and all this because they have been taught to look upon him as an enemy of God.

There is a class of religious persons against whom this vehemence has been especially directed. No one who can read the signs of the times can help perceiving that we are on the eve of great changes, perhaps a disruption of the Church of England. Unquestionably there has been a large secession to the Church of Rome.

Now what has been the position of those who are about to take this step? They have been taunted with dishonest reception of the wages of the Church; a watch has been set over them: not a word they uttered in private, or in public, but was given to the world by some religious busy-body; there was not a visit which they paid, not a foolish dress which they adopted, but became the subject of bitter scrutiny and malevolent gossip. For years the religious press has denounced them with a vehemence as virulent, but happily more impotent than that of the Inquisition. There has been an anguish and an inward struggle little suspected, endured by men who felt themselves outcasts in their own society, and naturally looked for a home elsewhere.

We congratulate ourselves that the days of persecution are gone by; but persecution is that which affixes penalties upon *views held*, instead of upon *life led*. Is persecution *only* fire and sword? But suppose a man of sensitive feeling says, The sword is less sharp to me than the slander: fire is less intolerable than the refusal of sympathy!

Now let us bring this home; you rejoice that the faggot and the stake are given up;—*you* never persecuted—you leave that to the wicked Church of Rome. Yes, you never burned a human being alive—you never clapped your hands as the death-shriek proclaimed that the lion's fang had gone home into the most vital part of the victim's frame; but did you never rob him of his friends?—gravely shake your head and oracularly insinuate that he was leading souls to hell?—chill the affections of his family?—take from him his good name? Did you never with delight see his Church placarded as the Man of Sin, and hear the platform denunciations which branded it with the spiritual abominations of the Apocalypse? Did you never find a malicious pleasure in repeating all the miserable gossip with which religious slander fastened upon his daily acts, his words, and even his uncommunicated thoughts? Did you never forget that for a man to "work out his own salvation with fear and trembling" is a matter difficult enough to be laid upon a human spirit, without intruding into the most sacred department of another's life—that namely, which lies between himself and God? Did you never say that "it was to be wished he should go to Rome," until at last life became intolerable,—until he was thrown more and more in upon himself; found himself, like his Redeemer, in this world alone, but unable like his Redeemer, calmly to repose upon the thought that his Father was with him? Then a stern defiant spirit took possession of his soul, and there burst from his lips, or heart, the wish for *rest*—rest at any cost,— peace anywhere, if even it is to be found only in the bosom of the Church of Rome!

II. The guilt of this license.

The first evil consequence is the harm that a man does himself: "so is the tongue among the members, that it defiles the whole body." It is not very obvious, in what way a man does himself harm by calumny. I will take the simplest form in which this injury is done; it effects a dissipation of spiritual energy. There are two ways in which the steam of machinery may find an outlet for its force: it may work, and if so it works silently; or it may escape, and that takes place loudly, in air and noise. There are two ways in which the spiritual energy of a man's soul may find its vent: it may express itself in action, silently; or in words, noisily: but just so much of force as is thrown into the one mode of expression, is taken from the other.

Few men suspect how much mere talk fritters away spiritual energy,—that which should be spent in action, spends itself in words. The fluent boaster is not the man who is steadiest before the enemy; it is well said to him that his courage is better kept till it is wanted. Loud utterance of virtuous indignation against evil from the platform, or in the drawing-room, do not characterize the spiritual giant: so much indignation as is expressed, has found vent, is wasted, is taken away from the work of coping with evil; the man has so much less left. And hence he who restrains that love of talk, lays up a fund of spiritual strength.

With large significance, St. James declares, "If any man offend not in word, the same is a perfect man, able also to bridle the whole body." He is entire, powerful, because he has not spent his strength. In these days of loud profession, and bitter, fluent condemnation, it is well for us to learn the divine force of silence. Remember Christ in the Judgment Hall, the very Symbol and Incarnation of spiritual strength; and yet when revilings were loud around Him and charges multiplied, "He held His peace."

2. The next feature in the guilt of calumny is its uncontrollable character: "the tongue can no man tame." You cannot arrest a calumnious tongue, you cannot arrest the calumny itself; you may refute a slanderer, you may trace home a slander to its source, you may expose the author of it, you may by that exposure give a lesson so severe as to make the repetition of the offence appear impossible; but

the fatal habit is incorrigible: to-morrow the tongue is at work again.

Neither can you stop the consequences of a slander; you may publicly prove its falsehood, you may sift every atom, explain and annihilate it, and yet, years after you had thought that all had been disposed of for ever, the mention of a name wakes up associations in the mind of some one who heard the calumny, but never heard or never attended to the refutation, or who has only a vague and confused recollection of the whole, and he asks the question doubtfully, " But were there not some suspicious circumstances connected with him?"

It is like the Greek fire used in ancient warfare, which burnt unquenched beneath the water, or like the weeds which when you have extirpated them in one place are sprouting forth vigorously in another spot, at the distance of many hundred yards; or, to use the metaphor of St. James himself, it is like the wheel which catches fire as it goes, and burns with a fiercer conflagration as its own speed increases; " it sets on fire the whole course of nature " (literally, the wheel of nature). You may tame the wild beast, the conflagration of the American forest will cease when all the timber and the dry underwood is consumed; but you cannot arrest the progress of that cruel word which you uttered carelessly yesterday or this morning,—which you will utter perhaps, before you have passed from this church one hundred yards: that will go on slaying, poisoning, burning beyond your own control, now and for ever.

3. The third element of guilt lies in the unnaturalness of calumny. " My brethren, these things ought not so to be;" *ought not*—that is, they are unnatural. That this is St. James's meaning is evident from the second illustration

which follows: "Doth a fountain send forth at the same place, sweet water and bitter?" "Can the fig tree, my brethren, bear olive berries, or a vine, figs?"

There is apparently in these metaphors little that affords an argument against slander; the motive which they suggest would appear to many far-fetched and of small cogency; but to one who looks on this world as a vast whole, and who has recognised the moral law as only a part of the great law of the universe, harmoniously blending with the whole, illustrations such as these are the most powerful of all arguments. The truest definition of evil is that which represents it as something contrary to nature: evil is evil, because it is unnatural; a vine which should bear olive berries, an eye to which blue seems yellow, would be diseased: an unnatural mother, an unnatural son, an unnatural act, are the strongest terms of condemnation. It is this view which Christianity gives of moral evil: the teaching of Christ was the recall of man to nature, not an infusion of something new into Humanity. Christ came to call out all the principles and powers of human nature, to restore the natural equilibrium of all our faculties; not to call us back to our own individual selfish nature, but to human nature as it is in God's ideal—the perfect type which is to be realised in us. Christianity is the regeneration of our whole nature, not the destruction of one atom of it.

Now the nature of man is to adore God and to love what is god-like in man. The office of the tongue is to bless. Slander is guilty because it contradicts this; yet even in slander itself, perversion as it is, the interest of man in man is still distinguishable. What is it but perverted interest which makes the acts, and words, and thoughts of his brethren, even in their evil, a matter of such strange delight? Remember therefore, this contradicts your nature and your destiny; to speak ill of others makes you a monster in God's world: get the habit of slander, and then there is not a stream which bubbles fresh from the heart of nature,—there is not a tree that silently brings forth its genial fruit in its appointed season,—which does not rebuke and proclaim you to be a monstrous anomaly in God's world.

4. The fourth point of guilt is the diabolical character of slander; the tongue " is set on fire of hell." Now, this is no mere strong expression—no mere indignant vituperation—it contains deep and emphatic meaning.

The apostle means literally what he says, slander is diabolical. The first illustration we give of this is contained in the very meaning of the word devil. "Devil," in the original, means traducer or slanderer. The first introduction of a demon spirit is found connected with a slanderous insinuation against the Almighty, implying that His command had been given in envy of His creature: "for God doth know that in the day ye eat thereof, then your eyes shall be opened, and ye shall be as gods, knowing good and evil."

In the magnificent imagery of the book of Job, the accuser is introduced with a demoniacal and malignant sneer, attributing the excellence of a good man to interested motives; "Doth Job serve God for naught?" There is another mode in which the fearful accuracy of St. James's charge may be demonstrated. There is one state only from which there is said to be no recovery—there is but one sin that is called unpardonable. The Pharisees beheld the works of Jesus. They could not deny that they were good works, they could not deny that they were miracles of beneficence, but rather than acknowledge that they were done by a good man through the co-operation of a Divine spirit, they preferred to account for them by the wildest and most incredible hypothesis; they said they were done by the power of Beelzebub, the prince of the devils. It was upon this occasion that our Redeemer said with solemn meaning, "For every idle word that men shall speak, they shall give account in the day of judgment." It was then that He said, for a word spoken against the Holy Ghost there is no forgiveness in this world, or in the world to come.

Our own hearts respond to the truth of this—to call evil, good, and good, evil—to see the Divinest good, and call it satanic evil—below this lowest deep there is *not* a lower still. There is no cure for mortification of the flesh—there is no remedy for ossification of the heart. Oh! that miserable state, when to the jaundiced eye all good transforms itself into evil, and the very instruments of health become the poison of disease. Beware of every approach of this!—Beware of that spirit which controversy fosters, of watching only for the evil in the character of an antagonist!—Beware of that habit which becomes the slanderer's life, of magnifying every speck of evil and closing the eye to goodness!—till at last men arrive at the state in which generous, universal love (which is heaven) becomes impossible, and a suspicious, universal hate takes possession of the heart, and *that* is hell!

There is one peculiar manifestation of this spirit to which I desire specially to direct your attention.

The politics of the community are guided by the political press. The religious views of a vast number are formed by that portion of the press which is called religious; it becomes, therefore, a matter of deepest interest to inquire what is the spirit of that "religious press." I am not asking you what are the views maintained—whether Evangelical, Anglican, or Romish—but what is the *spirit* of that fountain from which the religious life of so many is nourished?

Let any man cast his eye over the pages of this portion of the press—it matters little to which party the newspaper or the journal may belong—he will be startled to find the characters of those whom he has most deeply reverenced, whose hearts he knows, whose integrity and life are above suspicion, held up to scorn and hatred: the organ of one party is established against the organ of another, and it is the recognised office of each to point out with microscopic care the names of those whose views are to be shunned; and in order that these may be the more shrunk from, the characters of those who hold such opinions are traduced and vilified. There is no personality too mean—there is no insinuation too audacious or too false for the recklessness of these daring slanderers. I do not like to use the expression, lest it should appear to be merely one of theatrical vehemence; but I say it in all seriousness, adopting the inspired language of the Bible, and using it advisedly and with accurate meaning, the spirit which guides the "religious press" of this country, which dictates those personalities, which prevents controversialists from seeing what is good in their opponents, which attributes low motives to account for excellent lives, and teaches men whom to suspect, and shun, rather than point out where it is possible to admire and love—is a spirit "set on fire of hell."

Before we conclude, let us get at the root of the matter. "Man," says the Apostle James, "was made in the image of God:" to slander man is to slander God: to love what is good in man is to love it in God. Love is the only remedy for slander : no set of rules or restrictions can stop it; we may denounce, but we shall denounce in vain. The radical cure of it is Charity—" out of a pure heart and faith unfeigned," to feel what is great in the human character; to recognise with delight all high, and generous, and beautiful actions; to find a joy even in seeing the good qualities of your bitterest opponents, and to admire those qualities even in those with whom you have least sympathy—be it either the Romanist or the Unitarian—this is the only spirit which can heal the love of slander and of calumny. If we would bless God, we must *first* learn to bless man, who is made in the image of God.

II.

Preached May 5, 1850.

THE VICTORY OF FAITH.

"For whatsoever is born of God overcometh the world: and this is the victory that overcometh the world, even our faith. Who is he that overcometh the world, but he that believeth that Jesus is the Son of God?"—1 John v. 4·5.

THERE are two words in the system of Christianity which have received a meaning so new, and so emphatic, as to be in a way peculiar to it, and to distinguish it from all other systems of morality and religion; these two words are—the World, and Faith. We find it written in Scripture that to have the friendship of the world is to be the enemy of God—whereupon the question arises—The world?—did not God make the world? Did He not place us in the world? Are we not to love what God has made? And yet meeting this distinctly we have the inspired record, "Love not the World."

The object of the Statesman is, or ought to be, to produce as much worldly prosperity as possible — but Christianity, that is Christ, speaks little of this world's prosperity, underrates it — nay, speaks of it at times as infinitely dangerous.

The legislator prohibits crime—the moralist transgression—the religionist sin. To these Christianity superadds a new enemy—the world and the things of the world. " If any man love the world, the love of the Father is not in him."

The other word used in a peculiar sense is Faith. It is impossible for any one to have read his Bible ever so negligently, and not to be aware that the word Faith, or the grace of Faith, forms a large element in the Christian system. It is said to work miracles, remove mountains, justify the soul, trample upon impossibilities. Every apostle, in his way, assigns to faith a primary importance. Jude tells us to " build up ourselves in our most holy faith." John tells us that—" he that believeth that Jesus is the Christ, is the born of God ;" and Paul tells us that, not by merit nor by works, but by trust or reliance only, can be formed that state of soul by which man is reckoned just before God. In these expressions, the apostles only develope their Master's meaning, when He uses such words as these, "All things are possible to him that believeth :" "O thou of little faith, wherefore didst thou doubt?"

These two words are brought into diametrical opposition in the text, so that it branches into a two-fold line of thought.

I. The Christian's enemy, the World.
II. The victory of Faith.

In endeavouring to understand first what is meant by the world, we shall feel that the mass of evil which is comprehended under this expression, cannot be told out in any one sermon ; it is an expression used in various ways, sometimes meaning one thing, sometimes meaning another; but we will endeavour to explain its general principles—and these we will divide into three heads; first, the tyranny of the present; secondly, the tyranny of the sensual; and lastly, the spirit of society.

1. The tyranny of the present.

"Christ," says the Apostle Paul, "hath redeemed us from this present evil world;" and again, "Demas hath forsaken me, having loved this present world."

Let a stress be laid on the word *present*. Worldliness is the attractive power of something present, in opposition to something to come. It is this rule and tyranny of the present that constitutes Demas a worldly man.

In this respect, worldliness is the spirit of childhood carried on into manhood. The child lives in the present hour—to-day to him is everything. The holiday promised at a distant interval is no holiday at all—it must be either now or never. Natural in the child, and therefore pardonable, this spirit, when carried on into manhood, is coarse—is worldliness. The most distinct illustration given us of this, is the case of Esau. Esau came from the hunting-field worn and hungry; the only means of procuring the tempting mess of his brother's pottage was the sacrifice of his father's blessing, which in those ages carried with it a substantial advantage; but that birthright could be enjoyed only after *years*—the pottage was *present*, near, and certain; therefore he sacrificed a future and higher blessing, for a present and lower pleasure. For this reason Esau is the Bible type of worldliness: he is called in Scripture a profane, that is, not a distinctly vicious, but a secular or worldly person—an overgrown child; impetuous, inconsistent, not without gleams of generosity and kindliness, but ever accustomed to immediate gratification.

In this worldliness, moreover, is to be remarked the gamester's desperate play. There is a gambling spirit in human nature. Esau distinctly expresses this: "Behold I am at the point to die, and what shall my birthright profit me?" He might never live to enjoy his birthright; but the pottage was before him, present, certain, *there.*

Now, observe the utter powerlessness of mere preaching to cope with this tyrannical power of the present. Forty thousand pulpits throughout the land this day, will declaim against the vanity of riches, the uncertainty of life, the sin of worldliness—against the gambling spirit of human nature; I ask what *impression* will be produced by those forty thousand harangues? In every congregation it is reducible to a certainty that, before a year has passed, some will be numbered with the dead. Every man knows this, but he thinks the chances are that it will not be himself; he feels it a solemn thing for Humanity generally—but for himself there is more than a chance. Upon this chance he plays away life.

It is so with the child : you tell him of the consequences of to-day's idleness—but the sun is shining brightly, and he cannot sacrifice to-day's pleasure, although he knows the disgrace it will bring to-morrow. So it is with the intemperate man : he says—"Sufficient unto the day is the evil, and the good thereof; let me have my portion now." So that one great secret of the world's victory lies in the mighty power of saying "*Now.*"

2. The tyranny of the sensual.

I call it *tyranny*, because the evidences of the senses are all powerful, in spite of the protestations of the reason. In vain you try to persuade the child that *he* is moving, and not the trees which seem to flit past the carriage—in vain we remind ourselves that this apparently solid earth on which we stand, and which seems so immoveable, is in reality flying through the regions of space with an inconceivable rapidity—in vain philosophers would persuade us that the colour which the eye beholds, resides not in the object itself, but in our own perception; we are victims of the apparent, and the verdict of the senses is taken instead of the verdict of the reason.

Precisely so is it with the enjoyments of the world. The man who died yesterday, and whom the world called a successful man—for what did he live?—He lived for this world—he gained this world. Houses, lands, name, position in society—all that earth could give of enjoyments—he had: he was the man of whom the Redeemer said that his thoughts were occupied in planning how to pull down his barns and build greater. We hear men complain of the sordid love of gold, but gold is merely a medium of exchange for other things: gold is land, titles, name, comfort—all that the world can give. If the world be *all*, it is *wise* to live for gold. There may be some little difference in the degree of degradation in different forms of worldliness; it is possible that the ambitious man who lives for power is somewhat higher than he who merely lives for applause, and he again may be a trifle higher than the mere seeker after gold — but after all, looking closely at the matter, you will find that, in respect of the objects of their idolatry, they agree in this, that all belong to the present. Therefore, says the Apostle, all that is in the world—" the lust of the flesh, the lust of the eye, and the pride of life, is not of the Father, but of the world," and are only various forms of one great tyranny. And then when such a man is at the brink of death, the words said to the man in our Lord's parable must be said to him. " Thou fool, the houses thou hast built, the enjoyments thou hast prepared; and all those things which have formed thy life for years—when thy soul is taken from them, what shall they profit thee?"

3. The spirit of society.

The *World* has various meanings in Scripture; it does not always mean the Visible, as opposed to the Invisible; nor the Present, as opposed to the Future: it sometimes stands for the secular spirit of the day—the Voice of Society.

Our Saviour says, "If ye were of the world, the world would love his own." The apostle says, "Be not conformed to this world;" and to the Gentiles he writes, "In time past ye walked according to the course of this world, the spirit which now worketh in the children of disobedience." In these verses, a tone, a temper, a spirit is spoken of. There are two things—the Church and the World—two spirits pervading different bodies of men, brought before us in these verses—those called the Spirit-born, and those called the World, which is to be overcome by the Spirit-born, as in the text, "Whatsoever is born of God overcometh the world."

Let us understand what is meant by the Church of God. When we speak of the Church we generally mean a society to aid men in their progress God-wards; but the Church of God is by no means co-extensive in any age with that organized institution which we *call* the Church; sometimes it is nearly co-extensive—that is, nearly all on earth who are born of God are found within its pale, nearly all who are of the world are extraneous to it—but sometimes the born of God have been found distinct from the Institution called the Church, opposed to it—persecuted by it. The Institution of the Church is a blessed ordinance of God, organized on earth for the purpose of representing the Eternal Church and of extending its limits, but still ever subordinate to it.

The Eternal Church is "the general assembly and church of the first-born which are written in heaven;" the selected spirits of the most High, who are struggling with the evil of their day; sometimes alone, like Elijah, and like him, longing that their work was done; sometimes conscious of their union with each other. God is for ever raising up a succession of these—His brave, His true, His good. Apostolical succession, as taught sometimes, means simply this—a succession of miraculous powers flowing in a certain line. The true apostolic succession is—not a succession in an hereditary line, or line marked by visible signs which men can always identify, but a succession emphatically spiritual.

The Jews looked for an hereditary succession; they thought that because they were Abraham's seed, the spiritual succession was preserved; the Redeemer told them that "God was able of those stones to raise up children unto Abraham." Therefore is this ever a spiritual succession—in the hands of God alone; and they are here called the God-born, coming into the world variously qualified; sometimes baptized with the spirit which makes them, like James and John, the "Sons of Thunder," sometimes with a milder spirit, as Barnabas, which makes them "Sons of Consolation," sometimes having their souls indurated into an adamantine hardness, which makes them living stones—rocks like Peter, against which the billows of this world dash themselves in vain, and against which the gates of hell shall not prevail. But whether as apostles, or visitors of the poor, or parents of a family, born to do a work on earth, to speak a word, to discharge a mission which they themselves perhaps do not know till it is accomplished—these are the Church of God—the children of the Most High—the noble army of the Spirit-born! Opposed to this stands the mighty confederacy called the World. But beware of fixing on individual men in order to stigmatize *them* as the world. You may not draw a line and say—" We are the sons of God, ye are of the world." The world is not so much individual as it is a certain spirit ; the course of this world is "the spirit which now worketh in the children of disobedience." The world and the Church are annexed as inseparably as the elements which compose the atmosphere. Take the smallest portion of this that you will, in a cubic inch the same proportions are found as in a temple. In the ark there was a Ham ; in the small band of the twelve apostles there was a Judas.

The spirit of the world is for ever altering—impalpable ; for ever eluding, in fresh forms, your attempts to seize it. In the days of Noah, the spirit of the world was *violence.* In Elijah's day it was *idolatry.* In the day of Christ it was *power* concentrated and condensed in the government of Rome. In ours, perhaps, it is the *love of money.* It enters in different proportions into different bosoms ; it is found in a different form in contiguous towns ; in the fashionable watering place, and in the commercial city : it is this thing at Athens, and another in Corinth. This is the spirit of the world—a thing in my heart and yours : to be struggled against, not so much in the case of others, as in the silent battle to be done within our own souls. Pass we on now to consider—

II. The victory of faith.

Faith is a theological expression ; we are apt to forget that it has any other than a theological import ; yet it is the commonest principle of man's daily life, called in that region prudence, enterprise, or some such name. It is in effect the principle on which alone any human superiority can be gained. Faith, in religion, is the same principle as faith in worldly matters, differing only in its object: it rises through successive stages. When, in reliance upon your promise, your child gives up the half-hour's idleness of to-day for the holiday of to-morrow, he lives by faith; a future supersedes the present pleasure. When he abstains from over-indulgence of the appetite, in reliance upon your word that the result will be pain and sickness, sacrificing the present pleasure for fear of future punishment, he acts on faith: I do not say that this is a high exercise of faith—it is a very low one—but it *is* faith.

Once more: the same motive of action may be carried on into manhood; in our own times two religious principles have been exemplified in the subjugation of a vice. The habit of intoxication has been broken by an appeal to the principle of combination, and the principle of belief. Men were taught to feel that they were not solitary strugglers against the vice; they were enrolled in a mighty army, identified in principles and interests. Here was the principle of the Church—association for reciprocated strength; they were thus taught the inevitable result of the indulgence of the vice. The missionaries of temperance went through the country contrasting the wretchedness and the degradation and the filth of drunkenness with the domestic comfort, and the health, and the regular employment of those who were masters of themselves. So far as men believed this, and gave up the tyranny of the present for the hope of the future—so far they lived by faith.

Brethren, I do not say that this was a high triumph for the principle of faith; it was in fact, little more than selfishness; it was a high future balanced against a low present;

only the preference of a future and higher physical enjoyment to a mean and lower one. Yet still to be ruled by this influence raises a man in the scale of being: it is a low virtue, prudence, a form of selfishness; yet prudence *is* a virtue. The merchant, who forecasts, saves, denies himself systematically through years, to amass a fortune, is not a very lofty being, yet he is higher, as a man, than he who is sunk in mere bodily gratifications. You would not say that the intemperate man—who has become temperate in order, merely to gain by that temperance honour and happiness—is a great man, but you would say he was a higher and a better man than he who is enslaved by his passions, or than the gambler who improvidently stakes all upon a moment's throw. The worldly mother who plans for the advancement of a family, and sacrifices solid enjoyments for a splendid alliance, is only *worldly* wise, yet in that manœuvring and worldly prudence there is the exercise of a self-control which raises her above the mere giddy pleasure-hunter of the hour; for want of self-control is the weakness of our nature—to restrain, to wait, to control present feeling with a large foresight, is human strength.

Once more, instead of a faith like that of the child, which over-leaps a few hours, or that of the worldly man, which over-passes years, there may be a faith which transcends the whole span of life, and, instead of looking for temporal enjoyments, looks for rewards in a future beyond the grave, instead of a future limited to time.

This is again a step. The child has sacrificed a day; the man has sacrificed a little more. Faith has now reached a stage which deserves to be called religious; not that this however, is very grand; it does but prefer a happiness hereafter to a happiness enjoyed here—an eternal well-being instead of a temporal well-being; it is but prudence on a grand scale—another form of selfishness—an anticipation of infinite rewards instead of finite, and not the more noble because of the infinitude of the gain: and yet this is what is often taught as religion in books and sermons. We are told that sin is wrong, because it will make us miserable hereafter. Guilt is represented as the short-sightedness which barters for a home on earth—a home in heaven.

In the text-book of ethics studied in one of our universities, virtue is defined as that which is done at the command of God for the sake of an eternal reward. So then, religion is nothing more than a calculation of infinite and finite quantities; vice is nothing more than a grand imprudence; and heaven is nothing more than selfishness rewarded with eternal well-being!

Yet this you will observe, is a necessary step in the development of faith. Faith is the conviction that God is a rewarder of them who diligently seek Him; and there is a moment in human progress when the anticipated rewards and punishments must be of a Mahometan character—the happiness of the senses. It was thus that the Jews were disciplined; out of a coarse, rude, infantine state, they were educated by rewards and punishments to abstain from present sinful gratification: at first, the promise of the life which now is, afterwards the promise of that which is to come; but even then the rewards and punishments of a future state were spoken of, by inspiration itself, as of an arbitrary character; and some of the best of the Israelites, in looking to the recompense of reward, seemed to have anticipated, coarsely, recompense in exchange for duties performed.

The last step is that which alone deserves to be called Christian Faith—" Who is he that overcometh but he that believeth that Jesus is the Christ?" The difference between the faith of the Christian and that of the man of the world, or the mere ordinary religionist, is not a difference in mental operation, but in the object of the faith—to believe that Jesus is the Christ is the peculiarity of Christian faith.

The anticipated heaven of the Christian differs from the anticipated heaven of any other man, not in the distinctness with which its imagery is perceived, but in the kind of objects which are hoped for. The apostle has told us the character of heaven. "Eye hath not seen, nor ear heard, neither hath it entered into the heart of man to conceive the things which God hath prepared for them that love Him"—which glorious words are sometimes strangely misinterpreted, as if the apostle merely meant rhetorically to exalt the conception of the heavenly world, as of something beyond all power to imagine or to paint. The apostle meant something infinitely deeper: the heaven of God is not only that which "eye hath not seen," but that which eye can *never* see; its glories are not of that kind at all which can ever stream in forms of beauty on the eye, or pour in melody upon the enraptured ear—not such joys as genius in its most gifted hour (here called "the heart of man") can invent or imagine: it is something which these sensuous organs of ours never can appreciate—bliss of another kind altogether, revealed to the spirit of man by the Spirit of God—joys such as spirit alone can receive.

Do you ask what these are? "The fruits of the Spirit are love, joy, peace, long-suffering, gentleness, goodness, faith, meekness, temperance." That is heaven, and therefore the Apostle tells us that he alone who "believeth that Jesus is the Christ," and only he, feels that. What is it to believe that Jesus is the Christ?—That He is the Anointed

One, that His life is the anointed life, the only blessed life, the blessed life divine for thirty years?—Yes, but if so, the blessed Life still, continued throughout all eternity: unless you believe that, you do not believe that Jesus is the Christ.

What is the blessedness that you expect?—to have the joys of earth with the addition of the element of eternity? Men think that heaven is to be a compensation for earthly loss: the saints are earthly-wretched here, the children of this world are earthly-happy; but *that*, they think, shall be all reversed—Lazarus, beyond the grave, shall have the purple and the fine linen, and the splendour, and the houses, and the lands which Dives had on earth: the one had them for time, the other shall have them for eternity. That is the heaven that men expect—this earth sacrificed *now*, in order that it may be re-granted for *ever*.

Nor will this expectation be reversed except by a reversal of the nature. None can anticipate such a heaven as God has revealed, except they that are born of the Spirit; therefore to believe that Jesus is the Christ, a man must be born of God. You will observe that no other victory overcomes the world: for this is what St. John means by saying, "Who is he that overcometh the world, but he that believeth that Jesus is the Christ?" For then it comes to pass that a man begins to feel, that to do wrong is hell ; and that to love God, to be like God, to have the mind of Christ, is the only heaven. Until this victory is gained, the world retains its stronghold in the heart.

Do you think that the temperate man has overcome the world, who, instead of the short-lived rapture of intoxication, chooses regular employment, health, and prosperity? Is it not the world in another form, which has his homage?

Or do you suppose that the so-called religious man is really the world's conqueror by being content to give up seventy years of enjoyment in order to win innumerable ages of the very same species of enjoyment? Has he not only made earth a hell, in order that earthly things may be his heaven for ever?

Thus the victory of Faith proceeds from stage to stage: the first victory is, when the Present is conquered by the Future; the last, when the Visible and Sensual is despised in comparison of the Invisible and Eternal. Then earth has lost its power for ever; for if *all* that it has to give be lost eternally, the gain of faith is still infinite.

III.

Preached Whitsunday, May 19, 1850.

THE DISPENSATION OF THE SPIRIT.

"Now there are diversities of gifts, but the same Spirit."—1 Corinthians xii, 4.

ACCORDING to a view which contains in it a profound truth, the ages of the world are divisible into three dispensations, presided over by the Father, the Son, and the Spirit.

In the dispensation of the Father, God was known as a Creator; creation manifested His eternal power and Godhead, and the religion of mankind was the religion of Nature.

In the dispensation of the Son, God manifested Himself to Humanity through man; the Eternal Word spoke, through the inspired and gifted of the human race, to those that were uninspired and ungifted. This was the dispensation of the prophets—its climax was the advent of the Redeemer; it was completed when *perfect* Humanity manifested God to man. The characteristic of this dispensation was, that God revealed Himself by an authoritative Voice, speaking from without, and the highest manifestation of God whereof man was capable, was a Divine Humanity.

The age in which we at present live is the dispensation

of the Spirit, in which God has communicated Himself by the highest revelation, and in the most intimate communion, of which man is capable; no longer through Creation, no more as an authoritative Voice from without, but as a Law within—as a Spirit mingling with a spirit. This is the dispensation of which the prophet said of old, that the time should come when they should no longer teach every man his brother and every man his neighbour, saying, " Know the Lord "—that is, by a will revealed by external authority from other human minds—"for they shall all know him, from the least of them to the greatest." This is the dispensation, too, of whose close the Apostle Paul speaks thus: "Then shall the Son also be subject to Him that hath put all things under Him, that God may be all in all."

The outward humanity is to disappear, that the inward union may be complete. To the same effect, he speaks in another place, "Yea, though we have known Christ after the flesh, yet henceforth know we Him no more." For this reason, the Ascension was necessary before Pentecost could come: the Spirit was not given, we are told, because Jesus was not yet glorified. It was necessary for the Son to disappear as an outward authority, in order that he might re-appear as an inward principle of life. Our salvation is no longer God manifested in a Christ *without* us, but as a Christ *within* us, the hope of glory. To-day is the selected anniversary of that memorable day when the first proof was given to the senses, in the gift of Pentecost, that that spiritual dispensation had begun.

There is a twofold way in which the operations of the Spirit on mankind may be considered—His influence on the Church as a whole, and His influence on individuals;

both of these are brought together in the text. It branches, therefore, into a twofold division.

I. Spiritual gifts conferred on individuals.
II. Spiritual union of the Church.

Let us distinguish between the Spirit and the gifts of the Spirit: by the Spirit, the apostle meant the vital principle of new life from God, common to all believers — the animating Spirit of the Church of God; by the gifts of the Spirit, he meant the diversities of form in which He operates on individuals; its influence varied according to their respective peculiarities and characteristics. In the twenty-eighth verse of this chapter a full catalogue of gifts is found; looking at them generally, we discover two classes into which they may be divided—the first are natural, the second are supernatural: the first are those capacities which are originally found in human nature—personal endowments of mind, a character elevated and enlarged by the gift of the Spirit; the second are those which were created and called into existence by the sudden approach of the same influence.

Just as if the temperature of this Northern hemisphere were raised suddenly, and a mighty tropical river were to pour its fertilizing inundation over the country, the result would be the impartation of a vigorous and gigantic growth to the vegetation already in existence, and at the same time the development of life in seeds and germs which had long lain latent in the soil, incapable of vegetation in the unkindly climate of their birth. Exactly in the same way, the flood of a Divine life, poured suddenly into the souls of men, enlarged and ennobled qualities which had been used already, and at the same time *developed* powers which never could have become apparent in the cold, low temperature of natural life.

Among the natural gifts, we may instance these: teaching—healing—the power of government. Teaching is a gift, natural or acquired. To know, is one thing; to have the capacity of imparting knowledge, is another.

The physician's art again is no supernatural mystery; long and careful study of physical laws capacitate him for his task. To govern, again, is a natural faculty: it may be acquired by habit, but there are some who never could acquire it. Some men seem born to command: place them in what sphere you will, others acknowledge their secret influence, and subordinate themselves to their will. The faculty of organization, the secret of rule, need no supernatural power. They exist among the uninspired. Now the doctrine of the apostle was, that all these are transformed and renovated by the spirit of a new life in such a way as to become almost new powers, or, as he calls them, gifts of the Spirit. A remarkable illustration of this is his view of the human body. If there be anything common to us by nature, it is the members of our corporeal frame; yet the apostle taught that these, guided by the Spirit as its instruments and obeying a holy will, became transfigured; so that, in his language, the body becomes a temple of the Holy Ghost, and the meanest faculties, the lowest appetites, the humblest organs, are ennobled by the Spirit mind which guides them. Thus he bids the Romans yield themselves "unto God as those that are alive from the dead, and their members as instruments of righteousness unto God."

The second class of gifts are supernatural: of these we find two pre-eminent—the gift of tongues, and the gift of prophecy.

It does not appear that the gift of tongues was merely the imparted faculty of speaking foreign languages — it could not be that the highest gift of God to His Church merely made them rivals of the linguist; it would rather seem that the Spirit of God, mingling with the soul of man, supernaturally elevated its aspirations and glorified its conceptions, so that an entranced state of ecstacy was produced, and feelings called into energy, for the expression of which the ordinary forms of speech were found inadequate. Even in a far lower department, when a man becomes possessed of ideas for which his ordinary vocabulary supplies no sufficient expression, his language becomes broken, incoherent, struggling, and almost unnaturally elevated; much more was it to be expected that when divine and new feelings rushed like a flood upon the soul, the language of men would have become strange and extraordinary; but in that supposed case, wild as the expressions might appear to one coldly looking on and not participating in the feelings of the speaker, they would be quite sufficient to convey intelligible meaning to any one affected by the same emotions.

Where perfect sympathy exists, incoherent utterance—a word—a syllable—is quite as efficient as elaborate sentences. Now this is precisely the account given of the phenomenon which attended the gift of tongues. On the day of Pentecost, all who were in the same state of spiritual emotion as those who spoke, understood the speakers; each was as intelligible to all as if he spoke in their several tongues: to those who were coolly and sceptically watching, the effects appeared like those of intoxication. A similar account is given by the Apostle Paul: the voice appeared to unsympathetic ears as that of a barbarian; the uninitiated and unbelieving coming in, heard nothing that was articulate to them, but only what seemed to them the ravings of insanity.

The next was the gift of prophecy. Prophecy has

several meanings in Scripture; sometimes it means the power of predicting future events, sometimes an entranced state accompanied with ravings, sometimes it appears to mean only exposition; but prophecy, as the miraculous spiritual gift granted to the early Church, seems to have been a state of communion with the mind of God lower than that which was called the gift of tongues, at least less ecstatic, less rapt into the world to come, more under the guidance of the reason, more within the control of calm consciousness—as we might say, less supernatural.

Upon these gifts we make two observations:

1. Even the highest were not accompanied with spiritual faultlessness. Inspiration was one thing, infallibility another. The gifts of the Spirit were, like the gifts of Nature, subordinated to the will—capable of being used for good or evil, sometimes pure, sometimes mixed with human infirmity. The supernaturally gifted man was no mere machine, no automaton ruled in spite of himself by a superior spirit. Disorder, vanity, over-weening self-estimation, might accompany these gifts, and the prophetic utterance itself might be degraded to a mere brawling in the Church; therefore St. Paul established laws of control, declared the need of subjection and rule over spiritual gifts: the spirits of the prophets were to be subject to the prophets; if those in the ecstatic state were tempted to break out into utterance and unable to interpret what it meant, those so gifted were to hold their peace.

The prophet poured out the truths supernaturally imparted to his highest spirit, in an inspired and impassioned eloquence which was intelligible even to the unspiritual, and was one of the appointed means of convincing the unconverted. The lesson derivable from this is not obsolete even in the present day. There is nothing perhaps precisely identical in our own day with those gifts of the early Church; but genius and talent are uncommon gifts, which stand in a somewhat analogous relation—in a closer one certainly—than more ordinary endowments. The flights of genius, we know, appear like maniac ravings to minds not elevated to the same spiritual level. Now these are perfectly compatible with mis-use, abuse, and moral disorder. The most gifted of our countrymen has left this behind him as his epitaph, " The greatest, wisest, *meanest* of mankind." The most glorious gift of poetic insight—itself in a way divine—having something akin to Deity—is too often associated with degraded life and vicious character. Those gifts which elevate us above the rest of our species, whereby we stand aloof and separate from the crowd, convey no moral—nor even mental—infallibility: nay, they have in themselves a peculiar danger, whereas that gift which is common to us all as brethren, the animating spirit of a divine life, in whose soil the spiritual being of all is rooted, cannot make us vain; we *cannot* pride ourselves on *that*, for it is common to us all.

2. Again, the gifts which were higher in one sense were lower in another; as supernatural gifts they would rank thus —the gift of tongues before prophecy, and prophecy before teaching; but as blessings to be desired, this order is reversed: rather than the gift of tongues St. Paul bids the Corinthians desire that they might prophecy. Inferior again to prophecy was the quite simple, and as we should say, lower faculty of explaining truth. Now the principle upon which that was tried was that of utility—not utility in the low sense of the utilitarian, who measures the value of a thing by its susceptibility of application to the purpose of this present life, but a utility whose measure was love,

charity. The apostle considered *that* gift most desirable by which men might most edify one another. And hence that noble declaration of one of the most gifted of mankind—" I had rather speak five words with my understanding, that I might teach others also, than ten thousand words in an unknown tongue."

Our estimate is almost the reverse of this: we value a gift in proportion to its rarity, its distinctive character, separating its possessor from the rest of his fellow-men; whereas, in truth, those gifts which leave us in lonely majesty apart from our species, useless to them, benefiting ourselves alone, are not the most godlike, but the least so; because they are dissevered from that beneficent charity which is the very being of God. Your lofty incommunicable thoughts, your ecstacies, and aspirations, and contemplative raptures—in virtue of which you have estimated yourself as the porcelain of the earth, of another nature altogether than the clay of common spirits—tried by the test of Charity, what is there grand in these if they cannot be applied as blessings to those that are beneath you? One of our countrymen has achieved for himself extraordinary scientific renown; he pierced the mysteries of nature, he analysed her processes, he gave new elements to the world. The same man applied his rare intellect to the construction of a simple and very common instrument—that well-known lamp which has been the guardian of the miner's life from the explosion of fire. His discoveries are his nobility in this world, his trifling invention gives him rank in the world to come. By the former he shines as one of the brightest luminaries in the firmament of science, by the latter evincing a spirit animated and directed by Christian love, he takes his place as one of the Church of God.

And such is ever the true order of rank which graces occupy in reference to gifts. The most trifling act which is marked by usefulness to others is nobler in God's sight, than the most brilliant accomplishment of genius. To teach a few Sunday-school children, week after week, commonplace simple truths—persevering in spite of dullness and mean capacities—is a more glorious occupation than the highest meditations or creations of genius which edify or instruct only our own solitary soul.

II. The spiritual unity of the Church—" the same Spirit."

Men have formed to themselves two ideas of unity: the first is a sameness of form—of expression; the second an identity of spirit. Some of the best of mankind have fondly hoped to realize an unity for the Church of Christ which should be manifested by uniform expressions in everything: their imaginations have loved to paint, as the ideal of a Christian Church, a state in which the same liturgy should be used throughout the world, the same ecclesiastical government, even the same vestments, the same canonical hours, the same form of architecture. They could conceive nothing more entirely one than a Church so constituted that the same prayers, in the very same expressions, at the very same moment, should be ascending to the Eternal Ear.

There are others who have thrown aside entirely this idea as chimerical; who have not only ceased to hope it, but even to wish it; who if it could be realized, would consider it a matter of regret; who feel that the minds of men are various—their modes and habits of thought, their original capacities and acquired associations, infinitely diverse; and who, perceiving that the law of the universal system is manifoldness in unity, have ceased to expect any other oneness for the Church of Christ than that of a sameness of spirit, showing itself through diversities of gifts. Among these last was the Apostle Paul: his large and glorious mind rejoiced in the contemplation of the countless manifestations of spiritual nature beneath which he detected one and the same pervading Mind. Now let us look at this matter somewhat more closely.

1. All real unity is manifold. Feelings in themselves identical find countless forms of expression: for instance, sorrow is the same feeling throughout the human race; but the Oriental prostrates himself upon the ground, throws dust upon his head, tears his garments, is not ashamed to break out into the most violent lamentations. In the north, we rule our grief in public; suffer not even a quiver to be seen upon the lip or brow, and consider calmness as the appropriate expression of manly grief. Nay, two sisters of different temperament will show their grief diversely; one will love to dwell upon the theme of the qualities of the departed, the other feels it a sacred sorrow, on which the lips are sealed for ever; yet would it not be idle to ask which of them has the truest affection? Are they not both in their own way true? In the same East, men take off their sandals in devotion; we exactly reverse the procedure, and uncover the head. The Oriental prostrates himself in the dust before his sovereign; even before his God the Briton only kneels; yet would it not again be idle to ask which is the essential and proper form of reverence? Is not true reverence in all cases modified by the individualities of temperament and education? Should we not say, in all these forms worketh one and the same spirit of reverence?

Again in the world as God has made it, one law shows itself under diverse, even opposite manifestations; lead sinks in water, wood floats upon the surface. In former times men assigned these different results to different forces, laws, and gods. A knowledge of Nature has demonstrated that they are expressions of one and the same law; and the great difference between the educated and the uneducated man is this—the uneducated sees in this world nothing but an infinite collection of unconnected facts—a broken, distorted, and fragmentary system, which his mind can by no means reduce to order. The educated man, in proportion to his education, sees the number of laws diminished—beholds in the manifold appearances of Nature the expression of a few laws, by degrees fewer, till at last it becomes possible to his conception that they are all reducible to one, and that that which lies beneath the innumerable phenomena of Nature is the One Spirit—God.

2. All *living* unity is spiritual, not formal; not sameness, but manifoldness. You may have a unity shown in identity of form; but it is a lifeless unity. There is a sameness on the sea-beach—that unity which the ocean waves have produced by curling and forcibly destroying the angularities of individual form, so that every stone presents the same monotony of aspect, and you must fracture each again in order to distinguish whether you hold in your hand a mass of flint or fragment of basalt. There is no life in unity such as this.

But as soon as you arrive at a unity that is living, the form becomes more complex, and you search in vain for uniformity. In the parts, it must be found, if found at all, in the sameness of the pervading life. The illustration given by the apostle is that of the human body—a higher unity, he says, by being composed of many members, than if every member were but a repetition of a single type. It is conceivable that God might have moulded such a form for human life; it is conceivable that every cause, instead of producing in different nerves a variety of sensations, should have affected every one in a mode precisely similar; that instead of producing a sensation of sound—a sensation of colour—a sensation of taste—the outward causes of nature, be they what they may, should have given but one unvaried feeling to every sense, and that the whole universe should have been light or sound.

That would have been unity, if sameness be unity; but, says the apostle, "if the whole body were seeing, where were the hearing?" That uniformity would have been irreparable loss—the loss of every part that was merged into the one. What is the body's unity? Is it not this? The unity of a living consciousness which marvellously animates every separate atom of the frame, and reduces each to the performance of a function fitted to the welfare of the whole—its own, not another's: so that the inner spirit can say of the remotest, and in form most unlike, member, "That too, is myself."

3. None but a spiritual unity can preserve the rights both of the individual and the Church. All other systems of unity, except the apostolic, either sacrifice the Church to the individual, or the individual to the Church.

Some have claimed the right of private judgment in such a way that every individual opinion becomes truth, and every utterance of private conscience right: thus the Church is sacrificed to the individual; and the universal conscience, the common faith, becomes as nothing; the spirits of the prophets are not subject to the prophets.

Again, there are others, who, like the Church of Rome, would surrender the conscience of each man to the conscience of the Church, and coerce the particulars of faith into exact coincidence with a formal creed. Spiritual unity saves the right of both in God's system. The Church exists for the individual, just as truly as the individual for the Church. The Church is then most perfect when all its powers converge, and are concentrated on the formation and protection of individual character; and the individual is then most complete—that is, most a Christian—when he has practically learned that his life is not his own, but owed to others—"that no man liveth to himself, and no man dieth to himself."

Now, spiritual unity respects the sanctity of the individual conscience. How reverently the Apostle Paul considered its claims, and how tenderly! When once it became a matter of conscience, this was his principle laid down in matters of dispute: "Let every man be fully persuaded in his own mind." The belief of the whole world cannot make that thing true to me which to me seems false. The conscience of the whole world cannot make a thing right to me, if I in my heart believe it wrong. You may coerce the conscience, you may control men's belief, and you may produce a unity by so doing; but it is the unity of pebbles on the sea-shore—a lifeless identity of outward form with no cohesion between the parts—a dead sea-beach on which nothing grows, and where the very seaweed dies.

Lastly, it respected the sanctity of individual character. Out of eight hundred millions of the human race, a few features diversify themselves into so many forms of countenance, that scarcely two could be mistaken for each other. There are no two leaves on the same tree alike; nor two sides of the same leaf, unless you cut and kill it. There is a sacredness in individuality of character; each one born into this world is a fresh new soul intended by his Maker to develope himself in a new fresh way; we are what we are; we cannot be truly other than ourselves. We reach perfection not by copying, much less by aiming at originality; but by consistently and steadily working out the life which is common to us all, according to the character which God has given us.

And thus will the Church of God be one at last—will present an unity like that of heaven. There is one universe in which each separate star differs from another in glory; one Church in which a single Spirit, the Life of God, pervades each separate soul; and just in proportion as that Life becomes exalted does it enable every one to shine forth in the distinctness of his own separate individuality, like the stars of heaven.

IV.

Preached May 26, 1850.

THE TRINITY.

" And the very God of peace sanctify you wholly ; and I pray God your whole spirit and soul and body be preserved blameless unto the coming of our Lord Jesus Christ."— 1 Thess. v. 23.

THE knowledge of God is the blessedness of man. To know God, and to be known by Him—to love God, and to be loved by Him—is the most precious treasure which this life has to give ; properly speaking the only treasure ; properly speaking the only knowledge ; for all knowledge is valuable only so far as it converges towards and ends in the knowledge of God, and enables us to acquaint ourselves with God, and be at peace with Him. The doctrine of the Trinity is the sum of all that knowledge which has as yet been gained by man. I say gained *as yet.* For we presume not to maintain that in the ages which are to come hereafter, our knowledge shall not be superseded by a higher knowledge ; we presume not to say that in a state of existence future—yea even here upon this earth, at that period which is mysteriously referred to in Scripture as " the coming of the Son of Man "—there shall not be given to the soul an intellectual conception of the Almighty, a vision of the Eternal, in comparison with whose brightness and clearness our present knowledge of the Trinity shall be as rudimentary and as childlike as the knowledge of the Jew was in comparison with the knowledge of the Christian.

Now the passage which I have undertaken to expound to-day, is one in which the doctrine of the Trinity is brought into connection practically with the doctrine of our Humanity. Before entering into it brethren, let us lay down these two observations and duties for ourselves. In the first place, let us examine the doctrine of the Trinity ever in the spirit of charity.

A clear statement of the deepest doctrine that man can know, and the intellectual conception of that doctrine, are by no means easy. We are puzzled and perplexed by *words;* we fight respecting *words.* Quarrels are nearly always verbal quarrels. Words lose their meaning in the course of time; nay, the very words of the Athanasian creed which we read to-day mean not in this age, the same thing which they meant in ages past. Therefore it is possible that men, externally Trinitarians, may differ from each other though using the same words, as greatly as a Unitarian differs from a Trinitarian. There may be found in the same Church and in the same congregation, men holding all possible shades of opinion, though agreeing externally, and in words.

I speak within the limit of my own experience when I say that persons have been known and heard to express the language of bitter condemnation respecting Unitarianism, who when examined and calmly required to draw out verbally the meaning of their own conceptions, have been proved to be holding all the time—unconsciously—the very doctrine of Sabellianism. And this doctrine is condemned by the Church as distinctly as that of Unitarianism. Therefore let us learn from all this a large and catholic charity. There are in almost every congregation, themselves not knowing it, Trinitarians who are practically Tri-theists, worshipping three Gods; and Sabellians, or worshippers of one person under three different manifestations. To know God so that we may be said intellectually, to appreciate Him, is blessed: to be unable to do so is a misfortune. Be content with your own blessedness, in comparison with others' misfortunes. Do not give to that misfortune the additional sting of illiberal and unchristian vituperation.

The next observation we have to lay down for ourselves is, that we should examine this doctrine in the spirit of modesty. There are those who are inclined to sneer at the Trinitarian; those to whom the doctrine appears merely a contradiction—a puzzle—an entangled, labyrinthine enigma, in which there is no meaning whatever. But let all such remember, that though the doctrine may appear to them absurd, because they have not the proper conception of it, some of the profoundest thinkers, and some of the holiest spirits among mankind, have believed in this doctrine—have clung to it as a matter of life or death. Let them be assured of this, that whether the doctrine be true or false, it is not necessarily a doctrine self-contradictory. Let them be assured of this, in all modesty, that such men never could have held it unless there was latent in the doctrine a deep truth,—perchance the truth of God.

We pass on now to the consideration of this verse under the following divisions. In the first place, we shall view it as a triad in discord: "I pray God your whole spirit and soul and body be preserved blameless;" in the second place, as a Trinity in Unity: "the God of peace sanctify you wholly." We take then first of all for our consideration the triad in discord: "I pray God your whole body and soul and spirit be preserved blameless."

The apostle here divides human nature into a three-fold division; and here we have to observe again the difficulty often experienced in understanding words. Thus words in the Athanasian creed have become obsolete, or lost their meaning: so that in the present day the words "person," "substance," "procession," "generation," to an ordinary person, mean almost nothing. So this language of the apostle, when rendered into English, shows no difference whatever between "soul" and "spirit." We say, for instance, that the soul of a man has departed from him. We also say that the spirit of a man has departed from him. There is no distinct difference between the two; but in the original two very different kinds of thoughts—two very different modes of conception — are represented by the two English words "soul" and "spirit."

It is our business, therefore, in the first place, to understand what is meant by this threefold division. When the apostle speaks of the body, what he means is the animal life —that which we share in common with beasts, birds, and reptiles; for our life my Christian brethren—our sensational existence—differs but little from that of the lower animals. There is the same external form, the same material in the blood-vessels, in the nerves, and in the muscular system. Nay, more than that, our appetites and instincts are alike, our lower pleasures like their lower pleasures, our lower pain like their lower pain, our life is supported by the same means, and our animal functions are almost indistinguishably the same.

But, once more, the apostle speaks of what he calls the "soul." What the apostle meant by what is translated "soul," is the immortal part of man—the immaterial as distinguished from the material: those powers, in fact, which man has by nature—powers natural, which are yet to survive the grave. There is a distinction made in scripture by our Lord between these two things. "Fear not," says He, "them who can kill the body;" but rather fear Him who can destroy both body and soul in hell."

We have again, to observe respecting this, that what the apostle called the "soul," is not simply distinguishable from the body, but also from the spirit; and on that distinction I have already touched. By the soul the apostle means our powers natural—the powers which we have by nature. Herein is the soul distinguishable from the spirit. In the Epistle to the Corinthians we read—"But the natural man receiveth not the things of the Spirit of God; for they are foolishness unto him; neither can he know them, because they are spiritually discerned. But he that is spiritual judgeth all things." Observe, there is a distinction drawn between the natural man and the spiritual. What is there translated "natural" is derived from precisely the same word as that which is here translated "soul." So that we may read just as correctly: "The man under the dominion of the soul receiveth not the things of the Spirit of God; for they are foolishness unto him; neither can he know them because they are spiritually discerned. But he that is spiritual judgeth all things." And again, the apostle, in the same Epistle to the Corinthians, writes: "That is not first which is spiritual, but that which is natural:" that is, the endowments of the soul precede the endowments of the spirit. You have the same truth in other places. The powers that belong to the Spirit were not the first developed; but the powers which belong to the soul, that is the powers of nature. Again in the same chapter, reference is made to the natural and spiritual body. "There is a natural body and there is a spiritual body." Literally, there is a body governed by the soul—that is, powers natural: and there is a body governed by the Spirit—that is, higher nature.

Let then this be borne in mind, that what the apostle calls "soul" is the same as that which he calls, in another place, the "natural man." These powers are divisible into two branches—the intellectual powers and the moral sense. The intellectual powers man has by nature. Man need not be regenerated in order to possess the power of reasoning, or in order to invent. The intellectual powers belong to what the apostle calls the "soul." The moral sense distinguishes between right and wrong. The apostle tells us, in the Epistle to the Romans, that the heathen—manifestly natural men—had the "work of the law written in their hearts; their conscience also bearing witness."

The third division of which the apostle speaks, he calls the "spirit;" and by the spirit he means that life in man which, in his natural state, is in such an embryo condition, that it can scarcely be said to exist at all—that which is called out into power and vitality by regeneration—the perfection of the powers of human nature. And you will observe, that it is not merely the instinctive life, nor the intellectual life, nor the moral life, but it is principally our nobler affections—that existence, that state of being, which we call love. That is the department of human nature which the apostle calls the spirit; and accordingly, when the Spirit of God was given on the day of Pentecost, you will remember that another power of man was called out, differing from what he had before. That Spirit granted on the day of Pentecost did subordinate to Himself, and was intended to subordinate to Himself, the will, the understanding, and the affection of man; but you often find these spiritual powers were distinguished from the natural powers, and existed without them.

So in the highest state of religious life, we are told, men prayed in the spirit. Till the spirit has subordinated the understanding, the gift of God is not complete—has not done its work. It is abundantly evident that a new life was called out. It was not merely the sharpening of the intellectual powers; it was calling out powers of aspiration and love to God; those affections which have in them something boundless, that are not limited to this earth, but seek their completion in the mind of God Himself.

Now, what we have to say respecting this threefold state of man is, it is a state of discord. Let us take up a very simple, popular, every-day illustration. We hear it remarked frequently in conversation of a man, that if only his will were commensurate with his knowledge, he would be a great man. His knowledge is great—his powers are almost unbounded; he has gained knowledge from nearly every department of science; but somehow or other—you cannot tell why—there is such an indecision, such a vacillation about the man, that he scarcely knows what to do, and, perhaps does nothing in this world. You find it remarked, respecting another class of men, that their will is strong, almost unbounded in its strength—they have iron wills, yet there is something so narrow in their conceptions, something so bounded in their views, so much of stagnation in their thoughts, so much of prejudice in all their opinions, that their will is prevented from being directed to anything in a proper manner. Here is the discord in human nature. There is a distinction between the will and the understanding. And sometimes a feeble will goes with a strong

understanding, or a powerful will is found in connection
with great feebleness or ignorance of the understanding.

Let us however, go into this more specially. The first
cause of discord in this threefold state of man is the state in
which the body is the ruler; and this, my Christian brethren,
you find most visibly developed in the uneducated and irreligious poor. I say uneducated and irreligious, because it is
by no means education alone which can subordinate the
flesh to the higher man. The religious uneducated poor
man may be master of his lower passions; but in the uneducated and irreligious poor man, these show themselves in
full force; this discord—this want of unity—appears, as it
were, in a magnified form. There is a strong man—health
bursting, as it were, at every pore, with an athletic body;
but coarse, and rude, and intellectually weak—almost an
animal. When you are regarding the upper classes of
society, you see less distinctly the absence of the spirit,
unless you look with a spiritual eye. The coarseness has
passed away—the rudeness is no longer seen: there is a
refinement in the pleasures. But if you take the life led
by the young men of our country—strong, athletic, healthy
men—it is still the life of the flesh: the unthinking, and the
unprincipled life in which there is as yet no higher life
developed. It is a life which, in spite of its refinement, the
Bible condemns as the life of the sensualist.

We pass on now, to another state of discord—a state in
which the soul is ruined. Brethren, this is a natural result
—this is what might have been expected. The natural man
gradually subordinates the flesh, the body, to the soul. It
is natural in the development of individuals, it is natural in
the development of society: in the development of individuals, because that childlike, infantine life which exists at

first, and is almost entirely a life of appetites, gradually subsides. Higher wants, higher desires, loftier inclinations arise ; the passions of the young man gradually subside, and by degrees the more rational life comes : the life is changed —the pleasures of the senses are forsaken for those of the intellect.

It appears natural, again, in the development of society. Civilization will subordinate the flesh to the soul. In the savage state, you find the life of the animal. Civilization is teaching a man, on the principle of this world, to subordinate his appetites ; to rule himself ; and there comes a refinement, and a gentleness, and a polish, and an enjoyment of intellectual pleasures ; so that the man is no longer what the apostle calls a sensual man, but he becomes now what the apostle calls a natural man. We can see this character delineated in the Epistle to the Ephesians. "Then we were," says the apostle, "in our Gentile state, fulfilling the desires of the flesh and of the mind." Man naturally fulfils not merely the desires of the flesh, but the desires of the mind. "And were," says the apostle, "children of wrath."

One of the saddest spectacles is the decay of the natural man before the work of the Spirit has been accomplished in him. When the savage dies—when a mere infant dies— when an animal dies—there is nothing that is appalling or depressing there; but when the high, the developed intellect —when the cultivated man comes to the last hours of life, and the memory becomes less powerful, and the judgment fails, and all that belongs to nature and to earth visibly perishes, and the higher life has not been yet developed, though it is destined to survive the grave for ever—even the life of God—there is here ample cause for grief ; and it is no wonder that the man of genius merely should shed tears at the idea of decaying life.

We pass on to consider the Trinity in unity. All this is contained in that simple expression, "The God of peace." God is a God of unity. He makes one where before there were two. He is the God of peace, and therefore can make peace. Now this peace, according to the Trinitarian doctrine, consists in a threefold unity. Brethren, as we remarked respecting this first of all, the distinction in this Trinity is not a physical distinction, but a metaphysical one. The illustrations which are often given are illustrations drawn from material sources: if we take only those, we get into contradiction: for example, when we talk of personality, our idea is of a being bounded by space; and then to say in this sense that three persons are one, and one is three, is simply contradictory and absurd. Remember that the doctrine of the Trinity is a metaphysical doctrine. It is a trinity—a division in the mind of God. It is not three materials; it is three persons in a sense we shall explain by and by.

In the next place I will endeavour to explain the doctrine —not to prove it, but to show its rationality, and to explain what it is.

The first illustration we endeavour to give in this is taken from the world of matter. We will take any material substance: we find in that substance qualities; we will say three qualities—colour, shape, and size. Colour is not shape, shape is not size, size is not colour. They are three distinct essences, three distinct qualities, and yet they all form one unity, one single conception, one idea—the idea for example, of a tree.

Now we will ascend from that into the immaterial world;

and here to be something more distinct still. Hitherto we have had but three qualities; we now come to the mind of man, where we find something more than qualities. We will take three—the will, the affections, and the thoughts of man. His will is not his affections, neither are his affections his thoughts; and it would be imperfect and incomplete to say that these are mere qualities in the man. They are separate consciousnesses, living consciousnesses—as distinct, and as really sundered as it is possible for three things to be, yet bound together by one unity of consciousness. Now we have distincter proof than even this that these things are three. The anatomist can tell you that the localities of these powers are different. He can point out the seat of the nerve of sensation; he can localize the feeling of affection; he can point to a nerve and say, "There resides the locality of thought."

There are three distinct localities for three distinct qualities, personalities, consciousnesses; yet all these three are one.

Once more, we will give proof even beyond all that. The act that a man does is done by one particular part of that man. You may say it was a work of his genius, or of his fancy; it may have been a manifestation of his love, or an exhibition of his courage; yet that work was the work of the whole man: his courage, his intellect, his habits of perseverance, all helped towards the completion of that single work. Just in this way certain special works are attributed to certain personalities of the Deity; the work of Redemption being attributed to one, the work of Sanctification to another. And yet just as the whole man was engaged in doing that work, so does the whole Deity perform that work which is attributed to one essential.

Once more, let us remember that principle which we expounded last Sunday, that it is the law of Being that in proportion as you rise from lower to higher life, the parts are more distinctly developed, while yet the unity becomes more entire. You find for example, in the lowest forms of animal life one organ performs several functions, one organ being at the same time heart and brain and blood-vessels. But when you come to man, you find all these various functions existing in different organs, and every organ more distinctly developed; and yet the unity of a man is a higher unity than that of a limpet. When you come from the material world to the world immaterial, you find that the more society is cultivated—the more man is cultivated—the more marvellous is the power of developing distinct powers. In the savage life it is almost all one feeling; but in proportion as the higher education advances and the higher life appears, every power and faculty developes and distinguishes itself, and becomes distinct and separate. And yet just in proportion as in a nation every part is distinct, the unity is greater, and just in proportion as in an individual every power is most complete, and stands out most distinct, just in that proportion has the man reached the entireness of his Humanity.

Now brethren, we apply all this to the mind of God. The Trinitarian maintains against the Unitarian and the Sabellian, that the higher you ascend in the scale of being, the more distinct are the consciousnesses, and that the law of unity implies and demands a manifold unity. The doctrine of Sabellianism, for example, is this, that God is but one essence—but one person under different manifestations; and that when He made the world He was called the Father, when He redeemed the world He was called the

Son, and when He sanctified the world He was called the Holy Ghost. The Sabellian and the Unitarian maintain that the unity of God consists simply in a unity of person, and in opposition to this does the Trinitarian maintain that grandness, either in man or in God, must be a unity of manifoldness.

But we will enter into this more deeply. The first power or consciousness in which God is made known to us is as the Father, the Author of our being. It is written, "In Him we live, and move, and have our being." He is the Author of all life. In this sense He is not merely our Father as Christians, but the Father of mankind; and not merely the Father of mankind, but the Father of creation; and in this way the sublime language of the prophets may be taken as true literally, "The morning stars sang together, and all the sons of God shouted for joy;" and the language of the canticle which belongs to our morning service, "the deeps, the fountains, the wells," all unite in one hymn of praise, one everlasting hallelujah to God the Father, the Author of their being. In this respect, simply as the Author of life, merely as the supreme Being, God has reference to us in relation to the body. He is the Lord of life: in Him we live, and move, and have our being. In this respect God to us is as law—as the collected laws of the universe; and therefore to offend against law, and bring down the result of transgressing law, is said in Scripture language, because applied to a person, to be provoking the wrath of God the Father.

In the next place, the second way through which the personality and consciousness of God has been revealed to us is as the Son. Brethren, we see in all those writers who have treated of the Trinity, that much stress is laid upon this eternal generation of the Son, the everlasting sonship. It is this which we have in the Creed—the Creed which was read to-day—" God, of the substance of the Father, begotten before the worlds ;" and, again, in the Nicene Creed, that expression, which is so often wrongly read, " God of God, Light of Light, very God of very God," means absolutely nothing. There are two statements made there. The first is this, " The Son was God :" the second is this, " The Son was — *of* God," showing his derivation. And in that, brethren, we have one of the deepest and most blessed truths of revelation. The Unitarian maintains a divine Humanity—a blessed, blessed truth. There is a truth more blessed still—the Humanity of Deity. Before the world was, there was that in the mind of God which we may call the Humanity of His Divinity. It is called in Scripture the Word : the Son : the Form of God. It is in virtue of this that we have a right to attribute to Him our own feelings ; it is in virtue of this that Scripture speaks of His wisdom, His justice, His love. Love in God is what love is in man ; justice in God is what justice is in man ; creative power in God is what creative power is in man ; indignation in God is that which indignation is in man, barring only this, that the one is emotional, but the other is calm, and pure, and everlastingly still. It is through this Humanity in the mind of God, if I may dare so to speak of Deity, that a revelation became possible to man. It was the Word that was made flesh ; it was the Word that manifested Itself to man. It is in virtue of the connection between God and man, that God made man in His own image ; that through a long line of prophets the human truth of God could be made known to man, till it came forth developed most entirely and at large in the incarnation of the Redeemer.

Now in this respect, it will be observed that God stands connected with us in relation to the soul as "the Light which lighteth every man that cometh into the world."

Once more; there is a nearer, a closer, and a more enduring relation in which God stands to us—that is, the relation of the Spirit. It is to the writings of St. John that we have to turn especially, if we desire to know the doctrines of the Spirit. You will remember the strange way in which he speaks of God. It would almost seem as if the external God has disappeared to him; nay, as if an external Christ were almost forgotten, because the internal Christ has been formed. He speaks of God as kindred with us; he speaks of Christ as Christ *in* us; and "if we love one another," he says, "God dwelleth in us." If a man keep the commandments, "God dwelleth in him, and he in God." So that the spiritual manifestation of God to us is that whereby He blends Himself with the soul of man.

These then, my Christian brethren, are the three consciousnesses by which He becomes known to us. Three, we said, *known* to us. We do not dare to limit God; we do not presume to say that there are in God only three personalities—only three consciousnesses: all that we dare presume to say is this, that there are three in reference to us, and only three; that a fourth there is not; that perchance, in the present state a fourth you cannot add to these—Creator, Redeemer, Sanctifier.

Lastly, let us turn to the relation which the Trinity in unity bears to the triad in discord. It is intended for the entireness of our sanctification: "the very God of peace sanctify you wholly." Brethren, we dwell upon that expression "*wholly*." There is this difference between Christianity and every other system: Christianity proposes to ennoble the whole man; every other system subordinates parts to parts. Christianity does not despise the intellect, but it does not exalt the intellect in a one-sided way: it only dwells with emphasis on the third and highest part of man—his spiritual affections; and these it maintains are the chief and real seat of everlasting life, intended to subordinate the other to themselves.

Asceticism would crush the natural affections—destroy the appetites. Asceticism feels that there is a conflict between the flesh and the spirit, and it would put an end to that conflict; it would bring back unity by the excision of all our natural appetites, and all the desires and feelings which we have by nature. But when the apostle Paul comes forward to proclaim the will of God, he says it is not by the crushing of the body, but by the sanctification of the body: "I pray God your whole spirit and soul and body be preserved blameless unto the coming of our Lord Jesus Christ."

In this my Christian brethren, there is one of the deepest of all truths. Does a man feel himself the slave and the victim of his lower passions? Let not that man hope to subdue them merely by struggling against them. Let him not by fasting, by austerity, by any earthly rule that he can conceive, expect to subdue the flesh. The more he thinks of his vile and lower feelings, the more will they be brought into distinctness, and therefore into power; the more hopelessly will he beome their victim. The only way in which a man can subdue the flesh, is not by the extinction of those feelings, but by the elevation of their character. Let there be added to that character, sublimity of aim, purity of affection; let there be given grandeur, spiritual nobleness; and then, just as the strengthening of the whole constitution of the body makes any particular and local affection disappear, so by degrees, by the raising of the character, do these lower affections become, not extinguished or destroyed by excision, but ennobled by a new and loftier spirit breathed through them.

This is the account given by the apostle. He speaks of the conflict between the flesh and the spirit. And his remedy is to give vigour to the higher, rather than to struggle with the lower. "This I say then, Walk in the spirit, and ye *shall not* fulfil the lust of the flesh."

Once more; the apostle differs from the world in this, that the world would restore this unity, and sanctify man simply from the soul. It is this which civilization pretends to effect. We hear much in these modern days of "the progress of Humanity." We hear of man's invention, of man's increase of knowledge; and it would seem in all this, as if man were necessarily becoming better. Brethren, it always must be the case in that state in which God is looked upon as the Supreme Being merely, where the intellect of man is supposed to be the chief thing—that which makes him most kindred to his Maker.

The doctrine of Christianity is this—that unity of all this discord must be made. Man is to be made one with God, not by soaring intellect, but by lowly love. It is the Spirit which guides him to all truth; not merely by rendering more acute the reasoning powers, but by convincing of sin, by humbling the man. It is the graces of the Spirit which harmonize the man, and make him one; and that is the end, and aim, and object of all the Gospel: the entireness of sanctification to produce a perfectly developed man.

Most of us in this world are monsters, with some part of our being bearing the development of a giant, and others showing the proportions of a dwarf: a feeble, dwarfish will—mighty, full-blown passions; and therefore it is that there is to be visible through the Trinity in us, a noble manifold unity; and when the triune power of God shall so have done its work on the entireness of our Humanity, that the body, soul, and spirit have been sanctified, then shall there be exhibited, and only then, a perfect affection in man to his Maker, and body, soul, and spirit shall exhibit a Trinity in unity.

V.

Preached June 2, 1850.

ABSOLUTION.

"And the Scribes and the Pharisees began to reason, saying, Who is this which speaketh blasphemies? Who can forgive sins, but God alone?"—Luke v. 21.

THERE are questions which having been again and again settled, still from time to time, present themselves for *re*-solution; errors which having been refuted, and cut up by the roots, re-appear in the next century as fresh and vigorous as ever. Like the fabled monsters of old, from whose dissevered neck the blood sprung forth and formed fresh heads, multiplied and indestructible; or like the weeds, which, extirpated in one place, sprout forth vigorously in another.

In every such case it may be taken for granted that the root of the matter has not been reached; the error has been exposed, but the truth which lay at the bottom of the error has not been disengaged. Every error is connected with a truth; the truth being perennial, springs up again as often as circumstances foster it, or call for it, and the seeds of error which lay about the roots spring up again in the form of weeds, as before.

A popular illustration of this may be found in the belief in the appearance of the spirits of the departed. You may examine the evidence for every such alleged apparition; you may demonstrate the improbability; you may reduce it to an impossibility; still the popular feeling will remain; and there is a lurking superstition even among the enlightened, which in the midst of professions of incredulity, shows itself in a readiness to believe the wildest new tale, if it possess but the semblance of an authentication. Now two truths lie at the root of this superstition. The first is the reality of the spirit-world, and the instinctive belief in it. The second is the fact that there are certain states of health in which the eye creates the objects which it perceives. The death-blow to such superstition is only struck when we have not only proved that men have been deceived, but shown besides how they came to be deceived; when science has explained the optical delusion, and shown the physiological state in which such apparitions become visible. Ridicule will not do it. Disproof will not do it. So long as men feel that there is a spirit-world, and so long as to some the impression is vivid that they have seen it, you spend your rhetoric in vain. You must show the truth that lies below the error.

The principle we gain from this is that you cannot overthrow falsehood by negation, but by establishing the antagonistic truth. The refutation which is to last must be positive, not negative. It is an endless work to be uprooting weeds: plant the ground with wholesome vegetation, and then the juices which would have otherwise fed rankness will pour themselves into a more vigorous growth; the dwindled weeds will be easily raked out then. It is an endless task to be refuting error. Plant truth, and the error will pine away.

The instance to which all this is preliminary, is the pertinacious hold which the belief in a human absolving power retains upon mankind. There has perhaps never yet been known a religion without such a belief. There is not a savage in the islands of the South Pacific who does not believe that his priest can shield him from the consequences of sin. There was not a people in antiquity who had not dispensers of Divine favour. That same belief passed from Paganism into Romanism. It was exposed at the period of the Reformation. A mighty reaction was felt against it throughout Europe. Apparently the whole idea of human priesthood was proved, once and for ever, to be baseless; human mediation, in every possible form, was vehemently controverted; men were referred back to God as the sole absolver.

Yet now again, three centuries after, the belief is still as strong as ever. That which we thought dead is alive again, and not likely it seems, to die. Recent revelations have shown that confession is daily made in the country whose natural manners are most against it; private absolution asked by English men and given by English priests. A fact so significant might lead us well to pause, and ask ourselves whether we have found the true answer to the question. The negation we have got—the vehement denial; we are weary of its reiteration: but the positive truth which lies at the bottom of this craving—where is that?

Parliaments and pulpits, senators and clergymen, have vied with each other in the vehemence with which they declare absolution un-Christian, un-English. All that is most abominable in the confessional has been with unsparing and irreverent indelicacy forced before the public mind. Still, men and women, whose holiness and purity are beyond slander's reach, come and crave assurance of forgiveness. How shall we reply to such men? Shall we say, "Who is this that speaketh blasphemies? who can forgive sins, but God only?" Shall we say it is all blasphemy; an impious intrusion upon the prerogatives of the One Absolver? Well, we may; it is *popular* to say we ought; but you will observe, if we speak so, we do no more than the Pharisees in this text: we establish a negation; but a negation is only one side of truth.

Moreover, we have been asserting that for 300 years, with small fruits. We keep asserting, Man cannot give assurance that sin is pardoned; in other words, man cannot absolve: but still the heart craves human assurance of forgiveness. What truth have we got to supply that craving? We shall therefore, rather try to fathom the deeps of the positive truth which is the true reply to the error; we shall try to see whether there is not a real answer to the craving contained in the Redeemer's words, " The Son of Man hath power on earth to forgive sins." What power is there in human forgiveness? What does absolution mean in the lips of a son of man? These are our questions for to-day. We shall consider two points.

I. The impotency of the negation.
II. The power of the positive truth.

The Pharisees denied the efficacy of human absolution: they said, "None can forgive sins, but God only:" that was a negation. What did they effect by their system of negations? They conferred no peace; they produced no holiness. It would be a great error to suppose that the Pharisees were hypocrites in the ordinary sense of the term —that is, pretending to be anxious about religion when they knew that they felt no anxiety. They *were* anxious, in their way. They heard a startling free announcement of forgiveness by a man. To them it appeared license given to sin. If this new teacher, this upstart—in their own language, "this fellow—of whom every man knew whence he was," were to go about the length and breadth of the land, telling sinners to be at peace; telling them to forget the past, and to work onwards; bidding men's consciences be at rest; and commanding them not to *fear* the God whom they had offended, but to *trust* in Him—what would become of morality and religion? This presumptuous Absolver would make men careless about both. If the indispensable safeguards of penalty were removed, what remained to restrain men from sin?

For the Pharisees had no notion of any other goodness than that which is restrained; they could conceive no goodness free, but only that which is produced by rewards and punishments—law-goodness, law-righteousness: to dread God, not to love and trust Him, was their conception of religion. And this, indeed, is the *ordinary* conception of religion—the ordinary meaning implied to most minds by the word religion. The word religion means, by derivation, restriction or obligation—obligation to do, obligation to avoid. And this is the negative system of the Pharisees —scrupulous avoidance of evil, rather than positive and free pursuit of excellence. Such a system never produced anything but barren denial. "*This* is wrong;" "*that* is heresy;" "*that* is dangerous."

There was another class of men who denied human power of absolution. They were called Scribes or writers— pedants, men of ponderous learning and accurate definitions; from being mere transcribers of the law, they had risen to be its expounders. They could define the exact number of yards that might be travelled on the Sabbath-day without infringement of the law; they could decide, according to the most approved theology, the respective importance of each duty; they would tell you, authoritatively, which was the *great* commandment of the law. The Scribe is a man who turns religion into etiquette: his idea of God is that of a monarch, transgression against whom is an offence against statute law, and he the Scribe, is there to explain the prescribed conditions upon which the offence may be expiated; he has no idea of admission to the sovereign's presence, except by compliance with certain formalities which the Scribe is commissioned to declare.

There are therefore Scribes in all ages—Romish Scribes, who distinguish between venial and mortal sin, and apportion to each its appointed penance and absolution. There are Protestant Scribes, who have no idea of God but as an incensed judge, and prescribe certain methods of appeasing him—a certain price—in consideration of which He is willing to sell forgiveness; men who accurately draw the distinction between the different kinds of faith—faith historical and faith saving; who bewilder and confuse all natural feeling; who treat the natural love of relations as if it were an idolatry as great as bowing down to mammon; who make intelligible distinction between the work that *may* and the work that may *not* be done on the Sabbath-day; who send you into a perilous consideration of the workings of your own feelings, and the examination of your spiritual experiences, to ascertain whether you have the feelings which give you a right to call God a Father. They hate the Romish Scribe as much as the Jewish Scribe hated the Samaritan and called him heretic. But in their way they are true to the spirit of the Scribe.

Now the result of this is fourfold. Among the tender-minded, despondency; among the vainer, spiritual pride; in the case of the slavish, superstition; with the hard-minded, infidelity. Ponder it well, and you will find these four things rife amongst us: Despondency, Spiritual Pride, Superstition, and Infidelity. In this way we have been going on for many years. In the midst of all this, at last we are informed that the confessional is at work again; whereupon astonishment and indignation are loudly expressed. It is not to be borne that the priests of the Church of England should confess and absolve in private. Yet it is only what might have been expected.

With our Evangelicalism, Tractarianism, Scribeism, Pharisaism, we have ceased to front the *living fact*—we are as zealous as Scribes and Pharisees ever were for negatives; but in the meantime Human Nature, oppressed and overborne, gasping for breath, demands something real and living. It cannot live on controversies. It cannot be fed on protests against heresy, however vehement. We are trying who can protest loudest. Every book, every journal, rings with warnings. "Beware!" is written upon everything. Beware of Rome; beware of Geneva; beware of Germany; some danger on every side; Satan everywhere — God *nowhere;* everywhere some man to be shunned or dreaded— nowhere one to be loved freely and without suspicion. Is it any wonder if men and women, in the midst of negations, cry, "Ye warn me from the error, but who will guide me into truth? I want guidance. I am sinful, full of evil! I want forgiveness! Absolve me; tell me that I am pardoned; help me to believe it. Your quarrels do not help me; if you cannot do *that*, it matters little what you *can* do. You have restricted God's love, and narrowed the path to heaven;

you have hampered religion with so many mysterious questions and quibbles that I cannot find the way to God ; you have terrified me with so many snares and pitfalls on every side, that I dare not tread at all. Give me peace; give me human guidance : I want a human arm to lean on."

This is a cry, I believe, becoming daily more passionate, and more common. And no wonder that all our information, public and private, is to the same effect—that the recent converts have found peace in Rome ; for the secret of the power of Rome is this—that she grounds her teaching, not on variable feelings and correct opinions, but on *facts*. God is not a highly probable God, but a *fact*. God's forgiveness is not a feeling, but a *fact;* and a material symbolic fact is the witness of the invisible one. Rome puts forward her absolution—her false, priestly, magical absolution—a visible fact, as a witness of the invisible. And her perversion prevails because founded on a truth.

II. The power of the positive truth.

Is it any wonder, if taught on every side distrust of man, the heart should by a violent reaction, and by an extravagant confidence in a priest, proclaim that its normal, natural state is not distrust, but trust ?

What is forgiveness?—It is God reconciled to us. What is absolution ?—It is the authoritative declaration that God is reconciled. Authoritative : that is a real power of conveying a sense and feeling of forgiveness. It is the power of the Son of Man *on earth* to forgive sins. It is man, God's image, representing, by his forgiveness on earth, God's forgiveness in heaven.

Now distinguish God's forgiveness of sin from an arresting of the consequences of sin. When God forgives a sin, it does

not follow that He stops its consequences: for example,
when He forgives the intemperate man whose health is
ruined, forgiveness does not restore his health. Divine
pardon does not interfere with the laws of the universe, for
it is itself one of those laws. It is a law that penalty follows
transgression. Forgiveness will not save from penalty; but
it alters the feelings with which the penalty is accepted.
Pain inflicted with a surgeon's knife for a man's good, is as
keen as that which results from the knife of the torturer;
but in the one case it is calmly borne, because remedial—in
the other it exasperates, because it is felt to be intended by
malevolence. So with the difference between suffering
which comes from a sin which we hope God has forgiven,
and suffering which seems to fall hot from the hand of an
angry God. It is a fearful truth, that so far as we know at
least, the consequences of an act are connected with it
indissolubly. Forgiveness does not arrest them; but by
producing softness and grateful penitence, it transforms them
into blessings. This is God's forgiveness; and absolution
is the conveyance to the conscience of the conviction of
forgiveness: to absolve is to free—to comfort by strengthening—to afford repose from fear.

Now it was the way of the Redeemer to emancipate
from sin by the freeness of absolution. The dying thief, an
hour before a blasphemer, was unconditionally assured; the
moment the sinner's feelings changed towards God, He
proclaimed that God was reconciled to him: "This day
thou shalt be with me in Paradise." And hence, speaking
humanly, hence, from this absolving tone and spirit, came
His wondrous and unparalleled power with sinful, erring
hearts; hence the life and fresh impulse which He imparted
to the being and experience to those with whom He dealt.

Hence the maniac, freed from the legion, sat at His feet, clothed, and in his right mind. Hence the outcast woman, whom human scorn would have hardened into brazen effrontery, hearing an unwonted voice of human sympathy, "washed His feet with her tears, and wiped them with the hairs of her head."

And this is what we have forgotten: we have not yet learned to trust the power of redeeming love; we do not believe in the omnipotence of grace, and the might of an appeal to the better parts, and not the slavish parts of human nature. Settle it in your minds, the absolving power is the central secret of the Gospel. Salvation is unconditional; not an offer, but *a Gift;* not clogged with conditions, but free as the air we breathe. God welcomes back the prodigal. God loves without money and without price. To this men reply gravely, It is dangerous to speak thus; it is perilous to dispense with the safeguards of restriction. Law! law! there is nothing like law—a salutary fear—for making men holy. O blind Pharisee! had you ever known the spring, the life which comes from feeling *free*, the gush of gratitude with which the heart springs to duty when all chains are shattered, and it stands fearless and free in the Light, and in the Love of God—you would understand that a large trusting charity, which can throw itself on the better and more generous impulses of a laden spirit, is the safest as well as the most beautiful means of securing obedience.

So far however, there will not be much objection to the doctrine: it will be admitted that absolution is true in the lips of Christ, because of His Divinity. It will be said He was God, and God speaking on earth is the same thing as God speaking in heaven. No my brethren, it is *not* the same thing. Christ forgiving on earth is *a new truth* added to that of God's forgiving in heaven. It is not the same truth. The one is forgiveness by Deity; the other is the declaration of forgiveness by Humanity. He bade the palsied man walk, that they might know that "the Son of Man hath power on earth to forgive sins." Therefore we proceed a step further. The same power He delegated to His Church which He had exercised Himself. "Whosesoever sins ye remit, they are remitted." Now perhaps, it will be replied to this, that that promise belongs to the apostles; that they were supernaturally gifted to distinguish genuine from feigned repentance; to absolve therefore, was their natural prerogative, but that we have no right to say it extends beyond the apostles.

We therefore, bring the question to a point by referring to an instance in which an apostle did absolve. Let us examine whether St. Paul confined the prerogative to himself. "To whom ye forgive anything, I forgive also: for to whom I forgave anything for your sakes, forgave I it in the person of Christ."

Observe now: it is quite true here that the apostle absolved a man whose excommunication he had formerly required; but he absolved him because the congregation absolved him; not as a plenipotentiary supernaturally gifted to convey a mysterious benefit, but as himself an organ and representative of the Church. The power of absolution therefore, belonged to the Church, and to the apostle through the Church. It was a power belonging to *all* Christians: to the apostle, because he was a Christian, not because he was an apostle. A priestly power no doubt, because Christ has made all Christians kings and priests.

Now let us turn again, with this added light, to examine the meaning of that expression, "The Son of man hath power on earth to forgive sins." Mark that form of words— not Christ as God, but Christ as Son of man. It was manifestly said by Him, not solely as divine, but rather as human, as the Son of man; that is, as Man. For we may take it as a rule: when Christ calls himself Son of man, He is asserting His Humanity. It was said by the High Priest of Humanity in the name of the race. It was said on the principle that human nature is the reflection of God's nature: that human love is the image of God's love; and that human forgiveness is the type and assurance of divine forgiveness.

In Christ Humanity was the perfect type of Deity, and therefore Christ's absolution was always the exact measure and counterpart of God's forgiveness. Herein lies the deep truth of the doctrine of His eternal priesthood—the Eternal Son—the Humanity of the Being of God—the ever Human mind of God. The Absolver ever lives. The Father judgeth no man, but hath committed all judgment to the Son—hath given Him authority to execute judgment also, because He is the Son of man.

But further than this. In a subordinate, because less perfect degree, the forgiveness of a man as man carries with it an absolving power. Who has not felt the load taken from his mind when the hidden guilt over which he had brooded long has been acknowledged, and met by forgiving human sympathy, especially at a time when he expected to be treated with coldness and reproof? Who has not felt how such a moment was to him the dawn of a better hope, and how the merciful judgment of some wise and good human being seemed to be the type and the assurance of God's pardon, making it credible? Unconsciously it may be, but still in substance really, I believe some such reason-

Absolution.   73

ing as *this* goes on in the whispers of the heart—" He loves me, and has compassion on me—will not God forgive? He, this man, made in God's image, does not think my case hopeless. Well, then, in the larger love of God it is not hopeless." Thus, and only thus, can we understand the *ecclesiastical* act. Absolution, the prerogative of our humanity, is represented by a formal act of the Church.

Much controversy and angry bitterness has been spent on the absolution put by the Church of England into the lips of her ministers—I cannot think with justice—if we try to get at the root of these words of Christ. The priest proclaims forgiveness authoritatively as the organ of the congregation—as the voice of the Church, in the name of Man and God. For human nature represents God. The Church represents what human nature is and ought to be. The minister represents the Church. He speaks therefore, in the name of our godlike, human nature. He declares a divine fact, he does not create it. There is no magic in his absolution: he can no more forgive whom God has not forgiven, by the formula of absolution, or reverse the pardon of him whom God has absolved by the formula of excommunication, than he can transfer a demon into an angel by the formula of baptism. He declares what every one has a right to declare, and ought to declare by his lips and by his conduct: but being a minister, he declares it authoritatively in the name of every Christian who by his Christianity is a priest to God; he specializes what is universal; as in baptism, he seals the universal Sonship on the individual by name, saying, "The Sonship with which Christ has redeemed all men, I hereby proclaim for this child;" so by absolution he specializes the universal fact of the love of God to those who are listening then and there, saying, " The Love of God the Absolver, I authoritatively proclaim to be *yours.*"

In the Service for the Visitation of the Sick, the Church of England puts into the lips of her ministers words quite unconditional : " I absolve thee from all thy sins." You know that passage is constantly objected to as Romish and superstitious. I would not give up that precious passage. I love the Church of England, because she has dared to claim her inheritance—because she has courage to assert herself as what she ought to be—God's representative on earth. She says to her minister, Stand there before a darkened spirit, on whom the shadows of death have begun to fall : in human flesh and blood representing the Invisible,—with words of human love making credible the Love Eternal. Say boldly, I am here to declare not a perhaps, *but a fact.* I forgive thee in the name of Humanity. And so far as Humanity represents Deity, that forgiveness is a type of God's. She does not put into her ministers' lips words of incantation. He cannot bless whom God has not blessed—he cannot curse whom God has not cursed. If the Son of absolution be there, his absolution will rest. If you have ever tried the slow and apparently hopeless task of ministering to a heart diseased, and binding up the wound that *will* bleed afresh, to which no assurances can give comfort, because they are not authoritative, it must have crossed your mind that such a power as that which the Church of England claims, if it were believed, is exactly the remedy you want. You must have felt that even the formula of the Church of Rome would be a blessed power to exercise, could it but once be accepted as a pledge that all the past was obliterated, and that from that moment a free untainted future lay before the soul—you must have *felt* that; you must have wished you had dared to *say* it. My whole spirit has absolved my erring brother. Is God less merciful than I? Can I—dare I—say or think it conditionally? Dare I say, I hope? May I not, must I not, say, *I know* God has forgiven you?

Every man whose heart has truly bled over another's sin, and watched another's remorse with pangs as sharp as if the crime had been his own, *has* said it. Every parent has said it who ever received back a repentant daughter, and opened out for her a new hope for life. Every mother has said it who ever by her hope against hope for some profligate, protested for a love deeper and wider than that of society. Every man has said it who forgave a deep wrong. See then, *why* and *how* the church absolves. She only exercises that power which belongs to every son of man. If society were Christian—if society, by its forgiveness and its exclusion, truly represented the mind of God—there would be no necessity for a Church to speak; but the absolution of society and the world does not represent by any means God's forgiveness. Society absolves those whom God has *not* absolved—the proud, the selfish, the strong, the seducer; society refuses return and acceptance to the seduced, the frail, and the sad penitent whom God has accepted; therefore it is necessary that a selected body, through its appointed organs, should do in the name of Man what man, as such, does not. The Church is the ideal of Humanity. It represents what God intended man to be—what man is in God's sight as beheld in Christ by Him; and the minister of the Church speaks as the representative of that ideal Humanity. Church absolution is an eternal protest, in the name of God the Absolver, against the false judgments of society.

One thing more. Beware of making this a dead formula.

If absolution be not a living truth, it becomes a monstrous falsehood ; if you take absolution as a mystical gift conveyed to an individual man called a priest, and mysteriously efficacious in *his* lips, and his *alone*, you petrify a truth into death and unreality. I have been striving to show that absolution is not a Church figment, invented by priestcraft, but a living, blessed, human power. It is a power delegated to you and to me, and just so far as we exercise it lovingly and wisely, in our lives, and with our lips, we help men away from sin : just so far as we do not exercise it, or exercise it falsely, we drive men to Rome. For if the heart cannot have a truth it will take a counterfeit of truth. By every magnanimous act, by every free forgiveness with which a pure man forgives, or pleads for mercy, or assures the penitent, he proclaims this truth, that " the Son of man hath power on earth to forgive sins "—he exhibits the priestly power of humanity—*he does* absolve ; let theology say what it will of absolution, he gives peace to the conscience—he is a type and assurance of what God is—he breaks the chains and lets the captive go free.

VI.

Preached June 9, 1850.

THE ILLUSIVENESS OF LIFE.

"By faith Abraham, when he was called to go out into a place which he should after receive for an inheritance, obeyed; and he went out, not knowing whither he went. By faith he sojourned in the land of promise, as in a strange country, dwelling in tabernacles with Isaac and Jacob, the heirs with him of the same promise: for he looked for a city which hath foundations, whose builder and maker is God."—Hebrews xi. 8-10.

LAST Sunday we touched upon a thought which deserves further development. God promised Canaan to Abraham, and yet Abraham never inherited Canaan: to the last he was a wanderer there; he had no possession of his own in its territory: if he wanted even a tomb to bury his dead, he could only obtain it by purchase. This difficulty is expressly admitted in the text, "In the land of promise he sojourned as in a strange country;" he dwelt there in tents—in changeful, moveable tabernacles—not permanent habitations; he had no home there.

It is stated in all its startling force, in terms still more explicit, in the 7th chapter of the Acts, 5th verse, "And He gave him none inheritance in it, no, not so much as to set his foot on: yet He promised that He would give it to him for a possession, and to his seed after him, when as yet he had no child."

Now the surprising point is that Abraham, deceived, as you might almost say, did not complain of it as a deception; he was even grateful for the non-fulfilment of the promise: he does not seem to have expected its fulfilment; he did not look for Canaan, but for "a city which had foundations;" his faith appears to have consisted in disbelieving the letter, almost as much as in believing the spirit of the promise.

And herein lies a principle, which, rightly expounded, can help us to interpret this life of ours. God's promises never are fulfilled in the sense in which they seem to have been given. Life is a deception; its anticipations, which are God's promises to the imagination, are never realized; they who know life best, and have trusted God most to fill it with blessings, are ever the first to say that life is a series of disappointments. And in the spirit of this text we have to say that it is a wise and merciful arrangement which ordains it thus.

The wise and holy do not expect to find it otherwise—would not wish it otherwise; their wisdom consists in disbelieving its promises. To develope this idea would be a glorious task; for to justify God's ways to man, to expound the mysteriousness of our present being, to interpret God,—is not this the very essence of the ministerial office? All that I can hope however to-day, is not to exhaust the subject, but to furnish hints for thought. Over-statements may be made, illustrations may be inadequate, the new ground of an almost untrodden subject may be torn up too rudely; but remember, we are here to live and die; in a few years it will be all over; meanwhile, what we have to do is to try to understand, and to help one another to understand, what it all means—what this strange and contradictory thing, which we call Life, contains within it.

Do not stop to ask therefore, whether the subject was satisfactorily worked out; let each man be satisfied to have received a germ of thought which he may develope better for himself.

I. The deception of life's promise.
II. The meaning of that deception.

Let it be clearly understood in the first place, the promise never was fulfilled. I do not say the fulfilment was delayed. I say it *never* was fulfilled. Abraham had a few feet of earth, obtained by purchase—beyond that nothing; he died a stranger and a pilgrim in the land. Isaac had a little. So small was Jacob's hold upon his country that the last years of his life were spent in Egypt, and he died a foreigner in a strange land. His descendants came into the land of Canaan, expecting to find it a land flowing with milk and honey; they found hard work to do—war and unrest, instead of rest and peace.

During one brief period, in the history of Israel, the promise may seem to have been fulfilled. It was during the later years of David and the earlier years of Solomon; but we have the warrant of Scripture itself for affirming, that even then the promise was not fulfilled. In the Book of Psalms, David speaks of a hope of entering into a *future* rest. The writer of the Epistle to the Hebrews, quoting this passage, infers from it that God's promise had not been exhausted nor fulfilled, by the entrance into Canaan; for he says, "If Joshua had given them rest then would he not have spoken of another day." Again in this very chapter, after a long list of Hebrew saints—" These *all* died in faith, not having received the promises." To none therefore, had the promise been fulfilled. Accordingly writers on prophecy, in order to get over this difficulty, take for granted that there must be a future fulfilment, because the first was inadequate.

They who believe that the Jews will be restored to their native land, expect it on the express ground that Canaan has never been actually and permanently theirs. A certain tract of country—300 miles in length, by 200 in breadth—must be given, or else they think the promise has been broken. To quote the expression of one of the most eloquent of their writers, "If there be nothing yet future for Israel, then the magnificence of the promise has been lost in the poverty of its accomplishment."

I do not quote this to prove the correctness of the interpretation of the prophecy, but as an acknowledgment which may be taken so far as a proof, that the promise made to Abraham has never been accomplished.

And such is life's disappointment. Its promise is, you shall have a Canaan; it turns out to be a baseless airy dream—toil and warfare—nothing that we can call our own; not the land of rest, by any means. But we will examine this in particulars.

1. Our senses deceive us; we begin life with delusion. Our senses deceive us with respect to distance, shape, and colour. That which afar off seems oval, turns out to be circular, modified by the perspective of distance; that which appears a speck, upon nearer approach becomes a vast body. To the earlier ages the stars presented the delusion of small lamps hung in space. The beautiful berry proves to be bitter and poisonous: that which apparently moves is really at rest: that which seems to be stationary is in perpetual motion: the earth moves: the sun is still. All experience is a correction of life's delusions—a modification, a reversal

of the judgment of the senses: and all life is a lesson on the falsehood of appearances.

2. Our natural anticipations deceive us—I say *natural* in contra-distinction to extravagant expectations. Every human life is a fresh one, bright with hopes that will never be realized. There may be differences of character in these hopes; finer spirits may look on life as the arena of successful deeds, the more selfish as a place of personal enjoyment.

With man the turning point of life may be a profession—with woman, marriage; the one gilding the future with the triumphs of intellect, the other with the dreams of affection; but in every case, life is not what any of them expects, but something else. It would almost seem a satire on existence to compare the youth in the outset of his career, flushed and sanguine, with the aspect of the same being when it is nearly done—worn, sobered, covered with the dust of life, and confessing that its days have been few and evil. Where is the land flowing with milk and honey?

With our affections it is still worse, because they promise more. Man's affections are but the tabernacles of Canaan—the tents of a night; not permanent habitations even for this life. Where are the charms of character, the perfection, and the purity, and the truthfulness, which seemed so resplendent in our friend? They were only the shape of our own conceptions—our creative shaping intellect projected its own fantasies on him: and hence we outgrow our early friendships; outgrow the intensity of all: we dwell in tents; we never find a home, even in the land of promise. Life is an unenjoyable Canaan, with nothing real or substantial in it.

3. Our expectations, resting on revelation, deceive us. The world's history has turned round two points of hope; one, the *first*—the other, the *second* coming of the Messiah.

The magnificent imagery of Hebrew prophecy had described the advent of the Conqueror; He came—"a root out of a dry ground, with no form or comeliness; and when they saw Him there was no beauty in Him that they should desire Him." The victory, predicted in such glowing terms, turned out to be the victory of Submission—the Law of our Humanity, which wins by gentleness and love. The promise in the letter was unfulfilled. For ages the world's hope has been the second advent. The early church expected it in their own day. "We, which are alive, and remain until the coming of our Lord."

The Saviour Himself had said, "This generation shall not pass till all things be fulfilled." Yet the Son of Man has never come; or rather, He has been *ever* coming. Unnumbered times the judgment eagles have gathered together over corruption ripe for condemnation. Times innumerable the separation has been made between good and bad. The promise has not been fulfilled, or it has been fulfilled, but in either case anticipation has been foiled and disappointed.

There are two ways of considering this aspect of life. One is the way of sentiment; the other is the way of faith. The sentimental way is trite enough. Saint, sage, sophist, moralist, and preacher, have repeated in every possible image, till there is nothing new to say, that life is a bubble, a dream, a delusion, a phantasm. The other is the way of faith: the ancient saints felt as keenly as any moralist could feel the brokenness of its promises; they confessed that they were strangers and pilgrims here; they said that they had here no continuing city; but they did not mournfully moralize on this; they said it cheerfully, and rejoiced that it was so. They felt that all was right; they knew that the promise itself had a deeper meaning : they looked undauntedly for "a city which hath foundations."

II. The second inquiry, therefore, is the meaning of this delusiveness.

1. It serves to allure us on. Suppose that a spiritual promise had been made at first to Israel; imagine that they had been informed at the outset that God's rest is inward; that the promised land is only found in the Jerusalem which is above—not material, but immaterial. That rude, gross people, yearning after the fleshpots of Egypt—willing to go back into slavery, so as only they might have enough to eat and drink—would they have quitted Egypt on such terms? Would they have begun one single step of that pilgrimage, which was to find its meaning in the discipline of ages?

We are led through life as we are allured upon a journey. Could a man see his route before him—a flat, straight road, unbroken by bush, or tree, or eminence, with the sun's heat burning down upon it, stretched out in dreary monotony— he could scarcely find energy to begin his task; but the uncertainty of what may be seen beyond the next turn keeps expectation alive. The view that may be seen from yonder summit—the glimpse that may be caught perhaps, as the road winds round yonder knoll—hopes like these, not far distant, beguile the traveller on from mile to mile, and from league to league.

In fact, life is an education. The object for which you educate your son is to give him strength of purpose, self-command, discipline of mental energies; but you do not reveal to your son this aim of his education; you tell him of his place in his class, of the prizes at the end of the year, of the honours to be given at college.

These are not the true incentives to knowledge, such incentives are not the highest—they are even mean, and partially injurious; yet these mean incentives stimulate and lead on, from day to day and from year to year, by a process the principle of which the boy himself is not aware of. So does God lead on, through life's unsatisfying and false reward, ever educating: Canaan first; then the hope of a Redeemer; then the millennial glory.

Now what is remarkable in this is, that the delusion continued to the last; they *all* died in faith, not having received the promises; all were hoping up to the very last, and all died in faith—not in realization; for thus God has constituted the human heart. It never will be believed that this world is unreal. God has mercifully so arranged it, that the idea of delusion is incredible. You may tell the boy or girl as you will that life is a disappointment; yet however you may persuade them to adopt your *tone*, and catch the language of your sentiment, they are both looking forward to some bright distant hope—the rapture of the next vacation, or the unknown joys of the next season—and throwing into it an energy of expectation which only a whole eternity is worth. You may tell the man who has received the heart-shock which in this world, he will not recover, that life has nothing left; yet the stubborn heart still hopes on, ever near the prize—" wealthiest when most undone:" he has reaped the whirlwind, but he will go on still, till life is over, sowing the wind.

Now observe the beautiful result which comes from this indestructible power of believing in spite of failure. In the first centuries, the early Christians believed that the millennial advent was close; they heard the warning of the apostle, brief and sharp, "The time is short." Now suppose that, instead of this, they had seen all the dreary page of Church history unrolled; suppose that they had known that after two thousand years the world would have scarcely spelled out three letters of the meaning of Christianity, where would have been those gigantic efforts,—that life spent as on the very brink of eternity, which characterize the days of the early Church,—and which was after all, only the true life of man in time? It is thus that God has led on His world. He has conducted it as a father leads his child, when the path homeward lies over many a dreary league. He suffers him to beguile the thought of time, by turning aside to pluck now and then a flower, to chase now a butterfly; the butterfly is crushed, the flower fades, but the child is so much nearer home, invigorated and full of health, and scarcely wearied yet.

2. This non-fulfilment of promise fulfils it in a *deeper* way. The account we have given already, were it to end there, would be insufficient to excuse the failure of life's promise; by saying that it allures us would be really to charge God with deception. Now life is not deception, but illusion. We distinguish between illusion and delusion. We may paint wood so as to be taken for stone, iron, or marble; this is delusion: but you may paint a picture, in which rocks, trees, and sky are never mistaken for what they seem, yet produce all the emotion which real rocks, trees, and sky would produce. This is illusion, and this is the painter's art: never for one moment to deceive by attempted imitation, but to produce a mental state in which the feelings are suggested which the natural objects themselves would create. Let us take an instance drawn from life.

To a child a rainbow is a real thing—substantial and palpable; its limb rests on the side of yonder hill; he believes that he can appropriate it to himself; and when, instead of gems and gold hid in its radiant bow, he finds nothing but damp mist—cold, dreary drops of disappointment—that disappointment tells that his belief has been delusion.

To the educated man that bow is a blessed illusion, yet it never once deceives; he does not take it for what it is not, he does not expect to make it his own; he feels its beauty as much as the child could feel it, nay infinitely more—more even from the fact that he knows that it will be transient; but besides and beyond this, to him it presents a deeper loveliness; he knows the laws of light, and the laws of the human soul which gave it being. He has linked it with the laws of the universe, and with the invisible mind of God; and it brings to him a thrill of awe, and the sense of a mysterious, nameless beauty, of which the child did not conceive. It is illusion still; but it has fulfilled the promise. In the realm of spirit, in the temple of the soul, it is the same. All is illusion; "but we look for a city which hath foundations;" and in this the promise is fulfilled.

And such was Canaan to the Israelites. To some doubtless it was delusion. They expected to find their reward in a land of milk and honey. They were bitterly disappointed, and expressed their disappointment loudly enough in their murmurs against Moses, and their rebellion against his successors. But to others, as to Abraham, Canaan was the bright illusion which never deceived, but for ever shone before as the type of something more real. And even taking the promise literally, though they built in tents, and could not call a foot of land their own, was not its beauty theirs? Were not its trellised vines, and glorious pastures, and rich olive-fields, ministers to the enjoyment of those who had all in God, though its milk, and oil, and honey, could not be enjoyed with exclusiveness of appropriation? Yet over and above and beyond this, there was a more blessed fulfilment of the promise; there was "a city which had foundations"—built and made by God—toward which the anticipation of this Canaan was leading them. The Kingdom of God was forming in their souls, for ever disappointing them by the unreal, and teaching them that what is spiritual, and belongs to mind and character alone can be eternal.

We will illustrate this principle from the common walks of life. The principle is, that the reward we get is not the reward for which we worked, but a deeper one; deeper and more permanent. The merchant labours all his life, and the hope which leads him on is perhaps wealth: well, at sixty years of age he attains wealth; is that the reward of sixty years of toil? Ten years of enjoyment, when the senses can enjoy no longer—a country seat, splendid plate, a noble establishment? Oh, no! a reward deeper than he dreamed of. Habits of perseverance: a character trained by industry: that is his reward. He was carried on from year to year by, if he were wise, illusion; if he were unwise, delusion; but he reaped a more enduring substance in himself.

Take another instance: the public man, warrior, or statesman, who has served his country, and complains at last in bitter disappointment, that his country has not fulfilled his expectations in rewarding him—that is, it has not given him titles, honours, wealth. But titles, honours, wealth—are these the rewards of well-doing? can they reward it? would it be well-doing if they could? To *be* such a man, to have the power of *doing* such deeds, what could be added to that reward by having? This same apparent contradiction, which was found in Judaism, subsists too in Christianity; we will state it in the words of an apostle: "Godliness is profitable for all things; having the promise of the life that now is, as well as of that which is to come." Now for the fulfilment: "If in this life only we have hope in Christ, then are we of all men most miserable."

Godliness is profitable; but its profit it appears, consists in finding that all is loss: yet in this way you teach your son. You will tell him that if he will be good all men will love him. You say that "Honesty is the best policy," yet in your heart of hearts you know that you are leading him on by a delusion. Christ was good. Was he loved by all? In proportion as he—your son—is like Christ, he will be loved, not by the many, but by the few. Honesty is *not* the best *policy;* the commonplace honesty of the market-place may be—the vulgar honesty which goes no further than paying debts accurately; but that transparent Christian honesty of a life which in every act is bearing witness to the truth, that is not the way to *get on* in life—the reward of such a life is the Cross. Yet you were right in teaching your son this: you told him what was true; truer than he could comprehend. It *is* better to be honest and good; better than he can know or dream: better even in this life; better by so much as *being* good is better than *having* good. But, in a rude coarse way, you must express the blessedness on a level with his capacity; you must state the truth in a way which he will inevitably interpret falsely. The true interpretation nothing but experience can teach.

And this is what God does. His promises are true, though illusive; far truer than we at first take them to be. We work for a mean, low, sensual happiness, all the while He is leading us on to a spiritual blessedness—unfathomably deep. This is the life of faith. We live by faith, and not by sight.

We do not preach that all is diappointment—the dreary creed of sentimentalism; but we preach that *nothing* here is disappointment, if rightly understood. We do not comfort the poor man, by saying that the riches that he has not now he will have hereafter—the difference between himself and the man of wealth being only this, that the one has for time what the other will have for eternity; but what we say is, that that which you have failed in reaping here, you never will reap, if you expected the harvest of Canaan. God has no Canaan for His own; no milk and honey for the luxury of the senses: for the city which hath foundations is built in the soul of man. He in whom Godlike character dwells, has all the universe for his own—"All things," saith the apostle, "are yours; whether life or death, or things present, or things to come; if ye be Christ's, then are ye Abraham's seed, and heirs according to the *promise*."

VII.

Preached June 23, 1850.

THE SACRIFICE OF CHRIST.

"For the love of Christ constraineth us; because we thus judge, that if one died for all, then were all dead; and that He died for all that they which live should not henceforth live unto themselves, but unto Him which died for them, and rose again."—2 Corinthians v. 14, 15.

IT may be, that in reading these verses some of us have understood them in a sense foreign to that of the apostle. It may have seemed that the arguments ran thus —Because Christ died upon the cross for *all*, therefore all must have been in a state of spiritual death before; and if they were asked what doctrines are to be elicited from this passage they would reply, "the doctrine of universal depravity, and the constraining power of the gratitude due to Him who died to redeem us from it." There is, however, in the first place, this fatal objection to such an interpretation, that the death here spoken of is used in two diametrically opposite senses. In reference to Christ, death literal—in reference to all, death spiritual. Now, in the thought of St. Paul, the death of Christ was always viewed as liberation from the power of evil: "in that he died, he died unto sin once," and again, "he that is dead is free from sin." The literal death then in one clause, means *freedom* from sin; the spiritual death of the next is *slavery*

The Sacrifice of Christ.   91

to it. Wherein then, lies the cogency of the apostle's reasoning? How does it follow that because Christ died to evil, all before that must have died to God? Of course that doctrine is true in itself, but it is *not* the doctrine of the text.

In the next place, the ambiguity belongs only to the English word—it is impossible to make the mistake in the original: the word which stands for *were*, is a word which does not imply a continued state, but must imply a single finished act. It cannot by any possibility imply that before the death of Christ men *were* in a state of death—it can only mean, they became dead at the moment when Christ died. If you read it thus, the meaning of the English will emerge—"if one died for all, then all died;" and the apostle's argument runs thus, that if one acts as the representative of all, then his act is the act of all. If the ambassador of a nation makes reparation in a nation's name, or does homage for a nation, that reparation, or that homage, is the nation's act—if *one* did it *for* all, then *all* did it. So that instead of inferring that because Christ died for all, therefore before that all were dead to God, his natural inference is that therefore all are now dead to sin.

Once more, the conclusion of the apostle is exactly the reverse of that which this interpretation attributes to him: he does not say that Christ died in order that men might *not* die, but exactly for this very purpose, that they *might* die; and this death he represents in the next verse by an equivalent expression—the life of unselfishness: "that they which live might henceforth live not unto themselves." The "dead" of the first verse are "they that live" of the second.

The form of thought finds its exact parallel in Romans vi. 10, 11. Two points claim our attention:—

    I. The vicarious sacrifice of Christ.
    II. The influence of that sacrifice on man.

    I. The vicariousness of the sacrifice is implied in the word "for." A vicarious act is an act done for another. When the Pope calls himself the vicar of Christ, he implies that he acts for Christ. The vicar or viceroy of a kingdom is one who acts for the king—a vicar's act therefore is virtually the act of the principal whom he represents; so that if the Papal doctrine were true, when the vicar of Christ *pardons*, Christ has pardoned. When the viceroy of a kingdom has published a proclamation or signed a treaty, the sovereign himself is bound by those acts.

    The truth of the expression *for all*, is contained in this fact, that Christ is the representative of Humanity—properly speaking, the representative of human nature. This is the truth contained in the emphatic expression, "Son of Man." What Christ did *for* Humanity was done by Humanity, because in the name of Humanity. For a truly vicarious act does not supersede the principal's duty of performance, but rather implies and acknowledges it. Take the case from which this very word of vicar has received its origin. In the old monastic times, when the revenues of a cathedral or a cure fell to the lot of a monastery, it became the duty of that monastery to perform the religious services of the cure. But inasmuch as the monastery was a corporate body, they appointed one of their number, whom they denominated their vicar, to discharge those offices for them. His service did not supersede theirs, but was a perpetual and standing acknowledgement that they, as a whole and individually, were under the obligation to perform it. The act of Christ is the act of Humanity—that which all Humanity is bound to do. His righteousness does not supersede our righteousness, nor does His sacrifice supersede our sacrifice. It is the representation of human life and human sacrifice—vicarious for all, yet binding upon all.

That He died for all is true—

1. Because He was the victim of the sin of all. In the peculiar phraseology of St. Paul, he died unto sin. He was the victim of Sin—He died by sin. It is the appalling mystery of our redemption that the Redeemer took the attitude of subjection to evil. There was scarcely a form of evil with which Christ did not come in contact, and by which He did not suffer. He was the victim of false friendship and ingratitude, the victim of bad government and injustice. He fell a sacrifice to the vices of all classes—to the selfishness of the rich and the fickleness of the poor:—intolerance, formalism, scepticism, hatred of goodness, were the foes which crushed Him.

In the proper sense of the word He was a victim. He did not adroitly wind through the dangerous forms of evil, meeting it with expedient silence. Face to face, and front to front, He met it, rebuked it, and defied it; and just as truly as he is a voluntary victim whose body opposing the progress of the car of Juggernaut is crushed beneath its monstrous wheels, was He a victim to the world's sin: because pure, He was crushed by impurity; because just and real and true, He waked up the rage of injustice, hypocrisy, and falsehood.

Now this sin was the sin of all. Here arises at once a difficulty: it seems to be most unnatural to assert that in any one sense He was the sacrifice of the sin of all. We did not betray Him—that was Judas's act—Peter denied Him—Thomas doubted—Pilate pronounced sentence—it must be a figment to say that these were our acts; we did not watch Him like the Pharisees, nor circumvent Him like the Scribes and lawyers; by what possible sophistry can we be involved in the complicity of that guilt? The savage of New Zealand who never heard of Him, the learned Egyptian and the voluptuous Assyrian who died before He came; how was it the sin of all?

The reply that is often given to this query is wonderfully unreal. It is assumed that Christ was conscious, by His Omniscience, of the sins of all mankind; that the duplicity of the child, and the crime of the assassin, and every unholy thought that has ever passed through a human bosom, were present to His mind in that awful hour as if they were His own. This is utterly unscriptural. Where is the single text from which it can be, except by force, extracted? Besides this, it is fanciful and sentimental; and again it is dangerous, for it represents the whole Atonement as a fictitious and shadowy transaction. There is a mental state in which men have felt the burthen of sins which they did not commit. There have been cases in which men have been mysteriouly excruciated with the thought of having committed the unpardonable sin. But to represent the mental phenomena of the Redeemer's mind as in any way resembling this—to say that His conscience was oppressed with the responsibility of sins which He had not committed—is to confound a state of sanity with the delusions of a half lucid mind, and the workings of a healthy conscience with those of one unnatural and morbid.

There is a way however, much more appalling and much

more true, in which this may be true, without resorting to any such fanciful hypothesis. Sin has a great power in this world: it gives laws like those of a sovereign, which bind us all, and to which we are all submissive. There are current maxims in church and state, in society, in trade, in law, to which we yield obedience. For this obedience every one is responsible; for instance in trade, and in the profession of law, every one is the servant of practices the rectitude of which his heart can only half approve—every one complains of them, yet all are involved in them. Now, when such sins reach their climax, as in the case of national bankruptcy or an unjust acquittal, there may be some who are in a special sense, the actors in the guilt; but evidently, for the bankruptcy, each member of the community is responsible in that degree and so far as he himself acquiesced in the duplicities of public dealing; every careless juror, every unrighteous judge, every false witness, has done his part in the reduction of society to that state in which the monster injustice has been perpetrated. In the riot of a tumultuous assembly by night, a house may be burnt, or a murder committed; in the eye of the law, all who are aiding and abetting there are each in his degree responsible for that crime; there may be difference in guilt, from the degree in which he is guilty who with his own hand perpetrated the deed, to that of him who merely joined the rable from mischievous curiosity—degrees from that of wilful murder to that of more or less excusable homicide.

The Pharisees were declared by the Saviour to be guilty of the blood of Zacharias, the blood of righteous Abel, and of all the saints and prophets who fell before He came. But how were the Pharisees guilty? They built the sepulchres of the prophets, they honoured and admired them; but they were guilty, in that they were the children of those that slew the prophets; children in this sense, that they inherited their *spirit*, they opposed the good in the form in which it showed itself in *their day*, just as their fathers opposed the form displayed to theirs; therefore He said that they belonged to the same confederacy of evil, and that the guilt of the blood of all who had been slain should rest on that generation. Similarly we are guilty of the death of Christ. If you have been a false friend, a sceptic, a cowardly disciple, a formalist, selfish, an opposer of goodness, an oppressor, whatever evil you have done, in that degree and so far you participate in the evil to which the Just One fell a victim—you are one of that mighty rabble which cry, " Crucify Him, Crucify Him!" for your sin He died; His blood lies at your threshold.

Again, He died for all, in that His sacrifice represents the sacrifice of all. We have heard of the doctrine of "imputed righteousness;" it is a theological expression to which meanings foolish enough are sometimes attributed, but it contains a very deep truth, which it shall be our endeavour to elicit.

Christ is the realized idea of our Humanity. He is God's idea of Man completed. There is every difference between the ideal and the actual—between what a man aims to be and what he is; a difference between the race as it is, and the race as it existed in God's creative idea when he pronounced it very good.

In Christ, therefore, God beholds Humanity; in Christ He sees perfected every one in whom Christ's spirit exists in germ. He to whom the possible is actual, to whom what will be already *is*, sees all things *present*, gazes on the imperfect, and sees it in its perfection. Let me venture an illustration. He who has never seen the vegetable world except in Arctic regions, has but a poor idea of the majesty of vegetable life,—a microscopic red moss tinting the surface of the snow, a few stunted pines, and here and there perhaps a dwindled oak; but to the botanist who has seen the luxuriance of vegetation in its tropical magnificence, all that wretched scene presents another aspect; to him those dwarfs are the representatives of what might be, nay, what has been in a kindlier soil and a more genial climate; he fills up by his conception the miserable actuality presented by these shrubs, and attributes to them—imputes, that is, to them—the majesty of which the undeveloped germ exists already.

Now the difference between those trees seen in themselves, and seen in the conception of their nature's perfectness which has been previously realized, is the difference between man seen in himself and seen in Christ. We are feeble, dwarfish, stunted specimens of Humanity. Our best resolves are but withered branches, our holiest deeds unripe and blighted fruit; but to the Infinite Eye, who sees in the perfect One the type and assurance of that which shall be, this dwindled Humanity of ours is divine and glorious. Such are we in the sight of God the Father as is the very Son of God Himself. This is what theologians, at least the wisest of them, meant by "imputed righteousness." I do not mean that all who have written or spoken on the subject had this conception of it, but I believe they who thought truly meant this; they did not suppose that in imputing righteousness there was a kind of figment, a self-deception in the mind of God; they did not mean that by an act of will He chose to consider that every act which Christ did was done by us; that He imputed or reckoned to us the baptism in Jordan and the victory in the wilderness, and the agony in the garden, or that He believed, or acted as if He believed, that when Christ died, each one of us died: but He saw Humanity submitted to the law of self-sacrifice; in the light of that idea He beholds us as perfect, and is satisfied. In this sense the apostle speaks of those that are imperfect, yet "by one offering He hath perfected for ever them that are sanctified." It is true again, that He died for us, in that we present His sacrifice as ours. The value of the death of Christ consisted in the surrender of self-will. In the fortieth Psalm, the value of every other kind of sacrifice being first denied, the words follow, "then said I, Lo, I come to do thy will, O God." The profound idea contained, therefore, in the death of Christ is the duty of self-surrender.

But in *us* that surrender scarcely deserves the name; even to use the word self-sacrifice covers us with a kind of shame. Then it is that there is an almost boundless joy in acquiescing in the life and death of Christ, recognizing it as ours, and representing it to ourselves and God as what we aim at. If we cannot understand how in this sense it can be a sacrifice for us, we may partly realize it by remembering the joy of feeling how art and nature realize for us what we cannot realize for ourselves. It is recorded of one of the world's gifted painters that he stood before the master-piece of the great genius of his age—one which he could never hope to equal, nor even rival—and yet the infinite superiority, so far from crushing him, only elevated his feeling, for he saw realized those conceptions which had floated before him, dim and unsubstantial; in every line and touch he felt a spirit immeasurably superior yet kindred, and he is reported to have exclaimed, with dignified humility, "And I too am a painter!"

We must all have felt, when certain effects in nature, combinations of form and colour, have been presented to us, our own idea speaking in intelligible and yet celestial language; when for instance, the long bars of purple, "edged with intolerable radiance," seemed to float in a sea of pale pure green, when the whole sky seemed to reel with thunder, when the night wind moaned. It is wonderful how the most commonplace men and women, beings who, as you would have thought, had no conception that rose beyond a commercial speculation, or a fashionable entertainment, are elevated by such scenes; how the slumbering grandeur of their nature wakes and acknowledges kindred with the sky and storm. "I cannot speak," they would say, "the feelings which are in me; I have had emotions, aspirations, thoughts; I cannot put them into words. Look there! listen now to the storm! That is what I meant, only I never could say it out till now." Thus do art and nature speak for us, and thus do we adopt them as our own. This is the way in which His righteousness becomes righteousness for us. This is the way in which the heart presents to God the sacrifice of Christ; gazing on that perfect Life we, as it were, say, "There, that is my religion—that is my righteousness—what I want to be, which I am not—that is my offering, my life as I would wish to give it, freely and not checked, entire and perfect." So the old prophets, their hearts big with unutterable thoughts, searched "what or what manner of time the spirit of Christ which was in them did signify, when it testified beforehand of the sufferings of Christ, and of the glory which should follow;" and so with us, until it passes into prayer: "My Saviour, fill up the blurred and blotted sketch which my clumsy hand has drawn of a divine life, with the fullness of Thy perfect picture. I feel the beauty which I cannot realize :—robe me in Thine unutterable purity :—

> " Rock of ages cleft for me,
> Let me hide myself in Thee."

II. The influence of that Sacrifice on man is the introduction of the principle of self-sacrifice into his nature,—" then were all dead." Observe again, not He died that we might not die, but that in His death we might be dead, and that in His sacrifice we might become each a sacrifice to God. Moreover, this death is identical with life. They who in the first sentence, are called dead, are in the second denominated " they who live." So in another place, " I am crucified with Christ, nevertheless I live ; " death, therefore—that is the sacrifice of self—is equivalent to life. Now, this rests upon a profound truth. The death of Christ was a representation of the life of God. To me this is the profoundest of all truths, that the whole of the life of God is the sacrifice of self. God is Love ; love is sacrifice—to give rather than to receive—the blessedness of self-giving. If the life of God were not such it would be a falsehood, to say that God is Love ; for even in our human nature, that which seeks to enjoy all instead of giving all, is known by a very different name from that of love. All the life of God is a flow of this divine self-giving charity. Creation itself is sacrifice—the self-impartation of the divine Being. Redemption too, is sacrifice, else it could not be love ; for which reason we will not surrender one iota of the truth that the death of Christ was the sacrifice of God—the manifestation once in time of that which is the eternal law of His life.

If man therefore, is to rise into the life of God, he must be absorbed into the spirit of that sacrifice—he must die with Christ if he would enter into his proper life. For sin is the withdrawing into self and egotism, out of the vivifying life of God, which alone is our true life. The moment the man sins he dies. Know we not how awfully true that sentence is, "Sin revived, and I died?" The vivid life of sin is the death of the man. Have we never felt that our true existence has absolutely in that moment disappeared, and that *we* are not?

I say therefore, that real human life is a perpetual completion and repetition of the sacrifice of Christ—"all are dead;" the explanation of which follows, "to live not to themselves, but to Him who died for them and rose again." This is the truth which lies at the bottom of the Romish doctrine of the mass. Rome asserts that in the mass a true and proper sacrifice is offered up for the sins of all—that the offering of Christ is for ever repeated. To this Protestantism has objected vehemently, that there is but one offering once offered—an objection in itself entirely true; yet the Romish doctrine contains a truth which it is of importance to disengage from the gross and material form with which it has been overlaid. Let us hear St. Paul, "I fill up that which is behindhand of the sufferings of Christ, in my flesh, for His body's sake, which is the Church." Was there then, something behindhand of Christ's sufferings remaining uncompleted, of which the sufferings of Paul could be in any sense the complement? He says there was. Could the sufferings of Paul for the Church in any form of correct expression be said to eke out the sufferings that were complete? In one sense it is true to say that there is one offering once offered *for* all. But it is equally true to say that that one offering is valueless, except so far as it is completed and repeated in the life and self-offering *of* all.

This is the Christian's sacrifice. Not mechanically completed in the miserable materialism of the mass, but spiritually in the life of all in whom the Crucified lives. The sacrifice of Christ is done over again in every life which is lived, not to self but, to God.

Let one concluding observation be made—self-denial, self-sacrifice, self-surrender! Hard doctrines, and impossible! Whereupon, in silent hours, we sceptically ask, Is this possible? is it natural? Let preacher and moralist say what they will, I am not here to sacrifice myself for others. God sent me here for happiness, not misery. Now introduce one sentence of this text of which we have as yet said nothing, and the dark doctrine becomes illuminated—"the *love* of Christ constraineth us." Self-denial, for the sake of self-denial, does no good; self-sacrifice for its own sake is no religious act at all. If you give up a meal for the sake of showing power over self, or for the sake of self-discipline, it is the most miserable of all delusions. You are not more religious in doing this than before. This is mere self-culture, and self-culture being occupied for ever about self, leaves you only in that circle of self from which religion is to free you; but to give up a meal that one you love may have it, is properly a religious act—no hard and dismal duty, because made easy by affection. To bear pain for the sake of bearing it has in it no moral quality at all, but to bear it rather than surrender truth, or in order to save another, is positive enjoyment as well as ennobling to the soul. Did you ever receive even a blow meant for another in order to shield that other? Do you not know that there was actual pleasure in the keen pain far beyond the most rapturous thrill of nerve which could be gained from pleasure in the midst of painlessness? Is not the mystic yearning of love expressed in words most purely thus, Let me suffer for him?

This element of love is that which makes this doctrine an intelligible and blessed truth. So sacrifice alone, bare and unrelieved, is ghastly, unnatural, and dead; but self-sacrifice, illuminated by love, is warmth and life; it is the death of Christ, the life of God, the blessedness, and only proper life of man.

VIII.

Preached June 30, 1850.

THE POWER OF SORROW.

"Now I rejoice, not that ye were made sorry, but that ye sorrowed to repentance: for ye were made sorry after a godly manner, that ye might receive damage by us in nothing. For godly sorrow worketh repentance to salvation not to be repented of: but the sorrow of the world worketh death."—2 Corinthians vii. 9, 10.

THAT which is chiefly insisted on in this verse, is the distinction between sorrow and repentance. To grieve over sin is one thing, to repent of it is another.

The apostle rejoiced, not that the Corinthians sorrowed, but that they sorrowed unto repentance. Sorrow has two results; it may end in spiritual life, or in spiritual death; and in themselves, one of these is as natural as the other. Sorrow may produce two kinds of reformation—a transient, or a permanent one—an alteration in habits, which originating in emotion, will last so long as that emotion continues, and then after a few fruitless efforts, be given up,—a repentance which will be repented of; or again, a permanent change, which will be reversed by no after thought—a repentance not to be repented of. Sorrow is in itself, therefore, a thing neither good nor bad: its value depends on the spirit of the person on whom it falls. Fire will inflame straw, soften iron, or harden clay; its effects are determined by the object with which it comes in contact. Warmth developes the energies of life, or helps the progress of decay. It is a great power in the hot-house, a great power also in the coffin; it expands the leaf, matures the fruit, adds precocious vigour to vegetable life: and warmth too developes, with tenfold rapidity, the weltering process of dissolution. So too with sorrow. There are spirits in which it developes the seminal principle of life; there are others in which it prematurely hastens the consummation of irreparable decay. Our subject therefore is the twofold power of sorrow.

I. The fatal power of the sorrow of the world.
II. The life-giving power of the sorrow that is after God.

The simplest way in which the sorrow of the world works death, is seen in the effect of mere regret for worldly loss. There are certain advantages with which we come into the world. Youth, health, friends, and sometimes property. So long as these are continued we are happy; and because happy, fancy ourselves very grateful to God. We bask in the sunshine of His gifts, and this pleasant sensation of sunning ourselves in life we call religion; that state in which we all are before sorrow comes, to test the temper of the metal of which our souls are made, when the spirits are unbroken and the heart buoyant, when a fresh morning is to a young heart what it is to the skylark. The exuberant burst of joy seems a spontaneous hymn to the Father of all blessing, like the matin carol of the bird; but this is not religion: it is the instinctive utterance of happy feeling, having as little of moral character in it, in the happy human being, as in the happy bird.

Nay more—the religion which is only sunned into being by happiness, is a suspicious thing : having been warmed by joy, it will become cold when joy is over; and then when these blessings are removed, we count ourselves hardly treated, as if we had been defrauded of a right; rebellious hard feelings come; then it is you see people become bitter, spiteful, discontented. At every step in the solemn path of life, something must be mourned which will come back no more; the temper that was so smooth becomes rugged and uneven; the benevolence that expanded upon all, narrows into an ever dwindling selfishness—we are alone; and then that death-like loneliness deepens as life goes on. The course of man is-downwards, and he moves with slow and ever more solitary steps, down to the dark silence—the silence of the grave. This is the death of heart; the sorrow of the world has worked death.

Again there is a sorrow of the world, when sin is grieved for in a worldly spirit. There are two views of sin: in one it is looked upon as wrong—in the other, as producing loss —loss for example, of character. In such cases, if character could be preserved before the world, grief would not come; but the paroxysms of misery fall upon our proud spirit when our guilt is made public. The most distinct instance we have of this is in the life of Saul. In the midst of his apparent grief, the thing still uppermost was that he had forfeited his kingly character: almost the only longing was, that Samuel should honour him before his people. And hence it comes to pass, that often remorse and anguish only begin with exposure. Suicide takes place, not when the act of wrong is done, but when the guilt is known, and hence too, many a one becomes hardened who would otherwise have remained tolerably happy; in consequence of which we blame the exposure, not the guilt; we say if it had hushed up, all would have been well; that the servant who robbed his master was ruined by taking away his character; and that if the sin had been passed over, repentance might have taken place, and he might have remained a respectable member of society. Do not think so. It is quite true that remorse was produced by exposure, and that the remorse was fatal; the sorrow which worked death arose from that exposure, and so far exposure may be called the cause: had it never taken place, respectability, and comparative peace, might have continued; but outward respectability is not change of heart.

It is well known that the corpse has been preserved for centuries in the iceberg, or in antiseptic peat; and that when atmospheric air was introduced to the exposed surface it crumbled into dust. Exposure worked dissolution, but it only manifested the death which was already there; so with sorrow, it is not the living heart which drops to pieces, or crumbles into dust, when it is revealed. Exposure did not work death in the Corinthian sinner, but life.

There is another form of grief for sin, which the apostle would not have rejoiced to see; it is when the hot tears come from pride. No two tones of feeling, apparently similar, are more unlike than that in which Saul exclaimed, "I have played the fool exceedingly," and that in which the Publican cried out, "God be merciful to me a sinner." The charge of folly brought against oneself only proves that we feel bitterly for having lost our own self-respect. It is a humiliation to have forfeited the idea which a man had formed of his own character—to find that the very excellence on which he prided himself, is the one in which he has failed. If there were a virtue for which Saul was conspicuous, it was generosity;

yet it was exactly in this point of generosity in which he discovered himself to have failed, when he was overtaken on the mountain, and his life spared by the very man whom he was hunting to the death, with feelings of the meanest jealousy. Yet there was no real repentance there; there was none of that in which a man is sick of state and pomp. Saul could still rejoice in regal splendour, go about complaining of himself to the Ziphites, as if he was the most ill-treated and friendless of mankind; he was still jealous of his reputation, and anxious to be well thought of. Quite different is the tone in which the Publican, who felt himself a sinner, asked for mercy. He heard the contumelious expression of the Pharisee, "this Publican." With no resentment, he meekly bore it as a matter naturally to be taken for granted—"he did not so much as lift up his eyes to heaven;" he was as a worm which turns in agony, but not revenge, upon the foot which treads it into the dust.

Now this sorrow of Saul's too, works death: no merit can restore self-respect; when once a man has found himself out, he cannot be deceived again. The heart is as a stone: a speck of canker corrodes and spreads within. What on this earth remains, but endless sorrow, for him who has ceased to respect himself, and has no God to turn to?

II. The divine power of sorrow.

1. It works repentance. By repentance is meant, in Scripture, change of life, alteration of habits, renewal of heart. This is the aim and meaning of all sorrow. The consequences of sin are meant to wean from sin. The penalty annexed to it is in the first instance, corrective, not penal. Fire burns the child, to teach it one of the truths of

this universe—the property of fire to burn. The first time it cuts its hand with a sharp knife, it has gained a lesson which it never will forget. Now, in the case of pain, this experience is seldom, if ever, in vain. There is little chance of a child forgetting that fire will burn, and that sharp steel will cut; but the moral lessons contained in the penalties annexed to wrong-doing are just as truly intended, though they are by no means so unerring in enforcing their application. The fever in the veins and the headache which succeed intoxication, are meant to warn against excess. On the first occasion they are simply corrective; in every succeeding one they assume more and more a penal character in proportion as the conscience carries with them the sense of ill desert.

Sorrow then, has done its work when it deters from evil; in other words when it works repentance. In the sorrow of the world, the obliquity of the heart towards evil is not cured; it seems as if nothing cured it: heartache and trials come in vain; the history of life at last is what it was at first. The man is found erring where he erred before. The same course, begun with the certainty of the same desperate end which has taken place so often before.

They have reaped the whirlwind, but they will again sow the wind. Hence I believe, that life-giving sorrow is less remorse for that which is irreparable, than anxiety to save that which remains. The sorrow that ends in death hangs in funeral weeds over the sepulchres of the past. Yet the present does not become more wise. Not one resolution is made more firm, nor one habit more holy. Grief is all. Whereas sorrow avails *only* when the past is converted into experience, and from failure lessons are learned which never are to be forgotten.

2. Permanence of alteration; for after all, a steady

reformation is a more decisive test of the value of mourning than depth of grief.

The susceptibility of emotion varies with individuals. Some men feel intensely, others suffer less keenly; but this is constitutional, belonging to nervous temperament, rather than to moral character. *This* is the characteristic of the divine sorrow, that it is a repentance " not repented of;" no transient, short-lived resolutions, but sustained resolve.

And the beautiful law is, that in proportion as the repentance increases the grief diminishes. " I rejoice," says Paul, that " I made you sorry, though it were but for a time." Grief for a time, repentance for ever. And few things more signally prove the wisdom of this apostle than his way of dealing with this grief of the Corinthian. He tried no artificial means of intensifying it—did not urge the duty of dwelling upon it, magnifying it, nor even of gauging and examining it. So soon as grief had done its work, the apostle was anxious to dry useless tears—he even feared lest haply such an one should be swallowed up with overmuch sorrow. "A true penitent," says Mr. Newman, "never forgives himself." O false estimate of the gospel of Christ, and of the heart of man! A proud remorse does not forgive itself the forfeiture of its own dignity; but it is the very beauty of the penitence which is according to God, that at last the sinner, realizing God's forgiveness, does learn to forgive himself. For what other purpose did St. Paul command the Church of Corinth to give ecclesiastical absolution, but in order to afford a symbol and assurance of the Divine pardon, in which the guilty man's grief should not be overwhelming, but that he should become reconciled to himself? What is meant by the Publican's going *down to his house* justified, but that he felt at peace with himself and God?

3. It is sorrow with God—here called godly sorrow; in the margin sorrowing according to God.

God sees sin not in its consequences but in itself: a thing infinitely evil, even if the consequences were happiness to the guilty instead of misery. So sorrow according to God, is to see sin as God sees it. The grief of Peter was as bitter as that of Judas. He went out and wept bitterly; how bitterly none can tell but they who have learned to look on sin as God does. But in Peter's grief there was an element of hope; and that sprung precisely from this—that he saw God in it all. Despair of self did not lead to despair of God.

This is the great, peculiar feature of this sorrow: God is there, accordingly self is less prominent. It is not a microscopic self-examination, nor a mourning in which self is ever uppermost: *my* character gone; the greatness of *my* sin; the forfeiture of *my* salvation. The thought of God absorbs all that. I believe the feeling of true penitence would express itself in such words as these:—There *is* a righteousness, though I have not attained it. There is a purity, and a love, and a beauty, though my life exhibits little of it. In that I can rejoice. Of that I can feel the surpassing loveliness. My doings? They are worthless, I cannot endure to think of them. I am not thinking of them. I have something else to think of. There, there; in that Life I see it. And so the Christian—gazing not on what he is, but on what he desires to be—dares in penitence to say, That righteousness is mine: dares, even when the recollection of his sin is most vivid and most poignant, to say with Peter, thinking less of himself than of God, and sorrowing as it were with God—"Lord, Thou knowest all things, Thou knowest that I love Thee."

IX.

Preached August 4, 1850.

SENSUAL AND SPIRITUAL EXCITEMENT.

"Wherefore be ye not unwise, but understanding what the will of the Lord is. And be not drunk with wine, wherein is excess; but be filled with the Spirit."—Ephesians v. 17, 18.

THERE is evidently a connection between the different branches of this sentence—for ideas cannot be properly contrasted which have not some connection—but what that connection is, is not at first sight clear. It almost appears like a profane and irreverent juxtaposition to contrast fulness of the Spirit with fulness of wine. Moreover, the structure of the whole context is antithetical. Ideas are opposed to each other in pairs of contraries; for instance, "fools" is the exact opposite to "wise;" "unwise," as opposed to "understanding," its proper opposite.

And here again, there must be the same true antithesis between drunkenness and spiritual fulness. The propriety of this opposition lies in the intensity of feeling produced in both cases. There is one intensity of feeling produced by stimulating the senses, another by vivifying the spiritual life within. The one commences with impulses from without, the other is guarded by forces from within. Here then is the similarity, and here the dissimilarity, which constitutes the propriety of the contrast. One is ruin, the other salvation. One degrades, the other exalts. This contrast then is our subject for to-day.

I. The effects are similar. On the day of Pentecost, when the first influences of the Spirit descended on the early Church, the effects resembled intoxication. They were full of the Spirit, and mocking bystanders said, "These men are full of new wine;" for they found themselves elevated into the ectasy of a life higher than their own, possessed of powers which they could not control; they spoke incoherently and irregularly; to the most part of those assembled, unintelligibly.

Now compare with this the impression produced upon savage nations — suppose those early ages in which the spectacle of intoxication was presented for the first time. They saw a man under the influence of a force different from and in some respects inferior to, their own. To them the bacchanal appeared a being half inspired; his frenzy seemed a thing for reverence and awe, rather than for horror and disgust; the spirit which possessed him must be they thought, divine; they deified it, worshipped it under different names as a god; even to a clearer insight the effects are wonderfully similar. It is almost proverbial among soldiers that the daring produced by wine is easily mistaken for the self-devotion of a brave heart.

The play of imagination in the brain of the opium-eater is as free as that of genius itself, and the creations produced in that state by the pen or pencil are as wildly beautiful as those owed to the nobler influences. In years gone by, the oratory of the statesman in the senate has been kindled by semi-intoxication, when his noble utterances were set down by his auditors to the inspiration of patriotism.

It is this very resemblance which deceives the drunkard: he is led on by his feelings as well as by his imagination. It is not the sensual pleasure of the glutton that fascinates him; it is those fine thoughts and those quickened sensibilities which were excited in that state, which he is powerless to produce out of his own being, or by his own powers, and which he expects to reproduce by the same means. The experience of our first parent is repeated in him: at the very moment when he expects to find himself as the gods, knowing good and evil, he discovers that he is unexpectedly degraded, his health wrecked, and his heart demoralized. Hence it is almost as often the finer as the baser spirits of our race which are found the victims of such indulgence. Many will remember while I speak, the names of the gifted of their species, the degraded men of genius who were the victims of these deceptive influences. The half-inspired painter, poet, musician, who began by soothing opiates to calm the over-excited nerves, or stimulate the exhausted brain, who mistook the sensation for somewhat half divine, and became morally and physically wrecks of manhood, degraded even in their mental conceptions. It was therefore, no mere play of words which induced the apostle to bring these two things together. That which might else seem irreverent appears to have been a deep knowledge of human nature; he contrasts, because his rule was to distinguish two things which are easily mistaken for each other.

2. The second point of resemblance is the necessity of intense feeling. We have fulness—fulness, it may be, produced by outward stimulus, or else by an inpouring of the Spirit. What we want is life, "more life, and fuller." To

escape from monotony, to get away from the life of mere routine and habits, to feel that we are alive—with more of surprise and wakefulness in our existence. To have less of the gelid, torpid, tortoise-like existence. "To feel the years before us." To be consciously existing.

Now this desire lies at the bottom of many forms of life which are apparently as diverse as possible. It constitutes the fascination of the gambler's life: money is not what he wants—were he possessed of thousands to-day he would risk them all to-morrow—but it is that being perpetually on the brink of enormous wealth and utter ruin, he is compelled to realize at every moment the possibility of the extremes of life. Every moment is one of feeling. This too, constitutes the charm of all those forms of life in which the gambling feeling is predominant—where a sense of skill is blended with a mixture of chance. If you ask the statesman why it is, that possessed as he is of wealth, he quits his princely home for the dark metropolis, he would reply, "That he loves the excitement of a political existence." It is this too, which gives to the warrior's and the traveller's existence such peculiar reality; and it is this in a far lower form which stimulates the pleasure of a fashionable life—which sends the votaries of the world in a constant round from the capital to the watering place, and from the watering place to the capital; what they crave for is the power of feeling intensely.

Now the proper and natural outlet for this feeling is the life of the Spirit. What is religion but fuller life? To live in the Spirit, what is it but to have keener feelings and mightier powers—to rise into a higher consciousness of life? What is religion's self but feeling? The highest form of religion is charity. Love is of God, and he that loveth is born of God, and knoweth God. This is an intense feeling, too intense to be excited, profound in its calmness, yet it rises at times in its higher flights into that ecstatic life which glances in a moment intuitively through ages. These are the pentecostal hours of our existence, when the Spirit comes as a mighty rushing wind, in cloven tongues of fire, filling the soul with God.

II. The dissimilarity or contrast in St. Paul's idea. The one fulness begins from without, the other from within. The one proceeds from the flesh and then influences the emotions. The other reverses this order. Stimulants like wine, inflame the senses, and through them set the imaginations and feelings on fire; and the law of our spiritual being is, that that which begins with the flesh, sensualizes the Spirit—whereas that which commences in the region of the Spirit, spiritualizes the senses in which it subsequently stirs emotion. But the misfortune is that men mistake this law of their emotions; and the fatal error is, when having found spiritual feelings existing in connection, and associated with, fleshly sensations, men expect by the mere irritation of the emotions of the frame to reproduce those high and glorious feelings.

You might conceive the recipients of the Spirit on the day of Pentecost acting under this delusion; it is conceiveable that having observed certain bodily phenomena—for instance, incoherent utterances and thrilled sensibilities coexisting with those sublime spiritualities—they might have endeavoured, by a repetition of those incoherencies, to obtain a fresh descent of the Spirit. In fact, this was exactly what was tried in after ages of the Church. In those events of church history which are denominated revivals, in the camp of the Methodist and the Ranter, a direct attempt was made to arouse the emotions by exciting addresses and vehement language. Convulsions, shrieks, and violent emotions, were produced, and the unfortunate victims of this mistaken attempt to produce the cause by the effect, fancied themselves, and were pronounced by others, converted. Now the misfortune is, that this delusion is the more easy from the fact that the results of the two kinds of causes resemble each other. You may galvanize the nerve of a corpse till the action of a limb startles the spectator with the appearance of life. It is not life, it is only a spasmodic hideous mimicry of life. Men having seen that the spiritual is always associated with forms, endeavour by reproducing the forms to recall spirituality; you do produce thereby a something that looks like spirituality, but it is a resemblance only. The worst case of all occurs in the department of the affections. That which begins in the heart ennobles the whole animal being, but that which begins in the inferior departments of our being is the most entire degradation and sensualizing of the soul.

Now it is from this point of thought that we learn to extend the apostle's principle. Wine is but a specimen of a class of stimulants. All that begins from *without* belongs to the same class. The stimulus may be afforded by almost any enjoyment of the senses. Drunkenness may come from anything wherein is excess: from over-indulgence in society, in pleasure, in music, and in the delight of listening to oratory, nay, even from the excitement of sermons and religious meetings. The prophet tells us of those who are drunken, and not with wine.

The other point of difference is one of effect. Fulness of the Spirit calms; fulness produced by excitement satiates and exhausts. They who know the world of fashion tell us that the tone adopted there is, either to be, or to affect to be, sated with enjoyment, to be proof against surprise, to have lost all keenness of enjoyment, and to have all keenness of wonder gone. That which ought to be men's shame becomes their boast—unsusceptibility of any fresh emotion.

Whether this be real or affected matters not; it is, in truth, the real result of the indulgence of the senses. The law is this: the "crime of sense is avenged by sense which wears with time;" for it has been well remarked that the terrific punishment attached to the habitual indulgence of the senses is, that the incitements to enjoyment increase in proportion as the power of enjoyment fades.

Experience at last forbids even the hope of enjoyment; the sin of the intoxicated soul is loathed, detested, abhorred; yet it is done. The irritated sense, like an avenging fury, goads on with a restlessness of craving, and compels a reiteration of the guilt though it has ceased to charm.

To this danger our own age is peculiarly exposed. In the earlier and simpler ages, the need of keen feeling finds a natural and safe outlet in compulsory exertions. For instance, in the excitement of real warfare, and in the necessity of providing the sustenance of life, warlike habits and healthy labour stimulate, without exhausting life. But in proportion as civilization advances, a large class of the community are exempted from the necessity of these, and thrown upon a life of leisure. Then it is that artificial life begins, and artificial expedients become necessary to sharpen the feelings amongst the monotony of existence; every amusement and all literature become more pungent in their character; life is no longer a thing proceeding from powers *within*, but sustained by new impulses from without.

There is one peculiar form of this danger to which I would specially direct your attention. There is one nation in Europe which, more than any other, has been subjected to these influences. In ages of revolution, nations live fast; centuries of life are passed in fifty years of time. In such a state, individuals become subjected more or less to the influences which are working around them. Scarcely an enjoyment or a book can be met with which does not bear the impress of this intensity. Now, the particular danger to which I allude is French novels, French romances, and French plays. The overflowings of that cup of excitement have reached our shores. I do not say that these works contain anything coarse or gross—better if it were so: evil which comes in a form of grossness is not nearly so dangerous as that which comes veiled in gracefulness and sentiment. Subjects which are better not touched upon at all are discussed, examined, and exhibited in all the most seductive forms of imagery. You would be shocked at seeing your son in a fit of intoxication; yet, I say it solemnly, better that your son should reel through the streets in a fit of drunkenness, than that the delicacy of your daughter's mind should be injured, and her imagination inflamed with false fire. Twenty-four hours will terminate the evil in the one case. Twenty-four hours will not exhaust the effects of the other; you must seek the consequences at the end of many, many years.

I speak that which I do know; and if the earnest warning of one who has seen the dangers of which he speaks realized, can reach the heart of one Christian parent, he will put a ban on all such works, and not suffer his children's hearts to be excited by a drunkenness which is worse than that of wine. For the worst of it is, that the men of our time are not yet alive to this growing evil; they are elsewhere—in their studies, counting-houses, professions—not knowing the food, or rather poison, on which their wives' and daughters' intellectual life is sustained. It is precisely those who are most unfitted to sustain the danger, whose feelings need restraint instead of spur, and whose imaginations are most inflammable, that are specially exposed to it.

On the other hand, spiritual life calms while it fills. True it is that there are pentecostal moments when such life reaches the stage of ecstasy. But these were given to the Church to prepare her for suffering, to give her martyrs a glimpse of blessedness, which might sustain them afterwards in the terrible struggles of death. True it is that there are pentecostal hours when the soul is surrounded by a kind of glory, and we are tempted to make tabernacles upon the Mount, as if life were meant for rest; but out of that very cloud there comes a voice telling of the Cross, and bidding us descend into the common world again, to simple duties and humble life. This very principle seems to be contained in the text. The apostle's remedy for this artificial feeling is—"Speaking to one another in psalms and hymns, and spiritual songs."

Strange remedy! Occupation fit for children — too simple far for men : as astonishing as the remedy prescribed by the prophet to Naaman—to wash in simple water, and be clean; yet therein lies a very important truth. In ancient medical phraseology, herbs possessed of healing natures were called simples: in God's laboratory, all things that heal are simple—all natural enjoyments—all the deepest—are simple too. At night, man fills his banquet-hall with the glare of splendour which fevers as well as fires the heart; and at the very same hour, as if by intended contrast, the quiet stars of God steal forth, shedding, together with the deepest feeling, the profoundest sense of calm. One from whose knowledge of the sources of natural feeling there lies almost no appeal, has said that to him,

"The meanest flower that blows can give
Thoughts that too often lie too deep for tears."

This is exceedingly remarkable in the life of Christ. No contrast is more striking than that presented by the thought, that that deep and beautiful Life was spent in the midst of mad Jerusalem. Remember the Son of man standing quietly in the porches of Bethesda, when the streets all around were filled with the revelry of innumerable multitudes, who had come to be present at the annual feast. Remember Him pausing to weep over his country's doomed metropolis, unexcited, while the giddy crowd around Him were shouting "Hosanna to the Son of David!" Remember Him in Pilate's judgment-hall, meek, self-possessed, standing in the serenity of Truth, while all around Him was agitation—hesitation in the breast of Pilate, hatred in the bosom of the Pharisees, and consternation in the heart of the disciples.

And this in truth, is what we want: we want the vision of a calmer and simpler Beauty, to tranquillize us in the midst of artificial tastes—we want the draught of a purer spring to cool the flame of our excited life;—we want in other words, the Spirit of the Life of Christ, simple, natural, with power to calm and soothe the feelings which it rouses: the fulness of the Spirit which can never intoxicate!

X.

Preached August 11, 1850.

PURITY.

"Unto the pure all things are pure: but unto them that are defiled and unbelieving is nothing pure; but even their mind and conscience is defiled."—Titus i. 15.

FOR the evils of this world there are two classes of remedies—one is the world's, the other is God's. The world proposes to remedy evil by adjusting the circumstances of this life to man's desires. The world says, give us a perfect set of *circumstances*, and then we shall have a set of perfect men. This principle lies at the root of the system called Socialism. Socialism proceeds on the principle that all moral and even physical evil arises from unjust laws. If the cause be remedied, the effect will be good. But Christianity throws aside all that as merely chimerical. It proves that the fault is not in outward circumstances, but in ourselves. Like the wise physician, who, instead of busying himself with transcendental theories to improve the climate, and the outward circumstances of man, endeavours to relieve and get rid of the tendencies of disease which are from within, Christianity, leaving all outward circumstances to ameliorate themselves, fastens its attention on the spirit which has to deal with them. Christ has declared that the kingdom of heaven is from within. He said to the Pharisee, "Ye make clean the outside of the cup and platter, but within ye are full of extortion and excess." The remedy for all this is a large and liberal charity, so overflowing that "Unto the pure all things are pure." To internal purity all external things *become* pure. The principle that St. Paul has here laid down is, that each man is the creator of his own world; he walks in a universe of his own creation.

As the free air is to one out of health the cause of cold and diseased lungs, so to the healthy man it is a source of greater vigour. The rotten fruit is sweet to the worm, but nauseous to the palate of man. It is the same air and the same fruit acting differently upon different beings. To different men a different world—to one all pollution—to another all purity. To the noble all things are noble, to the mean all things are contemptible.

The subject divides itself into two parts.

I. The apostle's principle.
II. The application of the principle.

Here we have the same principle again; each man creates his own world. Take it in its simplest form. The eye creates the outward world it sees. We see not things as they are, but as God has made the eye to receive them.

In its strictest sense, the creation of a new man is the creation of a new universe. Conceive an eye so constructed as that the planets and all within them should be minutely seen, and all that is near should be dim and invisible like things seen through a telescope, or as we see through a magnifying glass the plumage of the butterfly, and the bloom upon the peach; then it is manifestly clear that we have called into existence actually a new *creation*, and not new objects. The mind's eye creates a world for itself.

Again, the visible world presents a different aspect to each individual man. You will say that the same things you see are seen by all—that the forest, the valley, the flood, and the sea, are the same to all; and yet all these things so seen, to different minds are a myriad of different universes. One man sees in that noble river an emblem of eternity; he closes his lips and feels that GOD is there. Another sees nothing in it but a very convenient road for transporting his spices, silks, and merchandise. To one this world appears useful, to another beautiful. Whence comes the difference? From the soul within us. It can make of this world a vast chaos—" a mighty maze without a plan;" or a mere machine—a collection of lifeless forces; or it can make it the Living Vesture of GOD, the tissue through which He can become visible to us. In the spirit in which we look on it the world is an arena for mere self-advancement, or a place for noble deeds, in which self is forgotten, and GOD is all.

Observe, this effect is traceable even in that produced by our different and changeful moods. We make and unmake a world more than once in the space of a single day. In trifling moods all seems trivial. In serious moods all seems solemn. Is the song of the nightingale merry or plaintive? Is it the voice of joy or the harbinger of gloom? Sometimes one, and sometimes the other, according to our different moods. We hear the ocean furious or exulting. The thunder-claps are grand, or angry, according to the different states of our mind. Nay, the very church bells chime sadly or merrily, as our associations determine. They speak the language of our passing moods. The young adventurer revolving sanguine plans upon the milestone, hears them speak to him as God did to Hagar in the wilderness, bidding him back to perseverance and greatness. The soul spreads its own hue over everything; the shroud or wedding-garment of nature is woven in the loom of our own feelings. This universe is the express image and direct counterpart of the souls that dwell in it. Be noble-minded, and all Nature replies—I am divine, the child of God—be thou too, His child, and noble. Be mean, and all Nature dwindles into a contemptible smallness.

In the second place, there are two ways in which this principle is true. To the pure, all things and all persons are pure, because their purity makes all seem pure.

There are some who go through life complaining of this world; they say they have found nothing but treachery and deceit; the poor are ungrateful, and the rich are selfish, Yet we do not find such the best men. Experience tells us that each man most keenly and unerringly detects in others the vice with which he is most familiar himself.

Persons seem to each man what he is himself. One who suspects hypocrisy in the world is rarely transparent; the man constantly on the watch for cheating is generally dishonest; he who suspects impurity is prurient. This is the principle to which Christ alludes when he says, "Give alms of such things as he have; and behold all things are clean unto you."

Have a large charity! Large "charity hopeth all things." Look at that sublime apostle who saw the churches of Ephesus and Thessalonica pure, because he saw them in his own large love, and painted them, not as they were, but as his heart filled up the picture; he viewed them in the light of his own nobleness, as representations of his own purity.

Once more, to the pure all *things* are pure, as well as all persons. That which is natural lies not in things, but in the minds of men. There is a difference between prudery and modesty. Prudery detects wrong where no wrong is; the wrong lies in the thoughts, and not in the objects. There is something of over-sensitiveness and over-delicacy which shows not innocence, but an inflammable imagination. And men of the world cannot understand that those subjects and thoughts which to them are full of torture, can be harmless, suggesting nothing evil to the pure in heart.

Here however, beware! No sentence of Scripture is more frequently in the lips of persons who permit themselves much license, than the text, " To the pure, all things are pure." Yes, all things natural, but not artificial—scenes which pamper the tastes, which excite the senses. Innocence feels healthily. To it all nature is pure. But, just as the dove trembles at the approach of the hawk, and the young calf shudders at the lion never seen before, so innocence shrinks instinctively from what is wrong by the same divine instinct. If that which is wrong seems pure, then the heart is not pure but vitiated. To the right minded all that is right in the course of this world seems pure. Abraham, looking forward to the destruction of Sodom and Gomorrah, entreated that it might be averted, and afterwards acquiesced! To the disordered mind "all things are out of course." This is the spirit which pervades the whole of the Ecclesiastes. There were two things which were perpetually suggesting themselves to the mind of Solomon; the intolerable sameness of this world, and the constant desire for change. And yet that same world, spread before the serene eye of God, was pronounced to be all "very good."

This disordered universe is the picture of your own mind. We make a wilderness by encouraging artificial wants, by creating sensitive and selfish feelings; then we project everything stamped with the impress of our own feelings, and we gather the whole of creation into our own pained being—"the whole creation groaneth and travaileth in pain together until now." The world you complain of as impure and wrong is not God's world, but your world; the blight, the dullness, the blank, are all your own. The light which is in you has become darkness, and therefore the light itself is dark.

Again, to the pure, all things not only seem pure, but are really so because they are made such.

1. As regards persons. It is a marvellous thing to see how a pure and innocent heart purifies all that it approaches. The most ferocious natures are soothed and tamed by innocence. And so with human beings, there is a delicacy so pure, that vicious men in its presence become almost pure; all of purity which is in them is brought out; like attaches itself to like. The pure heart becomes a centre of attraction, round which similar atoms gather, and from which dissimilar ones are repelled. A corrupt heart elicits in an hour all that is bad in us; a spiritual one brings out and draws to itself all that is best and purest. Such was Christ. He stood in the world, the Light of the world, to which all sparks of light gradually gathered. He stood in the presence of impurity, and men became pure. Note this in the history of Zaccheus. In answer to the invitation of the Son of man, he says, "Behold, Lord, the half of my goods I give to the poor, and if I have done wrong to any man I restore

him fourfold." So also the Scribe, " Well, Master, thou hast well said, there is one God, and there is none other than He." To the pure Saviour, all was pure. He was lifted up on high, and drew all men unto Him."

Lastly, all situations are pure to the pure. According to the world, some professions are reckoned honourable, and some dishonourable. Men judge according to a standard merely conventional, and not by that of moral rectitude. Yet it was in truth, the men who were in these situations which made them such. In the days of the Redeemer, the publican's occupation was a degraded one, merely because low base men filled that place. But since He was born into the world a poor, labouring man, poverty is noble and dignified, and toil is honourable. To the man who feels that "the king's daughter is all glorious within," no outward situation can seem inglorious or impure.

There are three words which express almost the same thing, but whose meaning is entirely different. These are, the gibbet, the scaffold, and the cross. So far as we know, none die on the gibbet but men of dishonourable and base life. The scaffold suggests to our minds the noble deaths of our greatest martyrs. The cross was once a gibbet, but it is now the highest name we have, because He hung on it. Christ has purified and ennobled the cross. This principle runs through life. It is not the situation which makes the man, but the man who makes the situation. The slave may be a freeman. The monarch may be a slave. Situations are noble or ignoble, as we make them.

From all this subject we learn to understand two things. Hence we understand the Fall. When man fell, the world fell with him. All creation received a shock. Thorns, briars, and thistles, sprang up. They were there before, but to the now restless and impatient hands of men they became obstacles and weeds. Death, which must ever have existed as a form of dissolution, a passing from one state to another, became a curse; the sting of death was sin—unchanged in itself, it changed in man. A dark, heavy cloud, rested on it—the shadow of his own guilty heart.

Hence too, we understand the Millennium. The Bible says that these things are not to be for ever. There are glorious things to come. Just as in my former illustration, the alteration of the eye called new worlds into being, so now nothing more is needed than to re-create the soul—the mirror on which all things are reflected. Then is realized the prophecy of Isaiah, " Behold, I create all things new," " new heavens and a new earth."

The conclusion of this verse proves to us why all these new creations were called into being—" wherein dwelleth righteousness." To be righteous makes all things new. We do not want a new world, we want *new hearts*. Let the Spirit of God purify society, and to the pure all things will be pure. The earth will put off the look of weariness and gloom which it has worn so long, and then the glorious language of the prophets will be fulfilled—" The forests will break out with singing, and the desert will blossom as the rose."

XI.

Preached February 9, 1851.

UNITY AND PEACE.

"And let the peace of God rule in your hearts, to the which also ye are called in one body; and be ye thankful."—Colossians iii. 15.

THERE is something in these words that might surprise us. It might surprise us to find that peace is urged on us as a duty. There can be no duty except where there is a matter of obedience; and it might seem to us that peace is a something over which we have no power. It is a privilege to have peace, but it would appear as if there were no power of control within the mind of a man able to ensure that peace for itself. "Yet," says the apostle, "let the peace of God rule in your hearts."

It would seem to *us* as if peace were as far beyond our own control as happiness. Unquestionably, we are not masters on our own responsibility of our own happiness. Happiness is the gratification of every innocent desire; but it is not given to us to ensure the gratification of every desire; therefore, happiness is not a duty, and it is nowhere written in the Scripture, "You must be happy." But we find it written by the apostle Paul, "Be ye thankful," implying therefore, that peace is a duty. The apostle says, "Let the peace of God rule in your hearts;" from which we infer that peace is attainable, and within the reach of our own wills ; that if there be not repose there is blame ; if there be not peace but discord in the heart, there is something wrong.

This is the more surprising when we remember the circumstances under which these words were written. They were written from Rome, where the apostle lay in prison, daily and hourly expecting a violent death. They were written in days of persecution, when false doctrines were rife, and religious animosities fierce; they were written in an epistle abounding with the most earnest and eager controversy, whereby it is therefore implied, that according to the conception of the Apostle Paul, it is possible for a Christian to live at the very point of death, and in the very midst of danger—that it is possible for him to be breathing the atmosphere of religious controversy—it is possible for him to be surrounded by bitterness, and even take up the pen of controversy himself—and yet his soul shall not lose its own deep peace, nor the power of the infinite repose and rest of God. Joined with the apostle's command to be at peace, we find another doctrine, the doctrine of the unity of the Church of Christ. "To the which ye are called in one body," in order that ye may be at peace ; in other words, the unity of the Church of Christ is the basis on which, and on which alone, can be built the possibility of the inward peace of individuals.

And thus, my Christian brethren, our subject divides itself into these two simple branches: in the first place, the unity of the Church of Christ; in the second place, the inward peace of the members of that Church.

The first subject then, which we have to consider, is the Unity of the Church of Christ.

And the first thing we have to do is both clearly to define and understand the meaning of that word "unity." I distinguish the unity of comprehensiveness from the unity of mere singularity. The word one, as oneness, is an ambiguous word. There is a oneness belonging to the army as well as to every soldier in the army. The army is one, and that is the oneness of unity; the soldier is one, but that is the oneness of the unit. There is a difference between the oneness of a body and the oneness of a member of that body. The body is many, and a unity of manifold comprehensiveness. An arm or a member of a body is one, but that is the unity of singularity. Without unity my Christian brethren, peace must be impossible. There can be no peace in the one single soldier of an army. You do not speak of the harmony of one member of a body. There is peace in an army, or in a kingdom joined with other kingdoms; there is harmony in a member united with other members. There is no peace in a unit, there is no possibility of the harmony of that which is but one in itself. In order to have peace you must have a higher unity, and therein consists the unity of God's own Being. The unity of God is the basis of the peace of God—meaning by the unity of God the comprehensive manifoldness of God, and not merely the singularity in the number of God's Being. When the Unitarian speaks of God as one, he means simply singularity of number. We mean that He is of manifold comprehensiveness—that there is unity between His various powers. Amongst the personalities or powers of His Being there is no discord, but perfect harmony, entire union; and that brethren, is repose, the blessedness of infinite rest, that belongs to the unity of God —"I and my Father are one."

The second thing which we observe respecting this

unity, is that it subsists between things not similar or alike, but things dissimilar or unlike. There is no unity in the separate atoms of a sand-pit; they are things similar; there is an aggregate or collection of them. Even if they be hardened in a mass they are not one, they do not form a unity: they are simply a mass. There is no unity in a flock of sheep: it is simply a repetition of a number of things similar to each other. If you strike off from a thousand five hundred, or if you strike off nine hundred, there is nothing lost of unity, because there never was unity. A flock of one thousand or a flock of five is just as much a flock as any other number.

On the other hand, let us turn to the unity of peace which the apostle speaks of, and we find it is something different; it is made up of dissimilar members, without which dissimilarity there could be no unity. Each is imperfect in itself, each supplying what it has in itself to the deficiencies and wants of the other members. So, if you strike off from this body any one member, if you cut off an arm, or tear out an eye, instantly the unity is destroyed; you have no longer an entire and perfect body, there is nothing but a remnant of the whole, a part, a portion; no unity whatever.

This will help us to understand the unity of the Church of Christ. If the ages and the centuries of the Church of Christ, if the different Churches whereof it was composed, if the different members of each Church, were similar—one in this, that they all held the same views, all spoke the same words, all viewed truth from the same side, they would have no unity; but would simply be an aggregate of atoms, the sand-pit over again—units, multiplied it may be to infinity, but you would have no real unity, and therefore, no peace.

No unity,—for wherein consists the unity of the Church of Christ? The unity of ages, brethren, consists it in this—that every age is merely the repetition of another age, and that which is held in one is held in another? Precisely in the same way, that is *not* the unity of the ages of the Christian Church.

Every century and every age has held a different truth, has put forth different fragments of the truth. In early ages for example, by martyrdom was proclaimed the eternal sanctity of truth, rather than give up which a man must lose his life. . . . . In our own age it is quite plain those are not the themes which engage us, or the truths which we put in force now. This age, by its revolutions, its socialisms, proclaims another truth—the brotherhood of the Church of Christ; so that the unity of ages subsists on the same principle as that of the unity of the human body: and just as every separate ray—the violet, the blue, and the orange—make up the white ray, so these manifold fragments of truth blended together make up the one entire and perfect white ray of Truth. And with regard to individuals, taking the case of the Reformation, it was given to one Church to proclaim that salvation is a thing received, and not local; to another to proclaim justification by faith; to another the sovereignty of God; to another the supremacy of the Scriptures; to another the right of private judgment, the duty of the individual conscience. Unite these all, and then you have the Reformation one—one in spite of manifoldness; those very varieties by which they have approached this proving them to be one. Disjoint them and then you have some miserable sect—Calvinism, or Unitarianism; the unity has dispersed. And so again with the unity of the Churches. Whereby would we produce unity? Would we force on other Churches our Anglicanism? Would we have our thirty-nine articles, our creeds, our prayers, our rules and regulations, accepted by every Church throughout the world? If that were unity, then in consistency you are bound to demand that in God's world there shall be but one colour instead of the manifold harmony and accordance of which this universe is full; that there should be but one chaunted note—the one which we conceive most beautiful. This is not the unity of the Church of God. The various Churches advance different doctrines and truths. The Church of Germany something different from those of the Church of England. The Church of Rome, even in its idolatry, proclaims truths which we would be glad to seize. By the worship of the Virgin, the purity of women; by the rigour of ecclesiastical ordinances, the sanctity and permanence of eternal order; by the very priesthood itself, the necessity of the guidance of man by man. Nay, even the dissenting bodies themselves—mere atoms of aggregates as they are—stand forward and proclaim at least this truth, the separateness of the individual conscience, the right of independence.

Peace subsists not between things exactly alike. We do not speak of peace in a single country. We say peace subsists between different countries where war *might* be. There can be no *peace* between two men who agree in everything; peace subsists between those who differ. There is no peace between Baptist and Baptist; so far as they are Baptists, there is perfect accordance and agreement. There may be peace between you and the Romanist, the Jew, or the Dissenter, because there are angles of sharpness which might come into collision if they were not subdued and softened by the power of love. It was given to the Apostle Paul to discern that this was the ground of unity.

In the Church of Christ he saw men with different views, and he said So far from that variety destroying unity, it was the only ground of unity. .There are many doctrines, all of them different, but let those varieties be blended together—in other words, let there be the peace of love, and then you will have unity.

Once more this unity, whereof the apostle speaks, consists in submission to one single influence or spirit. Wherein consists the unity of the body? Consists it not in this,—that there is one life uniting, making all the separate members one? Take away the life, and the members fall to pieces: they are no longer one; decomposition begins, and every element separates, no longer having any principle of cohesion or union with the rest.

There is not one of us who, at some time or other, has not been struck with the power there is in a single living influence. Have we never for instance, felt the power wherewith the orator unites and holds together a thousand men as if they were but one; with flashing eyes and throbbing hearts, all attentive to his words, and by the difference of their attitudes, by the variety of the expressions of their countenances testifying to the unity of that single living feeling with which he had inspired them? Whether it be indignation, whether it be compassion, or whether it be enthusiasm, that one living influence made the thousand for the time, one. Have we not heard how, even in this century in which we live, the various and conflicting feelings of the people of this country were concentrated into one, when the threat of foreign invasion had fused down and broken the edges of conflict and variance, and from shore to shore was heard one cry of terrible defiance, and the different classes and orders of this manifold and mighty England were as one? Have we not heard how the mighty winds hold together, as if one, the various atoms of the desert, so that they rush like a living thing, across the wilderness? And this, brethren, is the unity of the Church of Christ, the subjection to the one uniting spirit of its God.

It will be said, in reply to this, "Why this is mere enthusiasm. It may be very beautiful in theory, but it is impossible in practice. It is mere enthusiasm to believe, that while all these varieties of conflicting opinion remain, we can have unity; it is mere enthusiasm to think that so long as men's minds reckon on a thing like unity, there can be a thing like oneness." And our reply is, Give us the Spirit of God, and we shall be one. You cannot produce a unity by all the rigour of your ecclesiastical discipline. You cannot produce a unity by consenting in some form of expression such as this, "Let us agree to differ." You cannot produce a unity by Parliamentary regulations or enactments, bidding back the waves of what is called aggression. Give us the living Spirit of God, and we shall be one.

Once on this earth was exhibited, as it were, a specimen of perfect anticipation of such an unity, when the "rushing mighty wind" of Pentecost came down in the tongues of fire and sat on every man; when the Parthians, and Medes, and Elamites, and the dwellers in Mesopotamia, the "Cretes and Arabians," the Jew and the Gentile, each speaking one language, yet blended and fused into one unity by enthusiastic love, heard one another speak as it were, in one language, the manifold works of God; when the spirit of giving was substituted for the spirit of mere rivalry and competition, and no man said the things he had were his own, but all shared in common. Let that spirit come again, as come it will, and come it must; and then, beneath the influences of a mightier love, we shall have a nobler and a more real unity.

We pass on now, in the second place, to consider the *individual peace* resulting from this unity. As we have endeavoured to explain what is meant by unity, so now, let us endeavour to understand what is meant by peace. Peace then, is the opposite of passion, and of labour, toil, and effort. Peace is that state in which there are no desires madly demanding an impossible gratification; that state in which there is no misery, no remorse, no sting. And there are but three things which can break that peace. The first is discord between the mind of man and the lot which he is called on to inherit; the second is discord between the affections and powers of the soul; and the third is doubt of the rectitude, and justice, and love, wherewith this world is ordered. But where these things exist not, where a man is contented with his lot, where the flesh is subdued to the spirit, and where he believes and feels with all his heart that all is right, there is peace, and to this says the apostle, "ye are called,"—the grand, peculiar call of Christianity,—the call, "Come unto Me, all ye that labour and are heavy laden, and I will give you rest."

This was the dying bequest of Christ: "Peace I leave with you, my peace I give unto you: not as the world giveth give I unto you:" and therein lies one of the greatest truths of the blessed and eternal character of Christianity, that it applies to, and satisfies the very deepest want and craving of our nature. The deepest want of man is not a desire for happiness, but a craving for peace; not a wish for the gratification of every desire, but a craving for the repose of acquiescence in the will of God; and it is this which

Christianity promises. Christianity does not promise happiness, but it does promise peace. "In the world ye shall have tribulation," saith our Master, "but be of good cheer; I have overcome the world." Now, let us look more closely, into this peace.

The first thing we see respecting it is, that it is called God's peace. God is rest: the infinite nature of God is infinite repose. The "*I am*" of God is contrasted with the *I am become* of all other things. Everything else is in a state of *becoming*, God is in a state of *Being*. The acorn has become the plant, and the plant has become the oak. The child has become the man, and the man has become good, or wise, or whatever else it may be. God ever *is;* and I pray you once more to observe, that this peace of God, this eternal rest in the Almighty Being, arises out of His unity. Not because He is an unit, but because He is an unity. There is no discord between the powers and attributes of the mind of God; there is no discord between His justice and His love; there is no discord demanding some miserable expedient to unite them together, such as some theologians imagined when they described the sacrifice and atonement of our Redeemer by saying, it is the clever expedient whereby God reconciles His justice with His love. God's justice and love are one. Infinite justice must be infinite love. Justice is but another sign of love. The infinite rest of the "*I am*" of God arises out of the harmony of His attributes.

The next thing we observe respecting this divine peace which has come down to man on earth is, that it is a *living peace*. Brethren, let us distinguish. There are several things called peace which are by no means divine or Godlike peace. There is peace, for example, in the man who lives for and enjoys self, with no nobler aspiration goading him on to make him feel the rest of God; that is peace, but that is merely the peace of toil. There is rest on the surface of the caverned lake, which no wind can stir; but that is the peace of stagnation. There is peace amongst the stones which have fallen and rolled down the mountain's side, and lie there quietly at rest; but that is the peace of inanity. There is peace in the hearts of enemies who lie together, side by side, in the same trench of the battle-field, the animosities of their souls silenced at length, and their hands no longer clenched in deadly enmity against each other; but that is the peace of death. If our peace be but the peace of the sensualist satisfying pleasure, if it be but the peace of mental torpor and inaction, the peace of apathy, or the peace of the soul dead in trespasses and sins, we may whisper to ourselves, "Peace, peace," but there will be no peace; *there* is not the peace of unity nor the peace of God, for the peace of God is the living peace of love.

The next thing we observe respecting this peace is, that it is the manifestation of power—it is the peace which comes from an inward power: "Let the peace of God," says the Apostle, "rule within your hearts." For it is a power, the manifestation of strength. There is no peace except there is the possibility of the opposite of peace although now restrained and controlled. You do not speak of the peace of a grain of sand, because it cannot be otherwise than merely insignificant, and at rest. You do not speak of the peace of a mere pond; you speak of the peace of the sea, because there is the opposite of peace implied, there is power and strength. And this brethren, is the real character of the peace in the mind and soul of man. Oh! we make a great mistake when we say there is strength in passion, in the exhibition of emotion. Passion, and emotion, and all those outward manifestations, prove, not strength, but weakness. If the passions of a man are strong, it proves the man himself is weak, if he cannot restrain or control his passions. The real strength and majesty of the soul of man is calmness, the manifestation of strength; "the peace of God" ruling; the word of Christ saying to the inward storms "Peace!" and there is "a great calm."

Lastly, the peace of which the apostle speaks is the peace that is received—the peace of reception. You will observe, throughout this passage the apostle speaks of a something received, and not done: "Let the peace of God rule in your hearts." It is throughout receptive, but by no means inactive. And according to this, there are two kinds of peace; the peace of obedience—"Let the peace of God rule" you—and there is the peace of gratefulness—"Be ye thankful." Very great, brethren, is the peace of obedience: when a man has his lot fixed, and his mind made up, and he sees his destiny before him, and quietly acquiesces in it; his spirit is at rest. Great and deep is the peace of the soldier to whom has been assigned even an untenable position, with the command, "Keep that, even if you die," and he obediently remains to die.

Great was the peace of Elisha—very, very calm are those words by which he expressed his acquiescence in the divine will. "Knowest thou," said the troubled, excited, and restless men around him—"Knowest thou that the Lord will take away thy master from thy head to-day?" He answered, "Yea, I know it; hold ye your peace." Then there is the other peace, it is the peace of gratefulness: "Be ye thankful." It is that peace which the Israelites had when these words were spoken to them on the shores of the

Red Sea, while the bodies of their enemies floated past them, destroyed, but not by them: "Stand still and see the salvation of the Lord."

And here brethren, is another mistake of ours: we look on salvation as a thing to be done, and not received. In God's salvation we can do but little, but there is a great deal to be received. We are here, not merely to act, but to be acted upon. "Let the peace of God rule in your hearts;" there is a peace that will enter there, if you do not thwart it; there is a Spirit that will take possession of your soul, provided that you do not quench it. In this world we are recipients, not creators. In obedience and in gratefulness, and the infinite peace of God in the soul of man, is alone to be found deep calm repose.

XII.

Preached January 4, 1852.

THE CHRISTIAN AIM AND MOTIVE.

"Be ye therefore perfect, even as your Father which is in heaven is perfect."—Matthew v. 48.

THERE are two erroneous views held respecting the character of the Sermon on the Mount. The first may be called an error of worldly-minded men, the other an error of mistaken religionists. Worldly-minded men—men that is, in whom the devotional feeling is but feeble—are accustomed to look upon morality as the whole of religion; and they suppose that the Sermon on the Mount was designed only to explain and enforce correct principles of morality. It tells of human duties and human proprieties, and an attention to these, they maintain, is the only religion which is required by it. Strange my Christian brethren, that men, whose lives are least remarkable for superhuman excellence, should be the very men to refer most frequently to those sublime comments on Christian principle, and should so confidently conclude from thence, that themselves are right and all others are wrong. Yet so it is.

The other is an error of mistaken religionists. They sometimes regard the Sermon on the Mount as if it were a collection of moral precepts, and consequently, strictly speaking, not Christianity at all. To them it seems as if the chief value, the chief intention of the discourse, was to show the breadth and spirituality of the requirements of the law of Moses—its chief religious significance, to show the utter impossibility of fulfilling the law, and thus to lead to the necessary inference that justification must be by faith alone. And so they would not scruple to assert that, in the highest sense of that term, it is not Christianity at all, but only preparatory to it—a kind of spiritual Judaism; and that the higher and more developed principles of Christianity are to be found in the writings of the apostles. Before we proceed further, we would remark here that it seems extremely startling to say that He who came to this world expressly to preach the Gospel, should, in the most elaborate of all His discourses, omit to do so: it is indeed something more than startling, it is absolutely revolting to suppose that the letters of those who spoke *of* Christ, should contain a more perfectly-developed, a freer and fuller Christianity than is to be found in Christ's own words.

Now you will observe that these two parties, so opposed to each other in their general religious views, are agreed in this—that the Sermon on the Mount is nothing but morality. The man of the world says—" It is morality only, and that is the whole of religion." The mistaken religionist says—" It is morality only, not the entire essence of Christianity." In opposition to both these views, we maintain that the Sermon on the Mount contains the sum and substance of Christianity—the very chief matter of the gospel of our Redeemer.

It is not, you will observe, a pure and spiritualized Judaism; it is contrasted with Judaism again and again by Him who spoke it. Quoting the words of Moses, he affirmed,

"So was it spoken by them of old time, but *I say unto you—*" For example, "Thou shalt not forswear thyself, but shalt perform unto the Lord thine oaths." That is Judaism. "But I say unto you swear not at all, but let your yea be yea, and your nay nay." That is Christianity. And that which is the essential peculiarity of this Christianity lies in these two things. First of all, that the morality which it teaches is *disinterested* goodness—goodness not for the sake of the blessing that follows it, but for its own sake, and because it is right. "Love your enemies," is the Gospel precept. Why?—Because if you love them you shall be blessed; and if you do not cursed? No; but "Love your enemies, bless them that curse you, do good to them that hate you, and pray for them which despitefully use you and persecute you, that ye may be the children of"—that is, may be like—"your Father which is in Heaven." The second essential peculiarity of Christianity—and this, too, is an essential peculiarity of this Sermon—is, that it teaches and enforces the law of self-sacrifice. "If thy right eye offend thee pluck it out; if thy right hand offend thee cut it off." This, brethren, is the law of self-sacrifice—the very law and spirit of the blessed cross of Christ.

How deeply and essentially Christian, then, this Sermon on the Mount is, we shall understand if we are enabled in any measure to reach the meaning and spirit of the single passage which I have taken as my text. It tells two things —the Christian aim and the Christian motive.

1st. The Christian aim—perfection. 2nd. The Christian motive—because it is right and Godlike to be perfect.

I. The Christian aim is this—to be perfect. "Be ye therefore perfect." Now distinguish this, I pray you, from mere worldly morality. It is not conformity to a creed that is here required, but aspiration after a *state*. It is not demanded of us to perform a number of duties, but to yield obedience to a certain spiritual law. But let us endeavour to explain this more fully. What is the meaning of this expression, "Be ye perfect?" Why is it that in this discourse, instead of being commanded to perform religious duties, we are commanded to think of being like God? Will not that inflame our pride, and increase our natural vainglory? Now the nature and possibility of human perfection, what it is and how it is possible, are both contained in one single expression in the text. " Even as your Father which is in Heaven is perfect." The relationship between father and son implies consanguinity, likeness, similarity of character and nature. God *made* the insect, the stone, the lily; but God is not the Father of the caterpillar, the lily, or the stone.

When therefore, God is said to be our Father, something more is implied in this than that God created man. And so when the Son of Man came proclaiming the fact that we are the children of God, it was in the truest sense a revelation. He told us that the nature of God resembles the nature of man, that love in God is not a mere figure of speech, but means the same thing as love in us, and that divine anger is the same thing as human anger divested of its emotions and imperfections. When we are commanded to be like God, it implies that God has that nature of which we have already the germs. And this has been taught by the incarnation of the Redeemer. Things absolutely dissimilar in their nature cannot mingle. Water cannot coalesce with fire—water cannot mix with oil. If, then, Humanity and Divinity were united in the person of the Redeemer, it follows that there must be something kindred between the two, or else the incarnation had been impossible. So that the incarnation is the realization of man's perfection.

But let us examine more deeply this assertion, that *our* nature is kindred with that of God—for if man has not a nature kindred to God's, then a demand such as that, "Be ye the children of"—that is, like—" God," is but a mockery of man. We say then, in the first place, that in the truest sense of the word man can be a creator. The beaver *makes* its hole, the bee *makes* its cell; man alone has the power of *creating*. The mason *makes*, the architect *creates*. In the same sense that we say God created the universe, we say that man is also a creator. The creation of the universe was the Eternal Thought taking reality. And thought taking expression is also a creation. Whenever therefore, there is a living thought shaping itself in word or in stone, there is there a creation. And therefore it is, that the simplest effort of what we call genius is prized infinitely more than the most elaborate performances which are done by mere workmanship, and for this reason: that the one is produced by an effort of power which we share with the beaver and the bee, that of *making*, and the other by a faculty and power which man alone shares with God.

Here however, you will observe another difficulty. It will be said at once—there is something in this comparison of man with God which looks like blasphemy, because one is finite and the other infinite—man is bounded, God boundless; and to speak of resemblance and kindred between these two, is to speak of resemblance and kindred between two natures essentially different. But this is precisely the argument which is brought by the Socinians against the doctrine of the incarnation; and we are bound to add that the Socinian argument is right, unless there be the similarity of which we have been speaking. Unless there be something in man's nature which truly and properly partakes of the divine nature, there could be no incarnation, and the demand for perfection would be a mockery and an impossibility.

Let us then endeavour to find out the evidences of this infinitude in the nature of man. First of all we find it in this—that the desires of man are for something boundless and unattainable. Thus speaks our Lord—" What shall it profit a man if he should gain the whole world and lose his own soul?" Every schoolboy has heard the story of the youthful prince who enumerated one by one the countries he meant to conquer year after year; and when the enumeration was completed, was asked what he meant to do when all those victories were achieved, and he replied—to sit down, to be happy, to take his rest. But then came the ready rejoinder—Why not do so now? But it is not every schoolboy who has paused to consider the folly of the question. He who asked his son why he did not at once take the rest which it was his ultimate purpose to enjoy, knew not the immensity and nobility of the human soul. He could not *then* take his rest and be happy. As long as one realm remained unconquered, so long rest was impossible; he would weep for fresh worlds to conquer. And thus, that which was spoken by our Lord of one earthly gratification, is true of all—" Whosoever drinketh of this water shall thirst again." The boundless, endless, infinite void in the soul of man can be satisfied with nothing but God. Satisfaction lies not in *having*, but in *being*. There is no satisfaction even in *doing*. Man cannot be satisfied with his own performances. When the righteous young ruler came to Christ, and declared that in reference to the life gone by, he had kept all the commandments and fulfilled all the duties required by the Law, still came the question—"What lack I yet?"

The Scribes and Pharisees were the strictest observers of the ceremonies of the Jewish religion, "touching the righteousness which is by the Law" they were blameless, but yet they wanted something more than that, and they were found on the brink of Jordan imploring the baptism of John, seeking after a new and higher state than they had yet attained to,—a significant proof that man cannot be satisfied with his own works. And again, there is not one of us who has ever been satisfied with his own performances. There is no man whose doings are worth anything, who has not felt that he has not yet done that which he feels himself able to do. While he was doing it, he was kept up by the spirit of hope; but when done the thing seemed to him worthless. And therefore it is that the author cannot read his own book again, nor the sculptor look with pleasure upon his finished work. With respect to one of the greatest of all modern sculptors, we are told that he longed for the termination of his earthly career, for this reason—that he had been satisfied with his own performance : satisfied for the first time in his life. And this expression of his satisfaction was but equivalent to saying that he had reached the goal, beyond which there could be no progress. This impossibility of being satisfied with his own performances is one of the strongest proofs of our immortality—a proof of that perfection towards which we shall for ever tend, but which we can never attain.

A second trace of this infinitude in man's nature we find in the infinite capacities of the soul. This is true intellectually and morally. With reference to our intellectual capacities, it would perhaps be more strictly correct to say that they are indefinite, rather than infinite; that is we can affix to them no limit. For there is no man, however low his intellectual powers may be, who has not at one time or another felt a rush of thought, a glow of inspiration, which seemed to make all things possible, as if it were merely the effect of some imperfect organization which stood in the way of his doing whatever he desired to do. With respect to our moral and spiritual capacities, we remark that they are not only indefinite, but absolutely infinite. Let that man answer who has ever truly and heartily loved another. That man knows what it is to partake of the infinitude of God. Literally, in the emphatic language of the Apostle John, he has felt his immortality—"God in him and he in God." For that moment, infinitude was to him not a name, but a reality. He entered into the infinite of time and space, which is not measured by days, or months, or years, but is alike boundless and eternal.

Again, we perceive a third trace of this infinitude in man, in the power which he possesses of giving up self. In this, perhaps more than in anything else, man may claim kindred with God. Nor is this power confined to the best of mankind, but is possessed, to some extent at least, by all. There is no man, how low soever he may be, who has not one or two causes or secrets, which no earthly consideration would induce him to betray. There is no man who does not feel towards one or two at least, in this world, a devotion which all the bribes of the universe would not be able to shake. We have heard the story of that degraded criminal who, when sentence of death was passed upon him, turned to his accomplice in guilt, in whose favour a verdict of acquittal was brought in, and in glorious self-forgetfulness exclaimed —"Thank God, *you* are saved!" The savage and bar-

barous Indian whose life has been one unbroken series of cruelty and crime, will submit to a slow, lingering, torturing death, rather than betray his country. Now, what shall we say to these things? Do they not tell of an indestructible something in the nature of man, of which the origin is divine?—the remains of a majesty which, though it may be sullied, can never be entirely lost?

Before passing on let us observe, that were it not for this conviction of the divine origin, and consequent perfectibility of our nature, the very thought of God would be painful to us. God is so great, so glorious, that the mind is overwhelmed by, and shrinks from, the contemplation of His excellence, unless there comes the tender, ennobling thought that we are the children of God, who are to become like our Father in Heaven, whose blessed career it is to go on in an advance of love and duty towards Him, until we love Him as we are loved, and know Him almost as we are known.

II. We pass on, in the second place, to consider the Christian motive—"Even as your Father which is in Heaven is perfect." Brethren, worldly prudence, miscalled morality, says—"Be honest; you will find your gain in being so. Do right; you will be the better for it—even in this world you will not lose by it." The mistaken religionist only magnifies this on a large scale. "Your duty," he says, "is to save your soul. Give up this world to have the next. Lose *here*, that you may gain *hereafter*." Now this is but prudence after all—it is but magnified selfishness, carried on into eternity,—none the more noble for being *eternal* selfishness. In opposition to all such sentiments as these, thus speaks the Gospel—"Be ye perfect." Why? "Because your Father which is in Heaven is perfect." Do right, because it is God-like and right so to do. Here however, let us be understood. We do not mean to say that the Gospel ignores altogether the personal results of doing right. This would be unnatural—because God has linked together well-doing and blessedness. But we do say that this blessedness is not the motive which the Gospel gives us. It is true the Gospel says—" Blessed are the meek, for they shall inherit the earth; blessed are the merciful, for they shall obtain mercy; blessed are they which do hunger and thirst after righteousness, for they shall be filled." But when these are made our motives—when we become meek in order that we may inherit here—then the promised enjoyment will not come. If we are merciful merely that we may ourselves obtain mercy, we shall not have that in-dwelling love of God which is the result and token of His forgiveness. Such was the law and such the example of our Lord and Master.

True it is that in the prosecution of the great work of redemption He had " respect to the recompense of reward." True it is He was conscious—how could He but be conscious—that when His work was completed He should be " glorified with that glory which He had with the Father before the world began;" but we deny that this was the *motive* which induced Him to undertake that work; and that man has a very mistaken idea of the character of the Redeemer, and understands but little of His spirit, who has so mean an opinion of Him as to suppose that it was any consideration of personal happiness and blessedness which led the Son of God to die. " For this end was He born, and for this end came He into the world to bear witness unto the Truth," and " to finish the work which was given Him to do."

If we were asked, Can you select one text in which more than in any other this unselfish, disinterested feature comes forth, it should be this, "Love ye your enemies, do good and lend, hoping for nothing again." This is the true spirit of Christianity—doing right disinterestedly, not from the hope of any personal advantage or reward, either temporal or spiritual, but entirely forgetting self, "hoping for nothing again." When that glorious philanthropist, whose whole life had been spent in procuring the abolition of the slave-trade, was demanded of by some systematic theologian, whether in his ardour in this great cause he had not been neglecting his personal prospects, and endangering his own soul, this was his magnanimous reply —one of those which show the light of truth breaking through like an inspiration. He said, "I did not think about my own soul, I had no time to think about myself, I had forgotten all about my soul." The Christian is not concerned about his own happiness; he has not time to consider himself; he has not time to put that selfish question which the disciples put to their Lord, when they were but half baptized with His spirit, "Lo, we have left all and followed Thee, what shall we have therefore?"

In conclusion we observe, there are two things which are to be learned from this passage. The first is this, that happiness is not our end and aim. It has been said, and has since been repeated as frequently as if it were an indisputable axiom, that "Happiness is our being's end and aim." Brethren, happiness is *not* our being's end and aim. The Christian's aim is perfection, not happiness, and every one of the sons of God must have something of that spirit which marked their Master; that holy sadness, that peculiar unrest, that high and lofty melancholy which belongs to a spirit which strives after heights to which it can never attain.

The second thing we have to learn is this, that on this earth there can be no rest for man. By rest we mean the attainment of a state beyond which there can be no change. Politically, morally, spiritually, there can be no rest for man here. In one country alone has that system been fully carried out which, conservative of the past, excludes all desire of progress and improvement for the future: but it is not to China that we should look for the perfection of human society. There is one ecclesiastical system which carries out the same spirit, looking rather to the Church of the past than to the Church of the future; but it is not in the Romish that we shall find the model of a Christian Church. In Paradise it may have been right to be at rest, to desire no change, but ever since the Fall every system that tends to check the onward progress of mankind is fatally, radically, curelessly wrong. The motto on every Christian banner is "Forwards." There is no resting in the present, no satisfaction in the past.

The last thing we learn from this is the impossibility of obtaining that of which some men speak—the satisfaction of a good conscience. Some men write and speak as if the difference between the Christian and the worldly man was this, that in the one conscience is a self-reproaching hell, and in the other a self-congratulating heaven. Oh, brethren, is this the fact? Think you that the Christian goes home at night counting up the noble deeds done during the day, saying to himself, "Well done, good and faithful servant?" Brethren, that habit of looking forwards to the future prevents all pride and self-righteousness, and makes our best and only rest and satisfaction to consist in contemplating the future which is bringing us nearer and nearer home. Our motto, therefore, must be that striking one of the Apostle Paul, "Forgetting those things which are behind, and reaching forth to those things which are before, I press towards the mark for the prize of the high calling of God in Christ Jesus."

XIII.

Preached January 4, 1852.

CHRISTIAN CASUISTRY.

"Is any man called being circumcised? let him not become uncircumcised. Is any called in uncircumcision? let him not be circumcised. Circumcision is nothing, and uncircumcision is nothing, but the keeping of the commandments of God. Let every man abide in the same calling wherein he was called. Art thou called being a servant? care not for it : but if thou mayest be made free use it rather. For he that is called in the Lord, being a servant, is the Lord's freeman ; likewise also he that is called being free, is Christ's servant. Ye are bought with a price ; be not ye the servants of men. Brethren, let every man wherein he is called therein abide with God."—1 Corinthians, vii. 18—24.

THE whole of these seven chapters of the First Epistle of the Apostle Paul to the Corinthians, is occupied with questions of Christian casuistry. In the application of the principles of Christianity to the varying circumstances of life, innumerable difficulties had arisen, and the Corinthians upon these difficulties had put certain questions to the Apostle Paul. This seventh chapter contains the apostle's answer to many of these questions. There are however, two great divisions into which these answers generally fall. St. Paul makes a distinction between those things which he speaks by commandment and those which he speaks only by permission ; there is a distinction between what he says as from the Lord, and what only from himself; between that which he speaks to them as being taught of God, and that which he speaks only as a servant, "called of the Lord and faithful."

It is manifestly plain that there are many questions in which *right* and *wrong* are not variable, but indissoluble and fixed; while there are questions, on the other hand, where these terms are not fixed, but variable, fluctuating, altering, dependent upon circumstances. As, for instance, those in which the apostle teaches in the present chapter the several duties and advantages of marriage and celibacy. There may be circumstances in which it is the duty of a Christian man to be married, there are others in which it may be his duty to remain unmarried. For instance, in the case of a missionary it may be right to be married rather than unmarried; on the other hand, in the case of a pauper, not having the wherewithal to bring up and maintain a family, it may be proper to remain unmarried. You will observe however, that no fixed law can be laid down upon this subject. We cannot say marriage is a Christian duty, nor celibacy is a Christian duty; nor that it is in every case the duty of a missionary to be married, or of a pauper to be unmarried. All these things must vary according to circumstances, and the duty must be stated not universally, but with reference to those circumstances.

These therefore, are questions of casuistry, which depend upon the particular *case:* from which word the term "casuistry" is derived. On these points the apostle speaks not by commandment, but by permission; not as speaking by God's command, but as having the Spirit of God. A distinction has sometimes been drawn with reference to this chapter between that which the apostle speaks by inspiration, and what he speaks as a man uninspired. The distinction, however, is an altogether false one, and beside the question. For the real distinction is not between inspired and uninspired, but between a *decision* in matters of Christian duty, and *advice* in matters of Christian prudence. It is abundantly evident that God cannot give advice; He can only issue a command. God cannot say, "It is better to do this;" His perfections demand something absolute: "Thou shalt *do* this; thou shalt *not* do this." Whensoever therefore, we come to advice there is introduced the human element rather than the divine. In all such cases therefore, as are dependent upon circumstances the apostle speaks not as inspired, but as uninspired; as one whose judgment we have no right to find fault with or to cavil at, who lays down what is a matter of Christian prudence, and not a bounden and universal duty. The matter of the present discourse will take in various verses in this chapter—from the tenth to the twenty-fourth verse—leaving part of the commencement and the conclusion for our consideration, if God permit, next Sunday.

There are three main questions on which the apostle here gives his inspired decision. The first decision is concerning the sanctity of the marriage-bond between two Christians. His verdict is given in the tenth verse: "Unto the married I command, yet not I, but the Lord, Let not the wife depart from her husband." He lays down this principle, that the union is an indissoluble one.

Upon such a subject, Christian brethren, before a mixed congregation, it is manifestly evident that we can only speak in general terms. It will be sufficient to say that marriage is of all earthly unions almost the only one permitting of no change but that of death. It is that engagement in which man exerts his most awful and solemn power,—the power of responsibility which belongs to him as one that shall give account,—the power of abnegating the right to change,—the power of parting with his freedom,—the power of doing *that* which in this world can never be reversed. And yet it is perhaps that relationship which is spoken of most frivolously, and entered into most carelessly and most wantonly. It is not an union merely between two creatures, it is an union between two spirits; and the intention of that bond is to perfect the nature of both, by supplementing their deficiencies with the force of contrast, giving to each sex those excellencies in which it is naturally deficient; to the one strength of character and firmness of moral will, to the other sympathy, meekness, tenderness. And just so solemn, and just so glorious as these ends are for which the union was contemplated and intended, just so terrible are the consequences if it be perverted and abused. For there is no earthly relationship which has so much power to ennoble and to exalt. Very strong language does the apostle use in this chapter respecting it: "What knoweth thou, O wife, whether thou shalt *save* thy husband? or how knowest thou, O man, whether thou shalt save thy wife?" The very power of *saving* belongs to this relationship. And on the other hand, there is no earthly relationship which has so much power to wreck and ruin the soul. For there are two rocks in this world of ours on which the soul must either anchor or be wrecked. The one is God; the other is the sex opposite to itself. The one is the "Rock of Ages," on which if the human soul anchors it lives the blessed life of faith; against which if the soul be dashed and broken, there ensues the wreck of Atheism—the worst ruin of the soul. The other rock is of another character. Blessed is the man, blessed is the woman whose life-experience has taught a confiding belief in the excellencies of the sex opposite to their own—a blessedness second only to the blessedness of salvation. And the ruin in the other case is second only to the ruin of everlasting perdition—the same wreck and ruin of the soul.

These then, are the two tremendous alternatives: on the one hand the possibility of securing, in all sympathy and tenderness, the laying of that step on which man rises towards his perfection; on the other hand the blight of all sympathy, to be dragged down to earth, and forced to become frivolous and common-place; to lose all zest and earnestness in life, to have heart and life degraded by mean and perpetually-recurring sources of disagreement; these are the two alternatives, and it is the worst of these alternatives which the young risk when they form an inconsiderate union, excusably indeed—because through inexperience; and it is the worst of these alternatives which parents risk—not excusably but inexcusably—when they bring up their children with no higher view of what that tie is, than the merely prudential one of a rich and honourable marriage.

The second decision which the apostle makes respecting another of the questions proposed to him by the Corinthians, is as to the sanctity of the marriage bond between a Christian and one who is a heathen. When Christianity first entered into our world, and was little understood, it seemed to threaten the dislocation and alteration of all existing relationships. Many difficulties arose; such for instance, as the one here started. When of two heathen parties only one was converted to Christianity, the question arose, What in this case is the duty of the Christian? Is not the duty separation? Is not the marriage in itself null and void? as if it were an union between one dead and one living? And that perpetual contact with a heathen, and therefore an enemy of God, is not that in a relation so close and intimate, perpetual defilement? The apostle decides this with his usual inspired wisdom. He decides that the marriage-bond is sacred still. Diversities of religious opinion, even the farthest and widest diversity, cannot sanction separation. And so he decides in the 13th verse, "The woman which hath an husband that believeth not, if he be pleased to dwell with her, let her not leave him." And, "if any brother hath a wife that believeth not, and she be pleased to dwell with him, let him not put her away," v. 12.

Now for us in the present day, the decision on this point is not of so much importance as the reason which is adduced in support of it. The proof which the Apostle gives of the sanctity of the marriage is exceedingly remarkable. Practically it amounts to this;—If this were no marriage, but an unhallowed alliance, it would follow as a necessary consequence that the offspring could not be reckoned in any sense as the children of God; but, on the other hand, it is the instinctive, unwavering conviction of every Christian parent, united though he or she may be to a heathen, "My child is a child of God," or, in the Jewish form of expression, "My child is *clean*." So the apostle says, "the unbelieving husband is sanctified by the wife, and the unbelieving wife is sanctified by the husband: else were your children unclean; but now they are holy," for it follows if the children are holy in this sense of dedicated to God, and are capable of Christian relationship, then the marriage relation was not unhallowed, but sacred and indissoluble.

The value of this argument in the present day depends

on its relation to baptism. The great question we are deciding in the present day may be reduced to a very few words. This question—the Baptismal question—is this:— whether we are baptized because we *are* the children of God, or, whether we are the children of God because we are *baptized;* whether in other words, when the Catechism of the Church of England says that by baptism we are "made the children of God," we are to understand thereby that we are made something which we were not before—magically and mysteriously changed; or, whether we are to understand that we are made the children of God by baptism in the same sense that a sovereign is made a sovereign by coronation. Here the apostle's argument is full, decisive, and unanswerable. He does not say that these children were Christian, or clean, because they were *baptized*, but they were the children of God because they were the children of one Christian parent; nay more than that, such children could scarcely ever have been baptized, because, if the rite met with opposition from one of the parents, it would be an entire and perfect veto to the possibility of baptism. You will observe that the very fundamental idea out of which infant-baptism arises is, that the impression produced upon the mind and character of the child by the Christian parent, makes the child one of a Christian community; and, therefore, as Peter argued that Cornelius had received the Holy Ghost, and so was to be baptized, just in the same way, as they are adopted into the Christian family and receive a Christian impression, the children of Christian parents are also to be baptized.

Observe also the important truth which comes out collaterally from this argument—namely, the sacredness of the impression, which arises from the close connection between parent and child. Stronger far than education—going on before education can commence, possibly from the very first moments of consciousness, we begin to impress ourselves on our children. Our character, voice, features, qualities — modified, no doubt, by entering into a new human being, and into a different organization—are impressed upon our children. Not the inculcation of opinions, but much rather the formation of principles, and of the tone of character, the derivation of qualities. Physiologists tell us of the derivation of the mental qualities from the father, and of the moral from the mother. But be this as it may, there is scarcely one here who cannot trace back his present religious character to some impression, in early life, from one or other of his parents—a tone, a look, a word, a habit, or even, it may be, a bitter, miserable exclamation of remorse.

The third decision which the apostle gives, the third principle which he lays down, is but the development of the last. Christianity he says, does not interfere with existing relationships. First he lays down the principle, and then unfolds the principle in two ways, ecclesiastically and civilly. The principle he lays down in almost every variety of form. In the 17th verse, "As God hath distributed to every man, as the Lord hath called every one, so let him walk." In the 20th verse, "Let every man abide in the same calling wherein he was called." In the 24th verse, "Brethren, let every man wherein he is called therein abide with God." This is the principle. Christianity was not to interfere with existing relationships; Christian men were to remain in those relationships in which they were, and in them to develope the inward spirituality of the Christian life. Then he applies this principle in two ways. First of all, ecclesiastically. With respect to their church, or ecclesiastical affairs, he says—" Is any man called being circumcised? Let him not become uncircumcised. Is any man in uncircumcision? Let him not be circumcised." In other words, the Jews, after their conversion, were to continue Jews, if they would. Christianity required no change in these outward things, for it was not in *these* that the depth and reality of the kingdom of Christ consisted. So the Apostle Paul took Timothy and circumcised him; so, also, he used all the Jewish customs with which he was familiar, and performed a vow, as related in the Acts of the Apostles, "having shorn his head in Cenchrea; for he had a vow." It was not his opinion that it was the duty of a Christian to overthrow the Jewish system. He knew that the Jewish system could not last, but what he wanted was to vitalize the system—to throw into it not a Jewish, but a Christian feeling; and so doing, he might continue in it so long as it would hold together. And so it was no doubt, with all the other apostles. We have no evidence that before the destruction of the Jewish polity, there was any attempt made by them to overthrow the Jewish external religion. They kept the Jewish Sabbath, and observed the Jewish ritual. One of them, James, the Christian Bishop of Jerusalem, though a Christian, was even among the Jews remarkable and honourable for the regularity with which he observed all his Jewish duties. Now let us apply this to modern duties. The great desire among men now, appears to be to alter institutions, to have perfect institutions, as if *they* would make perfect men. Mark the difference between this feeling and that of the apostle, "Let every man abide in the same calling wherein he was called." We are called to be members of the Church of England—what is our duty now? What would Paul have done? Is this our duty—to put such questions to ourselves as these? "Is there any single, particular sentence in the service of my Church with which I do not entirely agree? Is there any single ceremony with which my whole soul does not go along? If so, then is it my duty to leave it at once?" No, my brethren, all that we have to do is to say, "All our existing institutions are those under which God has placed us, under which we are to mould our lives according to His will." It is our duty to vitalize our forms, to throw into them a holier, deeper meaning. My Christian brethren, surely no man will get true rest, true repose for his soul in these days of controversy, until he has learned the wise significance of these wise words—"Let every man abide in the same calling wherein he was called." He will but gain unrest, he will but disquiet himself, if he says, "I am sinning by continuing in this imperfect system," if he considers it his duty to change his calling if his opinions do not agree in every particular and special point with the system under which God has placed him.

Lastly, the apostle applies this principle civilly. And you will observe he applies it to that civil relationship which of all others, was the most difficult to harmonize with Christianity—slavery. "Art thou called," he says, "being a servant? Care not for it." Now, in considering this part of the subject we should carry along with us these two recollections. First, we should recollect that Christianity had made much way among this particular class, the class of slaves. No wonder that men cursed with slavery embraced with joy a religion which was perpetually teaching the worth and dignity of the human soul, and declaring that rich and poor, peer and peasant, master and slave, were equal in the sight of God. And yet, great as this growth was, it contained within it elements of danger. It was to be feared, lest men, hearing for ever of brotherhood and Christian equality, should be tempted and excited to throw off the yoke by *force*, and compel their masters and oppressors to do them right.

The other fact we are to keep in remembrance is this—that all this occurred in an age in which slavery had reached its worst and most fearful form, an age in which the emperors were accustomed, not unfrequently, to feed their fish with living slaves; when captives were led to fight in the amphitheatre with wild beasts or with each other, to glut the Roman appetite for blood upon a Roman holiday. And yet fearful as it was, the apostle says, "Care not for it." And fearful as war was in those days, when the soldiers came to John to be baptized, he did not recommend them to join some "Peace Association," to use the modern term; he simply exhorted them to be content with their wages.

And hence we understand the way in which Christianity was to work. It interferes indirectly and not directly with existing institutions. No doubt it will at length abolish war and slavery, but there is not one case where we find Christianity interfering with institutions, as such. Even when Onesimus ran away and came to Paul, the apostle sent him back to his master Philemon, not dissolving the connection between them. And then, as a consolation to the servant, he told him of a higher feeling—a feeling that would make him free, with the chain and shackle upon his arm. And so it was possible for the Christian then, as it is now, to be possessed of the highest liberty even under tyranny. It many times occurred that Christian men found themselves placed under an unjust and tyrannical government, and compelled to pay unjust taxes. The Son of Man showed his freedom not by refusing, but by paying them. His glorious liberty could do so without any feeling of degradation; obeying the laws, not because they were right, but because institutions are to be upheld with cordiality.

One thing in conclusion we have to observe. It is possible from all this to draw a most inaccurate conclusion. Some men have spoken of Christianity as if it was entirely indifferent about liberty and all public questions—as if with such things as these Christianity did not concern itself at all. This indifference is not to be found in the Apostle Paul. While he asserts that inward liberty is the only true liberty, he still goes on to say, " If thou mayst be free use it rather." For he well knew that although it was possible for a man to be a high and lofty Christian even though he were a slave, yet it was not probable that he would be so. Outward institutions are necessary partly to make a perfect Christian character; and thus Christianity works from what is internal to what is external. It gave to the slave the feeling of his dignity as a man, at the same time it gave to the Christian master a new view of his relation to his slave, and taught him to regard him "not now as a servant, but above a servant, a brother beloved." And so by degrees slavery passed into freed servitude, and freed servitude, under God's blessing, may pass into something else.

There are two mistakes which are often made upon this subject; one is, the error of supposing that outward institutions are unnecessary for the formation of character, and the other, that of supposing that they are *all* that is required to form the human soul. If we understand rightly the duty of a Christian man, it is this: to make his brethren free inwardly and outwardly; first inwardly, so that they may become masters of themselves, rulers of their passions, having the power of self-rule and self-control; and then outwardly, so that there may be every power and opportunity of developing the inward life; in the language of the prophet, "To break the rod of the oppressor and let the oppressed go free."

XIV.

Preached January 11, 1852.

MARRIAGE AND CELIBACY.

" But this I say, brethren, the time is short : it remaineth that both they that have wives be as though they had none ; and they that weep as though they wept not ; and they that rejoice as though they rejoiced not ; and they that buy, as though they possessed not ; and they that use this world as not abusing it : for the fashion of this world passeth away."—1 Corinthians vii. 29—31.

THE subject of our exposition last Sunday was an essential portion of this chapter. It is our duty to examine now the former and the latter portions of it. These portions are occupied entirely with the inspired apostolic decision upon this one question—the comparative advantages and merits of celibacy and marriage. One preliminary question, however, is to be discussed. How came it that such a question should be put at all to the apostle?

In the church at Corinth there were two different sections of society; first there were those who had been introduced into the church through Judaism, and afterwards those who had been converted from different forms of heathenism. Now it is well known, that it was the tendency of Judaism highly to venerate the marriage state, and just in the same proportion to disparage that of celibacy, and to place those who led a single life under a stigma and disgrace. Those converts therefore, entered into the Church of Christ carrying with them their old Jewish prejudices. On the other hand, many who had entered into the Christian Church had been converted to Christianity from different forms of heathenism. Among these prevailed a tendency to the belief (which originated primarily in the oriental schools of philosophy) that the highest virtue consisted in the denial of all natural inclinations, and the suppression of all natural desires; and looking upon marriage on one side only, and that the lowest, they were tempted to consider it as low, earthly, carnal, and sensual. It was at this time that Christianity entered into the world, and while it added fresh dignity and significance to the marriage relationship, it at the same time shed a splendour and a glory upon the other state. The virginity of the mother of Our Lord—the solitary life of John the Baptist—the pure and solitary youth of Christ Himself—had thrown upon celibacy a meaning and dignity which it did not possess before. No marvel therefore, that to men so educated, and but half prepared for Christianity, practices like these should have become exaggerations; for it rarely happens that any right ideas can be given to the world without suffering exaggeration. Human nature progresses, the human mind goes on; but it is rarely in a straight line, almost always through the medium of re-action, rebounding from extremes which produce contrary extremes. So it was in the Church of Corinth. There were two opposite parties holding views diametrically opposed to one another—one honouring the married and depreciating the unmarried life—the other attributing peculiar dignity and sanctity to celibacy, and looking down with contempt upon the married Christian state.

It is scarcely necessary to remind ourselves that this

diversity of sentiment has existed in the Church of Christ in almost all ages. For example in the early ages, in almost all the writings of the Fathers we have exaggerated descriptions of the dignity and glory of the state of celibacy. They speak as if the marriage state was low, carnal, and worldly; and the other the only one in which it is possible to attain to the higher spiritual life—the one the natural state, fit for man, the other the angelic, fit for angels. But ordinarily among men in general, in every age, the state of single life has been looked down upon and contemned. And then there comes to the parties who are so circumstanced a certain sense of shame, and along with this a disposition towards calumny and slander. Let us endeavour to understand the wise, inspired decision which the Apostle Paul pronounced upon this subject. He does not decide, as we might have been led to suppose he would, from his own peculiarity of disposition, upon one side only; but raises into relief the advantages and excellencies of both. He says that neither state has in itself any *intrinsic* merit— neither is in itself superior to the other. "I suppose, then," he says, "that this is good for the present distress. Art thou bound unto a wife? Seek not to be loosed. Art thou loosed from a wife? Seek not a wife. But and if thou marry, thou hast not sinned : and if a virgin marry, she hath not sinned. Nevertheless, such shall have trouble in the flesh: but I spare you." That is, I will spare you this trouble, in recommending a single, solitary life. You will observe that in these words he attributes no intrinsic merit or dignity to either celibacy or marriage. The comparative advantages of these two states he decides with reference to two considerations; first of all with respect to their comparative power in raising the character of the individual, and afterwards with reference to the opportunities which each respectively gives for the service of God.

I. With respect to the single life, he tells us that he had his own proper gift from God; in other words, he was one of those rare characters who have the power of living without personal sympathy. The feelings and affections of the Apostle Paul were of a strange and rare character—tending to expansiveness rather than concentration. Those sympathies which ordinary men expend upon a few, he extended to many. The members of the churches which he had founded at Corinth, and Ephesus, and Colosse, and Philippi, were to him as children; and he threw upon them all that sympathy and affection which other men throw upon their own domestic circle. To a man so trained and educated, the single life gave opportunities of serving God which the marriage state could not give. St. Paul had risen at once to that philanthropy—that expansive benevolence, which most other men only attain by slow degrees, and this was made, by God's blessing, a means of serving his cause. However we may sneer at the monastic system of the Church of Rome, it is unquestionable that many great works have been done by the monks which could not have been performed by men who had entered into the marriage relationship. Such examples of heroic Christian effort as are seen in the lives of St. Bernard, of Francis Xavier, and many others, are scarcely ever to be found except in the single state. The forlorn hope in battle, as well as in the cause of Christianity, must consist of men who have no domestic relationships to divide their devotion, who will leave no wife nor children to mourn over their loss.

Let this great truth bring its improvement to those who,

either of their own choice, or by the force of circumstances, are destined hereafter to live a single life on earth; and, instead of yielding to that feeling so common among mankind—the feeling of envy at another's happiness—instead of becoming gloomy, and bitter and censorious, let them remember what the Bible has to tell of the deep significance of the Virgin Mary's life—let them reflect upon the snares and difficulties from which they are saved—let them consider how much more time and money they can give to God—that they are called to the great work of serving Causes, of entering into public questions, while others spend their time and talents only upon themselves. The state of single life, however we may be tempted to think lightly of it, is a state that has peculiar opportunities of deep blessedness.

2. On the other hand, the Apostle Paul brings forward, into strong relief, the blessedness and advantages of the marriage state. He tells us that it is a type of the union between the Redeemer and the Church. But as this belongs to another part of the subject, we shall not enter into it now. But we observe, that men in general, must have their sympathies drawn out step by step, little by little. We do not rise to philanthropy all at once. We begin with personal, domestic, particular affections. And not only is it true that rarely can any man have the whole of his love drawn out except through this domestic state, but, also, it is to be borne in mind that those who have entered into this relationship have also their own peculiar advantages. It is true that in the marriage-life, interrupted as it is by daily cares and small trifles, those works of Christian usefulness cannot be so continuously carried on as in the other. But is there not a deep meaning to be learned from the old

expression—that celibacy is an *angelic* state? that it is preternatural, and not natural? that the goodness which is induced by it is not, so to speak, the natural goodness of Humanity, but such a goodness as God scarcely intended?

Who of us cannot recollect a period of his history when all his time was devoted to the cause of Christ; when all his money was given to the service of God; and when we were tempted to look down upon those who were less ardent than ourselves, as if they were not Christians? But now the difficulties of life have come upon us; we have become involved in the trifles and the smallness of social domestic existence; and these have made us less devoted perhaps, less preternatural, less angelic—but more human, better fitted to enter into the daily cares and small difficulties of our ordinary humanity. And this has been represented to us by two great lives—one human, the other divine—one, the life of John the Baptist, and the other, of Jesus Christ. In both these cases is verified the saying, that "Wisdom is justified of all her children." Those who are wisdom's children—the truly wise—will recognise an even wisdom in both these lives; they will see that there are cases in which a solitary life is to be chosen for the sake of God; while there are other cases in which a social life becomes our bounden duty. But it should be specially observed here that *that* Life which has been given to us as a specimen of life for all, was a social, a human Life. Christ did not refuse to mix with the common joys and common sorrows of Humanity. He was present at the marriage-feast, and by the bier of the widow's son. This of the two lives was the one which, because it was the most human, was the most divine; the most rare, the most difficult, the most natural—therefore, the most Christ-like.

II. Let us notice, in the second place, the principle upon which the apostle founds this decision. It is given in the text—" This I say, brethren, the time is short: it remaineth that both they that have wives be as though they had none," "for the fashion of this world passeth away." Now observe here, I pray you, the deep wisdom of this apostolic decision. In point of fact it comes to this: Christianity is a spirit, not a law; it is a set of principles, not a set of rules; it is not a saying to us—You shall do this, you shall not do that—you shall use this particular dress, you shall not use that—you *shall* lead, you shall *not* lead a married life—Christianity consists of principles, but the application of those principles is left to every man's individual conscience. With respect not only to this particular case, but to all the questions which had been brought before him, the apostle applies the same principle; the cases upon which he decided were many and various, but the large, broad principle of his decision remains the same in all. You may marry, and you have not sinned; you may remain unmarried, and you do not sin; if you are invited to a heathen feast, you may go, or you may abstain from going; you may remain a slave, or you may become free; in *these things* Christianity does not consist. But what it does demand is this: that whether married or unmarried, whether a slave or free, in sorrow or in joy, you are to live in a spirit higher and loftier than that of the world.

The apostle gives us in the text two motives for this Christian unworldliness. The first motive which he lays down is this—"The time is short." You will observe how frequently, in the course of his remarks upon the questions proposed to him, the apostle turns, as it were entirely away from the subject, as if worn-out and wearied by the comparatively trivial character of the questions—as if this balancing of one earthly condition or advantage with another, were but a solemn trifling compared with eternal things. And so here, he seems to turn away from the question before him, and speaks of the shortness of time. "The time is short!"

Time is short in reference to two things. First, it is short in reference to the person who regards it. That mysterious thing *Time* is a matter of sensation, and not a reality; a modification merely of our own consciousness, and not actual existence; depending upon the flight of ideas—long to one, short to another. The span granted to the butterfly, the child of a single summer, may be long; that which is given to the cedar of Lebanon may be short. The shortness of time, therefore is entirely relative—belonging to us not to God. Time is short in reference to *existence*, whether you look at it before or after. Time past seems nothing; time to come always seems long. We say this chiefly for the sake of the young. To them fifty or sixty years seem a treasure inexhaustible. But, my young brethren, ask the old man, trembling on the verge of the grave, what he thinks of Time and Life. He will tell you that the threescore years and ten, or even the hundred-and-twenty years of Jacob, are but "few and evil." And, therefore, if you are tempted to unbelief in respect to this question, we appeal to experience—experience alone can judge of its truth.

Once more, time is short with reference to its *opportunities*. For this is the emphatic meaning in the original—literally, "the opportunity is compressed, or shut in." Brethren, time may be long, and yet the opportunity may be very short. The sun in autumn may be bright and clear, but the seed which has not been sown until then will not vegetate. A man may have vigour and energy in manhood and maturity, but the work which ought to have been done in childhood and youth cannot be done in old age. A chance once gone in this world can never be recovered.

Brother men—have you learned the meaning of yesterday? Do you rightly estimate the importance of to-day? That there are duties to be done to-day which cannot be done to-morrow? This it is that throws so solemn a significance into your work. The time for working is short, therefore begin to-day; "for the night is coming when no man can work." Time is short in reference to *eternity*. It was especially with this reference that the text was written. In those days, and even by the apostles themselves, the day of the Lord's appearance and second advent seemed much nearer than it was. They believed that it would occur during their own lives. And with this belief came the feeling which comes sometimes to all. "Oh, in comparison with that vast Hereafter, this little life shrivels into nothing! What is to-day worth, or its duties or its cares?" All deep minds have thought that. The thought of Time is solemn and awful to all minds in proportion to their depth—and in proportion as the mind is superficial, the thought has appeared little, and has been treated with levity. Brethren, let but a man possess himself of that thought—the deep thought of the brevity of time; this thought—that time is short, and that eternity is long—and he has learned the first great secret of unworldliness.

2. The second motive which the apostle gives us is the changing character of the external world. "The fashion of this world passeth away"—literally "the *scenery* of this world,"

a dramatic expression, drawn from the Grecian stage. One of the deepest of modern thinkers has told us in words often quoted, "All the world's a stage." And a deeper thinker than he, because inspired, had said long before in the similar words of the text, " the *scenery* of this world passeth away."

There are two ways in which this is true. First, it is true with respect to all the things by which we are surrounded. It is only in poetry—the poetry of the Psalms for example —that the hills are called " everlasting." Go to the side of the ocean which bounds our country, and watch the tide going out, bearing with it the sand which it has worn from the cliffs; the very boundaries of our land are changing; they are not the same as they were when these words were written. Every day new relationships are forming around us; new circumstances are calling upon us to act—to act manfully, firmly, decisively, and up to the occasion, remembering that an opportunity once gone is gone for ever. Indulge not in vain regrets for the past, in vainer resolves for the future—act, act in the present.

Again, this is true with respect to ourselves. "The fashion of this world passeth away" in us. The feelings we have now are not those which we had in childhood. There has passed away a glory from the earth—the stars, the sun, the moon, the green fields have lost their beauty and significance—nothing remains as it was, except their repeated impressions on the mind, the impressions of time, space, eternity, colour, form; these cannot alter, but all besides has changed. Our very minds alter. There is no bereavement so painful, no shock so terrible, but time will remove or alleviate. The keenest feeling in this world time wears out at last, and our minds become like old monumental tablets which have lost the inscription once graven deeply upon them.

In conclusion, we have to examine the nature of this Christian unworldliness which is taught us in the text. The principle of unworldliness is stated in the latter portion of the text; in the former part the apostle makes an application of the principle to four cases of life. First, to cases of domestic relationship—"it remaineth that they that have wives be as though they had none." Secondly, to cases of sorrow—"and they that weep as though they wept not." Thirdly, to cases of joy—"and they that rejoice as though they rejoiced not." And, finally to cases of the acquisition of worldly property, "and they that buy as though they possessed not." Time will not allow us to go into these applications; we must confine ourselves to a brief consideration of the principle. The principle of Christian unworldliness, then is this, to "use this world as not abusing it." Here Christianity takes its stand, in opposition to two contrary principles. The spirit of the world says, "Time is short, therefore use it while you have it; take your fill of pleasure while you may." A narrow religion says, "Time is short, therefore temporal things should receive no attention : do not weep, do not rejoice; it is beneath a Christian." In opposition to the narrow spirit of religion, Christianity says, "*Use* this world;"—in opposition to the spirit of the world Christianity says, "Do not *abuse* it." A distinct duty arises from this principle to use the world. While in the world we are citizens of the world: it is our *duty* to share its joys, to take our part in its sorrows, not to shrink from its difficulties, but to mix ourselves with its infinite opportunities. So that if time be short, so far from that fact lessening their dignity or importance, it infinitely increases them; since upon these depend the destinies of our eternal being. Unworldliness is this—to hold things from God in the perpetual conviction that they will not last; to have the world, and not to let the world have us; to be the world's masters, and not the world's slaves.

XV.

Preached January 11, 1852.

THE CHRISTIAN CHURCH A FAMILY.

"Our Lord Jesus Christ, of whom the whole family in heaven and earth is named."—Ephesians iii. 14, 15.

IN the verses immediately before the text the Apostle Paul has been speaking of what he calls a mystery—that is, a revealed secret. And the secret was this, that the Gentiles would be "fellow-heirs and of the same body, and partakers of the promise in Christ by the gospel." It had been kept secret from the former ages and generations; it was a secret which the Jew had not suspected, had not even dreamt of. It appeared to him to be his duty to keep as far as possible from the Gentile. Circumcision, which taught him the duty of separation from the Gentile spirit, and Gentile practices, seemed to him to teach hatred towards Gentile *persons*, until at length, in the good pleasure and providence of God, in the fulness of time, through the instrumentality of men whose *hearts* rather than whose intellects were inspired by God, the truth came out distinct and clear, that God was the Father of the Gentiles as well as of the Jews, "for the same Lord over all is rich unto all that call upon Him."

In the progress of the months, my Christian brethren,

we have arrived again at that period of the year in which our Church calls upon us to commemorate the Epiphany, or manifestation of Jesus Christ to the Gentiles, and we know not that in the whole range of Scripture we could find a passage which more distinctly and definitely than this, brings before us the spirit in which it is incumbent upon us to enter upon this duty. In considering this passage we shall divide it into these two branches :—1st, the definition which the Apostle Paul here gives of the Church of Christ; and, 2ndly, the Name by which this Church is named.

I. In the first place, let us consider the definition given by the Apostle Paul of the Christian Church, taken in its entirety. It is this, "the whole family in heaven and earth." But in order to understand this fully, it will be necessary for us to break it up into its different terms.

1. First of all it is taught by this definition that the Church of Christ is a society founded upon natural affinities —a "family." A family is built on affinities which are natural, not artificial; it is not a combination, but a society. In ancient times an association of interest combined men in one guild or corporation for protecting the common persons in that corporation from oppression. In modern times identity of political creed or opinion has bound men together in one league, in order to establish those political principles which appeared to them of importance. Similarity of taste has united men together in what is called an association, or a society, in order by this means to attain more completely the ends of that science to which they had devoted themselves. But as these have been raised artificially, so their end is inevitably, dissolution. Society passes on, and guilds and corporations die; principles are

established, and leagues become dissolved; tastes change, and then the association or society breaks up and comes to nothing.

It is upon another principle altogether that that which we call a family, or true society, is formed. It is not built upon similarity of taste, nor identity of opinion, but upon affinities of nature. You do not *choose* who shall be your brother; you cannot exclude your mother or your sister; it does not depend upon choice or arbitrary opinion at all, but is founded upon the eternal nature of things. And precisely in the same way is the Christian Church formed—upon natural affinity, and not upon artificial combination. "The family, the whole family in heaven and earth;" not made up of those who *call* themselves brethren, but of those who *are* brethren; not founded merely upon the principles of combination, but upon the principles of affinity. That is not a church, or a family, or a society which is made up by men's choice, as when in the upper classes of life, men of fashion unite together, selecting their associates from their own *class*, and form what is technically called a society; it is a combination if you will, but a society it is not—a family it is not—a Church of Christ it cannot be.

And, again, when the Baptists or the Independents, or any other sectarians, unite themselves with men holding the same faith and entertaining the same opinions, there may be a *sect*, a *combination*, a *persuasion*, but a *Church* there cannot be. And so again, when the Jew in time past linked himself with the Jew, with those of the same nation, there you have what in ancient times was called Judaism, and in modern times is called Hebraicism—a system, a combination, but not a Church. The Church rises ever out of the family. First of all in the good providence of God, there is the family, then the tribe, then the nation ; and then the nation merges itself into Humanity. And the nation which refuses to merge its nationality in Humanity, to lose itself in the general interests of mankind, is left behind, and loses almost its religious nationality—like the Jewish people.

Such is the first principle. A man is born of the same family, and is not made such by an appointment, or by arbitrary choice.

2. Another thing which is taught by this definition is this, that the Church of Christ is a whole made up of manifold diversities. We are told here it is "the *whole* family," taking into it the great and good of ages past, now in heaven ; and also the struggling, the humble, and the weak now existing upon earth. Here again, the analogy holds good between the Church and the family. Never more than in the family is the true entirety of our nature seen. Observe how all the diversities of human condition and character manifest themselves in the family.

First of all, there are the two opposite poles of masculine and feminine, which contain within them the entire of our Humanity—which together, not separately, make up the whole of man. Then there are the diversities in the degrees and kinds of affection. For when we speak of family affection, we must remember that it is made up of many diversities. There is nothing more different than the love which the sister bears towards the brother, compared with that which the brother bears towards the sister. The affection which a man bears towards his father is quite distinct from that which he feels towards his mother; it is something quite different towards his sister; totally diverse again, towards his brother.

And then there are diversities of character. First the

mature wisdom and stern integrity of the father; then the exuberant tenderness of the mother. And then one is brave and enthusiastic, another thoughtful, and another tender. One is remarkable for being full of rich humour, another is sad, mournful, even melancholy. Again, besides these, there are diversities of condition in life. First, there is the heir, sustaining the name and honour of the family; then perchance the soldier, in whose career all the anxiety and solicitude of the family is centred; then the man of business, to whom they look up, trusting his advice, expecting his counsel; lastly perhaps, there is the invalid, from the very cradle trembling between life and death, drawing out all the sympathies and anxieties of each member of the family, and so uniting them all more closely, from their having one common point of sympathy and solicitude. Now, you will observe that these are not accidental, but absolutely essential to the idea of a family; for so far as any one of them is lost, so far the family is incomplete. A family made up of one sex alone, all brothers and no sisters; or in which all are devoted to one pursuit; or in which there is no diversity of temper and dispositions—the same monotonous repeated identity—a sameness in the type of character—this is not a family, it is only the fragment of a family.

And precisely in the same way all these diversities of character and condition are necessary to constitute and complete the idea of a Christian Church. For as in ages past it was the delight of the Church to canonize one particular class of virtues—as for instance, purity or martyrdom—so now, in every age, and in every individual bosom, there is a tendency to canonize, or honour, or reckon as Christian, only one or two classes of Christian qualities. For example, if you were to ask in the present day where you should find a type of the Christian character, many in all probability would point you to the man who keeps the Sabbath-day, is regular in his attendance upon the services of the Church, who loves to hear the Christian sermon. This is a phase of Christian character—that which is essentially and peculiarly the *feminine* type of religion. But is there in God's Church to be found no place for that type which is rather masculine than feminine?—which, not in litanies or in psalm-singing does the will of God, but by struggling for principles, and contending for the truth—*that* life whose prayer is action, whose aspiration is continual effort?

Or again, in every age, amongst all men, in the history of almost every individual, at one time or another, there has been a tendency towards that which has been emphatically named in modern times *hero-worship*—leading us to an admiration of the more singular, powerful, noble qualities of humanity. And wherever this tendency to hero-worship exists there will be found side by side with it a tendency to undervalue and depreciate excellences of an opposite character—the humble, meek, retiring qualities. But it is precisely for these that the Church of Christ finds place. "Blessed are the meek, blessed are the merciful, blessed are they that hunger and thirst after righteousness, blessed are the poor in spirit." In God's world there is a place for the wren and the violet, just as truly as there is for the eagle and the rose. In the Church of God there is a place—and that the noblest—for Dorcas making garments for the poor, and for Mary sitting at the feet of Jesus, just as truly as there is for Elijah confounding a false religion by his noble opposition; for John the Baptist making a king tremble on his throne; or for the Apostle Paul "compassing sea and land" by his wisdom and his heroic deeds.

Once more, there are ages, as well as times in our own individual experience, when we set up charity as if it were the one only Christian character. And wherever this tendency is found there will be found at the same time, and side by side with it, a tendency to admire the spurious form of charity, which is a sentiment and not a virtue; which can sympathize with crime, but not with law; which can be tender to savages, but has no respect, no care for national honour. And therefore, does this principle of the Apostle Paul call upon us to esteem also another form or type of character, and the opposite one; that which is remarkable for—in which predominates—not so much charity as *justice;* that which was seen in the warriors and prophets of old; who perchance, had a more strong recoil from vice than sympathy with virtue; whose indignation towards that which is wrong and hypocritical was more intense than their love for that which is good : the material, the character, out of which the reformer and the prophet, those who are called to do great works on earth, are made.

The Church of Christ takes not in one individual form of goodness merely, but every form of excellence that can adorn Humanity. Nor is this wonderful when we remember Who He was from whom this Church was named. It was He in whom centred all excellence—a righteousness which was entire and perfect. But when we speak of the perfection of righteousness, let us remember that it is made not of one exaggerated character, but of a true harmony, a due proportion of all virtues united. In Him were found therefore, that tenderness towards sinners which had no sympathy with sin; that humility which could be dignified, and was yet united with self-respect; that simplicity which is ever to be met with, side by side with true majesty; that love which could weep over Jerusalem at the very moment when He was pronouncing its doom; that truth and justice which appeared to stand as a protection to those who had been oppressed, at the same time that He scathed with indignant invective the Pharisees of the then existing Jews.

There are two, only two, *perfect* Humanities. One has existed already in the person of our Lord Jesus Christ, the other is to be found only in the collective Church. Once, only once, has God given a perfect representation of Himself, "the brightness of the Father's glory, and the express image of His person." And if we ask again for a perfect Humanity, the answer is, it is not in this Church or in that Church, or in this man or in that man, in this age or in that age, but in the collective blended graces and beauties, and humanities, which are found in every age, in all churches, but not in every separate man. So, at least, Paul has taught us, " Till we *all* come "—*collectively* not separately—" in the unity of the faith, and of the knowledge of the Son of God, unto a perfect man "—in other words, to a perfect *Humanity*—" unto the measure of the stature of the fulness of Christ."

3. The last thing which is taught us by this definition is, that the Church of Christ is a society which is for ever shifting its locality, and altering its forms. It is the *whole* church, "the *whole* family in heaven and earth." So then, those who were on earth, and are now in heaven, are yet members of the same family still. Those who had their home here, now have it there.

Let us see what it is that we should learn from this doctrine. It is this, that the dead are not lost to us. There is a sense in which the departed are ours more than they were before. There is a sense in which the Apostles Paul, or John, the good and great of ages past, belong to this age more than to that in which they lived, but in which they were not understood; in which the common-place and every-day part of their lives hindered the brightness and glory and beauty of their character from shining forth. So it is in the family. It is possible for men to live in the same house, and partake of the same meal from day to day, and from year to year, and yet remain strangers to each other, mistaking each other's feelings, not comprehending each other's character; and it is only when the Atlantic rolls between, and half a hemisphere is interposed, that we learn how dear they are to us, how all our life is bound up in deep anxiety with their existence. Therefore it is the Christian feels that the family is not broken. Think you that family can break or end?—that because the chair is empty, therefore he, your child, is no more? It may be so with the coarse, the selfish, the unbelieving, the superstitious; but the eye of faith sees there only a transformation. He is not there, he is risen. You see the place where he was, but he has passed to heaven. So at least the parental heart of David felt of old, "by faith and not by sight," when speaking of his infant child. "I shall go to him, but he shall not return to me."

Once more, the Church of Christ is a society ever altering and changing its external forms. "The *whole* family"— the Church of the Patriarchs, and of ages before them; and yet the same family. Remember, I pray you, the diversities of form through which, in so many ages and generations, this Church has passed. Consider the difference there was between the patriarchal Church of the time of Abraham and Isaac, and its condition under David; or the difference between the Church so existing and its state in the days of the apostles; and the marvellous difference between that and the same Church four or five centuries later; or, once again, the difference between that, externally one, and the Church as it exists in the present day, broken into so many fragments. Yet diversified as these states may be, they are not more so than the various stages of a family.

There is a time when the children are all in one room, around their mother's knee. Then comes a time, still further on, when the first separation takes place, and some are leaving their home to prepare for after life. Afterwards, when all in their different professions, trades, or occupations, are separate. At last comes the time when some are gone. And, perchance, the two survivors meet at last—an old, gray-haired man, and a weak, worn-out woman—to mourn over the last graves of a household. Christian brethren, which of these is the right form—the true, external pattern of a family? Say we not truly, it remains the same under all outward mutations? We must think of this, or else we may lose heart in our work. Conceive for instance, the feelings of a pious Jew, when Christianity entered this world; when all his religious system was broken up—the Temple service brought to a violent end; when that polity which he thought was to redeem and ennoble the world was cast aside as a broken and useless thing. Must they not have been as gloomy and as dreary as those of the disciples, when He was dead who they " trusted should have redeemed Israel?" In both cases the body was gone or was altered—the spirit had arisen.

And precisely so it is with our fears and unbelieving apprehensions now. Institutions pass—churches alter—old forms change—and high-minded and good men cling to these as if *they* were the only things by which God could regenerate the world. Christianity appears to some men to be effete and worn out. Men who can look back upon the times of Venn, and Newton, and Scott—comparing the degeneracy of their descendants with the men of those days — lose heart, as if all things were going wrong. "Things are not," they say, "as they were in our younger days." No my Christian brethren, things are not as they then were; but the Christian cause lives on—not in the successors of such men as those; the outward form is altered, but the spirit is elsewhere, is risen—risen just as truly as the spirit of the highest Judaism rose again in Christianity. And to mourn over old superstitions and effete creeds, is just as unwise as is the grief of the mother mourning over the form which was once her child. She cannot separate her affection from that form—those hands, those limbs, those features—are they not her child? The true answer is, her child is not there. It is only the form of her child. And it is as unwise to mourn over the decay of those institutions—the change of human forms—as it was unwise in Jonah to mourn with that passionate sorrow over the decay of the gourd which had sheltered him from the heat of the noontide sun. A worm had eaten the root of the gourd, and it was gone. But he who made the gourd the shelter to the weary—the shadow of those who are oppressed by the noontide heat of life—lived on: Jonah's God. And so brethren, all things change—all things outward change and alter; but the God of the Church lives on. The Church of God remains under fresh forms—the one, holy, entire family in heaven and earth.

II. Pass we on now, in the second place, to consider the name by which this Church is named. "Our Lord

Jesus Christ," the Apostle says, " of whom the whole family in heaven and earth is named."

Now, every one familiar with the Jewish modes of thought and expression, will allow here, that *name* is but another word to express being, actuality, and existence. So when Jacob desired to know the character and nature of Jehovah, he said—" Tell me now, I beseech thee, thy *name*." When the Apostle here says, " Our Lord Jesus Christ, of whom the whole family in heaven and earth is *named*," it is but another way of saying that it is He on Whom the Church depends—Who has given it substantive existence—without Whom it could not be at all. It is but another way of saying what he has expressed elsewhere—"that there is none other name under heaven given among men, whereby we may be saved." Let us not lose ourselves in vague generalities. Separate from Christ, there is no salvation; there can be no Christianity. Let us understand what we mean by this. Let us clearly define and enter into the meaning of the words we use. When we say that our Lord Jesus Christ is He " of whom the whole family in heaven and earth is named," we mean that the very being of the Church depends on Christ—that it could not be without Him. Now, the Church of Christ depends upon these three things—first, the recognition of a common Father; secondly, of a common Humanity; and thirdly, of a common Sacrifice.

1. First, the recognition of a common Father. That is the sacred truth proclaimed by the Epiphany. God revealed in Christ—not the Father of the Jew only, but also of the Gentile. The Father of a "whole family." Not the partial Father, loving one alone—the elder—but the younger son besides : the outcast prodigal who had spent his living with harlots and sinners, but the child still, and the child of a

Father's love. Our Lord taught this in His own blessed prayer—"*Our* Father;" and as we lose the meaning of that single word *our*, as we say *my* Father—the Father of *me* and of *my* faction—of *me* and *my* fellow believers—*my* Anglicanism or *my* Judaism—be it what it may—instead of *our* Father—the Father of the outcast, the profligate, of all who choose to claim a Father's love ; *so* we lose the meaning of the lesson which the Epiphany was designed to teach, and the possibility of building up a family to God.

2. The recognition of a common Humanity. He from whom the Church is named, took upon Him not the nature merely of the noble, of kings, or of the intellectual philosopher—but of the beggar, the slave, the outcast, the infidel, the sinner, and the nature of every one struggling in various ways. Let us learn then brother men, that we shall have no family in God, unless we learn the deep truth of our common Humanity, shared in by the servant and the sinner, as well as the sovereign. Without this we shall have no Church—no family in God.

3. Lastly, the Church of Christ proceeds out of, and rests upon, the belief in a common Sacrifice.   *   *

*   *   *   *   *   *

*   *   *   *   *   *

There are three ways in which the human race hitherto has endeavoured to construct itself into a family ; first, by the sword ; secondly, by an ecclesiastical system ; and thirdly, by trade or commerce. First, by the sword. The Assyrian, the Persian, the Greek, and the Roman, have done their work—in itself a most valuable and important one ;

but so far as the formation of mankind into a family was the object aimed at, the work of the sword has done almost nothing. Then there was the ecclesiastical system—the grand attempt of the Church of Rome to organize all men into one family, with one ecclesiastical, visible, earthly head. Being Protestants, it is not necessary for us to state our conviction that this attempt has been a signal and complete failure. We now come to the system of commerce and trade. We are told that that which chivalry and honour could not do—which an ecclesiastical system could not do—personal interest *will* do. Trade is to bind men together into one family. When they feel it their *interest* to be one, they will be brothers. Brethren, that which is built on selfishness cannot stand. The system of personal interest must be shivered into atoms. Therefore, we, who have observed the ways of God in the past, are waiting in quiet but awful expectation until he shall confound this system as he has confounded those which have gone before. And it may be effected by convulsions more terrible and more bloody than the world has yet seen. While men are talking of peace, and of the great progress of civilization, there is heard in the distance the noise of armies gathering rank on rank : east and west, north and south, are rolling towards us the crushing thunders of universal war.

Therefore there is but one other system to be tried, and that is the Cross of Christ—a system that is not to be built upon selfishness, nor upon blood, nor upon personal interest, but upon Love. Love, not self—the Cross of Christ, and not the mere working-out of the ideas of individual humanity.

One word only in conclusion. Upon this, the great truth of the Epiphany, the Apostle founds a prayer. He prays, "For this cause I bow my knees unto the Father of our Lord

Jesus Christ, of whom the whole family in heaven and earth is named, that he would grant you, according to the riches of His glory, to be strengthened with might by His Spirit in the inner man, that Christ may dwell in your hearts by faith." This manifestation of joy and good to the Gentiles was, according to him, the great mystery of Love. A Love, brighter, deeper, wider, higher than the largest human heart had ever yet dreamed of. But the Apostle tells us it is after all, but a glimpse of the love of God. How should we learn it more? How should we comprehend the whole meaning of the Epiphany? By sitting down to read works of theology? The Apostle Paul tells us—No. You must love, in order to understand love. "That ye, being rooted and grounded in love, may be able to comprehend with all saints what is the breadth and length, and depth and height; and to know the love of Christ which passeth knowledge." Brother men, one act of charity will teach us more of the love of God than a thousand sermons—one act of unselfishness, of real self-denial, the putting forth of one loving feeling to the outcast and "those who are out of the way," will tell us more of the meaning of the Epiphany than whole volumes of the wisest writers on theology.

XVI.

Preached January 25, 1852.

THE LAW OF CHRISTIAN CONSCIENCE.

"Howbeit there is not in every man that knowledge: for some, with conscience of the idol, unto this hour, eat it as a thing offered unto an idol; and their conscience being weak is defiled. But meat commendeth us not to God: for neither if we eat are we the better; neither if we eat not are we the worse. But take heed lest by any means this liberty of yours become a stumbling-block to them that are weak. For if any man see thee which hast knowledge, sit at meat in the idol's temple, shall not the conscience of him which is weak be emboldened to eat those things which are offered to idols; and through thy knowledge shall the weak brother perish for whom Christ died? But when ye sin so against the brethren and wound their weak conscience ye sin against Christ. Wherefore if meat make my brother to offend I will eat no flesh while the world standeth, lest I make my brother to offend."—1 Corinthians viii. 7—13.

WE have already divided this chapter into two branches —the former portion of it containing the difference between Christian knowledge and secular knowledge, and the second portion containing the apostolic exposition of the law of Christian conscience. The first of these we endeavoured to expound last Sunday, but it may be well briefly to recapitulate the principles of that discourse in a somewhat different form.

Corinth, as we all know and remember, was a city built on the sea coast, having a large and free communication

with all foreign nations; and there was also within it, and
going on amongst its inhabitants, a free interchange of
thought, and a vivid power of communicating the philosophy
and truths of those days to each other. Now it is plain,
that to a society in such a state, and to minds so educated,
the gospel of Christ must have presented a peculiar
attraction, presenting itself to them as it did, as a law of
Christian liberty. And so, in Corinth the gospel had " free
course and was glorified," and was received with great joy
by almost all men, and by minds of all classes and all sects;
and a large number of these attached themselves to the
teaching of the Apostle Paul as the most accredited ex-
pounder of Christianity—the " royal law of liberty." But
it seems, from what we read in this epistle, that a large
number of these men received Christianity as a thing
intellectual, and that alone—and not as a thing which
touched the conscience, and swayed and purified the affections. Thus this liberty became to them almost *all*—they
ran into sin or went to extravagance—they rejoiced in their
freedom from the superstitions, the ignorances, and the
scruples which bound their weaker brethren; but had no
charity—none of that intense charity which characterized
the Apostle Paul, for those still struggling in the delusions
and darkness from which they themselves were free.

More than that, they demanded their right, their Christian
liberty of expressing their opinions in the church, merely for
the sake of *exhibiting* the Christian graces and spiritual gifts
which had been showered upon them so largely; until by
degrees those very assemblies became a lamentable exhibition
of their own depravity, and led to numerous irregularities
which we find severely rebuked by the Apostle Paul. Their
women, rejoicing in the emancipation which had been given

to the Christian community, laid aside the old habits of attire which had been consecrated so long by Grecian and Jewish custom, and appeared with their heads uncovered in the Christian community. Still further than that, the Lord's Supper exhibited an absence of all solemnity, and seemed more a meeting for licentious gratification, where " one was hungry, and another was drunken"—a place in which earthly drunkenness, the mere enjoyment of the appetites, had taken the place of Christian charity towards each other.

And the same feeling—this love of mere liberty—liberty in itself—manifested itself in many other directions. Holding by this freedom, their philosophy taught that the body, that is the flesh, was the only cause of sin; that the soul was holy and pure; and that therefore, to be free from the body would be entire, perfect, Christian emancipation. And so came in that strange, wrong doctrine, exhibited in Corinth, where immortality was taught separate from, and in opposition to, the doctrine of the resurrection. And afterwards they went on with their conclusions about liberty, to maintain that the body, justified by the sacrifice of Christ, was no longer capable of sin; and that in the evil which was done by the body, the soul had taken no part. And therefore sin was to them but as a name, from which a Christian conscience was to be freed altogether. So that when one of their number had fallen into grievous sin, and had committed fornication, " such as was not so much as named among the Gentiles," so far from being humbled by it, they were " puffed up," as if they were exhibiting to the world an enlightened, true, perfect Christianity—separate from all prejudices.

To such a society and to such a state of mind, the Apostle Paul preached in all its length, breadth, and fulness, the humbling doctrines of the Cross of Christ. He taught that knowledge was one thing—that charity was *another* thing; that "knowledge puffeth up, but charity buildeth up." He reminded them that love was the perfection of knowledge. In other words, his teaching came to this: there are two kinds of knowledge; the one the knowledge of the intellect, the other the knowledge of the heart. Intellectually, God never can be known. He must be known by Love—for, "if any man love God, the same is known of Him." Here then, we have arrived in another way, at precisely the same conclusion at which we arrived last Sunday. Here are two kinds of knowledge, secular knowledge and Christian knowledge; and Christian knowledge is this—to know by Love.

Let us now consider the remainder of the chapter, which treats of the law of Christian conscience. You will observe that it divides itself into two branches—the first containing an exposition of the law itself, and the second the Christian applications which flow out of this exposition.

I. The way in which the apostle expounds the law of Christian conscience is this:—Guilt is contracted by the soul, in so far as it sins against and transgresses the law of God by doing that which it believes to be wrong: not so much what *is* wrong as what *appears* to *it* to be wrong. This is the doctrine distinctly laid down in the 7th and 8th verses. The apostle tells the Corinthians — these strong-minded Corinthians—that the superstitions of their weaker brethren were unquestionably wrong. "Meat," he says, "commendeth us not to God; for neither if we eat are we the better, neither if we eat not are we the worse." He then tells them further, that "there is not in every man that knowledge; for some with conscience of the idol, eat it as a thing offered unto an idol." Here then, is an ignorant, mistaken, ill-informed conscience; and yet he goes on to tell them that this conscience, so ill-informed, yet binds the possessor of it: "and their conscience being weak, is defiled." For example,—there could be no harm in eating the flesh of an animal that had been offered to an idol or false god; for a false god is nothing, and it is impossible for it to have contracted positive defilement by being offered to that which is a positive and absolute negation. And yet if any man thought it wrong to eat such flesh, to him it *was* wrong; for in that act there would be a deliberate act of transgression—a deliberate preference of that which was mere enjoyment, to that which was apparently, though it may be only apparently, sanctioned by the law of God. And so it would carry with it all the disobedience, all the guilt, and all the misery which belongs to the doing of an act altogether wrong; or as St. Paul expresses it, the conscience would become defiled.

Here then, we arrive at the first distinction—the distinction between absolute and relative right and wrong. Absolute right and absolute wrong, like absolute truth, can each be but *one* and unalterable in the sight of God. The one absolute *right*—the charity of God and the sacrifice of Christ—this, from eternity to eternity must be the sole measure of eternal right. But human right or human wrong, that is the merit or demerit of any action done by any particular man, must be measured, not by that absolute standard, but as a matter relative to his particular circumstances, the state of the age in which he lives, and his own knowledge of right and wrong. For we come into this world with a moral sense; or to speak more Christianly, with a conscience. And yet that will tell us but very little distinctly. It tells us broadly that which is right and that which is wrong, so that every child can understand this. That charity and self-denial are right—this we see recognised in almost every nation. But the boundaries of these two—when and how far self-denial is right—what are the bounds of charity—this it is for different circumstances yet to bring out and determine.

And so, it will be found that there is a different standard among different nations and in different ages. That for example, which was the standard among the Israelites in the earlier ages, and before their settlement in Canaan, was very different from the higher and truer standard of right and wrong recognised by the later prophets. And the standard in the third and fourth centuries after Christ, was truly and unquestionably an entirely different one from that recognised in the nineteenth century among ourselves.

Let me not be mistaken. I do not say that right and wrong are merely conventional, or merely chronological or geographical, or that they vary with latitude and longitude. I do not say that there ever was or ever can be a nation so utterly blinded and perverted in its moral sense as to acknowledge that which is wrong—seen and known to be wrong—as right; or on the other hand, to profess that which is seen and understood as right, to be wrong. But what I do say is this: that the form and aspect in which different deeds appear, so vary, that there will be for ever a change and alteration in men's opinions, and that which is really most generous may seem most base, and that which is really most base may appear most generous. So for example, as I have already said, there are two things universally recognised—recognised as right by every man whose conscience is not absolutely perverted—charity and self-denial. The charity of God, the sacrifice of Christ—these are the two grand, leading principles of the Gospel; and in some form or other you will find these lying at the roots of every profession and state of feeling in almost every age. But the form in which these appear, will vary with all the gradations which are to be found between the lowest savage state and the highest and most enlightened Christianity.

For example, in ancient Israel the law of love was expounded thus:—"Thou shalt love thy neighbour, and hate thine enemy." Among the American Indians and at the Cape, the only homage perchance given to self-denial, was the strange admiration given to that prisoner of war who bore with unflinching fortitude the torture of his country's enemies. In ancient India the same principle was exhibited, but in a more strange and perverted manner. The homage there given to self-denial, self-sacrifice, was this—that the highest form of religion was considered to be that exhibited by the devotee who sat in a tree until the birds had built their nests in his hair—until his nails, like those of the King of Babylon, had grown like birds' talons—until they had grown into his hands—and he became absorbed into the Divinity.

We will take another instance, and one better known. In ancient Sparta it was the custom to teach children to steal. And here there would seem to be a contradiction to our proposition—here it would seem as if right and wrong were matters merely conventional; for surely stealing can never be anything but wrong. But if we look deeper we shall see that there is no contradiction here. It was not stealing which was admired; the child was punished if the theft was discovered; but it was the dexterity which was admired, and that because it was a warlike virtue, necessary it may be to a people in continual rivalry with their neighbours. It was not that honesty was despised and dishonesty esteemed, but that honesty and dishonesty were made subordinate to that which appeared to them of higher importance, namely, the duty of concealment. And so we come back to the principle which we laid down at first. In every age, among all nations, the same broad principle remains; but the application of it varies. The conscience may be ill-informed, and in this sense only are right and wrong conventional—varying with latitude and longitude, depending upon chronology and geography.

The principle laid down by the Apostle Paul is this:— A man will be judged, not by the abstract law of God, not by the rule of absolute right, but much rather by the relative law of conscience. This he states most distinctly—looking at the question on both sides. That which seems to a man to be right is, in a certain sense, right to him; and that which seems to a man to be wrong, in a certain sense *is* wrong to him. For example: he says in his Epistle to the Romans (v. 14.) that, "sin is not imputed when there is no law," in other words, if a man does not really know a thing to be wrong there is a sense in which, if not right to him, it ceases to be so wrong as it would otherwise be. With respect to the other of these sides however, the case is still more distinct and plain. Here, in the judgment which the apostle delivers in the parallel chapter of the Epistle to the Romans (the 14th), he says, "I know, and am persuaded of the Lord Jesus, that there is nothing unclean of itself: but to him that esteemeth anything to be unclean, to him it is unclean." In other words, whatever may be the abstract merits of the question—however in God's jurisprudence any particular act may stand—to you, thinking it to be wrong, it manifestly *is* wrong, and your conscience will gather round it a stain of guilt if you do it.

In order to understand this more fully, let us take a few instances. There is a difference between *truth* and *veracity*. Veracity—mere veracity—is a small, poor thing. Truth is something greater and higher. Veracity is merely the correspondence between some particular statement and facts—truth is the correspondence between a man's whole soul and reality. It is possible for a man to say that which, unknown to him is false; and yet he may be true: because if deprived of truth he is deprived of it unwillingly. It is possible, on the other hand, for a man to utter veracities, and yet at the very time that he is uttering those veracities to be false to himself, to his brother, and to his God. One of the most signal instances of this is to be seen in the Book of Job. Most of what Job's friends said to him were veracious statements. Much of what Job said for himself was unveracious and mistaken. And yet those veracities of theirs were so torn from all connection with fact and truth, that they became falsehoods; and they were, as has been said, nothing more than "orthodox liars" in the sight of God. On the other hand, Job, blundering perpetually, and falling into false doctrine, was yet a true man—searching for and striving after the truth; and if deprived of it for a time, deprived of it with all his heart and soul unwillingly. And therefore it was that at last the Lord appeared out of the whirlwind, to confound the men of mere veracity, and to stand by and support the honour of the heartily true.

Let us apply the principle further. It is a matter of less importance that a man should state true views, than that he should state views truly. We will put this in its strongest form. Unitarianism is false—Trinitarianism is true. But yet in the sight of God, and with respect to a man's eternal destinies hereafter, it would surely be better for him earnestly, honestly, truly, to hold the doctrines of Unitarianism, than in a cowardly or indifferent spirit, or influenced by authority, or from considerations of interest, or for the sake of lucre, to hold the doctrines of Trinitarianism.

For instance:—Not many years ago the Church of Scotland was severed into two great divisions, and gave to this age a marvellous proof that there is still amongst us the power of living faith—when five hundred ministers gave up all that earth holds dear—position in the church they had loved; friendships and affections formed, and consecrated by long fellowship, in its communion; and almost their hopes of gaining a livelihood—rather than assert a principle which seemed to them to be a false one. Now my brethren, surely the question in such a case for us to consider is not this, merely—whether of the two sections held the abstract *right* —held the principle in its integrity—but surely far rather, this: who on either side was true to the light within, true to God, true to the truth as God had revealed it to his soul.

Now it is precisely upon this principle that we are enabled to indulge a Christian hope that many of those who in ancient times were persecutors, for example, may yet be justified at the bar of Christ. Nothing can make persecution right—it is wrong, essentially, eternally wrong in the sight of God. And yet, if a man sincerely and assuredly thinks that Christ has laid upon him a command to persecute with fire and sword, it is surely better that he should, in spite of all feelings of tenderness and compassion, cast aside the dearest affections at the command of his Redeemer, than that he should, in mere laxity and tenderness, turn aside from what seemed to him to be his duty. At least, this appears to be the opinion of the Apostle Paul. He tells us that he was "a blasphemer and a persecutor and injurious," that "he did many things contrary to the name of Jesus of Nazareth," that "being exceedingly mad against the disciples, he persecuted them even unto strange cities." But he tells us further that, "for this cause he obtained mercy, because he did it ignorantly in unbelief."

Now take a case precisely opposite. In ancient times the Jews did that by which it appeared to them that they would contract defilement and guilt—they spared the lives of the enemies which they had taken in battle. Brethren the eternal law is, that charity is right: and that law is eternally right which says, "Thou shalt love thine enemy." And had the Jews acted upon this principle they would have done well to spare their enemies: but they did it thinking it to be wrong, transgressing that law which commanded them to slay their idolatrous enemies—not from generosity, but in cupidity—not from charity, but from lax zeal. And so doing, the act was altogether wrong.

II. Such is the apostle's exposition of the law of Christian conscience. Let us now, in the second place, consider the applications both of a personal and of a public nature, which arise out of it.

1. The first application is a personal one. It is this:— Do what *seems* to *you* to be right: it is only so that you will at last learn by the grace of God to see clearly what *is* right. A man thinks within himself that it is God's law and God's will that he should act thus and thus. There is nothing possible for us to say—there is no advice for us to give, but this—"You *must* so act." He is responsible for the opinions he holds, and still more for the way in which he arrived at

them—whether in a slothful and selfish, or in an honest and truth-seeking manner; but being now his soul's convictions, you can give no other law than this—" You must obey your conscience." For no man's conscience gets so seared by doing what is wrong unknowingly, as by doing that which appears to be wrong to his conscience. The Jews' consciences did not get seared by their slaying the Canaanites, but they did become seared by their failing to do what appeared to them to be right. Therefore, woe to you if you do what others think right, instead of obeying the dictates of your own conscience; woe to you if you allow authority, or prescription, or fashion, or influence, or any other human thing, to interfere with that awful and sacred thing—responsibility. "Every man," said the apostle, "must give an account of himself to God."

2. The second application of this principle has reference to others. No doubt to the large, free, enlightened mind of the Apostle Paul, all these scruples and superstitions must have seemed mean, trivial, and small indeed. It was a matter to him of far less importance that truth should be *established* than that it should be arrived at truly—a matter of far less importance even, that right should be done, than that right should be done rightly. Conscience was far more sacred to him than even liberty—it was to him a prerogative far more precious to assert the rights of Christian conscience, than to magnify the privileges of Christian liberty. The scruple may be small and foolish, but it may be impossible to uproot the scruple without tearing up the feeling of the sanctity of conscience, and of reverence to the law of God, associated with this scruple. And therefore the Apostle Paul counsels these men to abridge their Christian liberty, and not to eat of those things which had been sacrificed to

idols, but to have compassion upon the scruples of their weaker brethren.

And this, for two reasons. The first of these is a mere reason of Christian feeling. It might cause exquisite pain to sensitive minds to see those things which appeared to them to be wrong, done by Christian brethren. Now you may take a parallel case. It may be, if you will, mere superstition to bow at the name of Jesus. It may be, and no doubt is, founded upon a mistaken interpretation of that passage in the Epistle to the Philippians (ii. 10), which says that "at the name of Jesus every knee shall bow." But there are many congregations in which this has been the long-established rule, and there are many Christians who would feel pained to see such a practice discontinued—as if it implied a declension from the reverence due to "that name which is above every name." Now what in this case is the Christian duty? Is it this—to stand upon our Christian liberty? Or is it not rather this—to comply with a prejudice which is manifestly a harmless one, rather than give pain to a Christian brother?

Take another case. It may be a mistaken scruple; but there is no doubt that it causes much pain to many Christians to see a carriage used on the Lord's day. But you, with higher views of the spirit of Christianity, who know that "the Sabbath was made for man, and not man for the Sabbath"—who can enter more deeply into the truth taught by our blessed Lord, that every day is to be dedicated to Him and consecrated to His service—upon the high principle of Christian liberty you can use your carriage—you can exercise your liberty. But if there are Christian brethren to whom this would give pain—then I humbly ask you, but most earnestly—What is the duty here? Is it not this—to abridge your Christian liberty—and to go through rain, and mud, and snow, rather than give pain to one Christian conscience?

To give one more instance. The words, and garb, and customs of that sect of Christians called Quakers may be formal enough; founded, no doubt, as in the former case, upon a mistaken interpretation of a passage in the Bible: But they are at least harmless; and have long been associated with the simplicity, and benevolence, and Christian humbleness of this body of Christians—the followers of one who, three hundred years ago, set out upon the glorious enterprise of making all men friends. Now would it be Christian, or would it not rather be something more than unchristian—would it not be gross rudeness and coarse unfeelingness to treat such words, and habits, and customs, with anything but respect and reverence?

Further: the apostle enjoined this duty upon the Corinthian converts, of abridging their Christian liberty, not merely because it might give pain to indulge it, but also because it might even lead their brethren into sin. For, if any man should eat of the flesh offered to an idol, feeling himself justified by his conscience, it were well: but if any man, overborne by authority or interest, were to do this, not according to conscience, but against it, there would be a distinct and direct act of disobedience—a conflict between his sense of right and the gratification of his appetites, or the power of influence; and then his compliance would as much damage his conscience and moral sense as if the act had been wrong in itself.

In the personal application of these remarks, there are three things which we have to say. The first is this:— Distinguish I pray you, between this tenderness for a brother's conscience and mere time-serving. This same apostle whom we here see so gracefully giving way upon the ground of expediency when Christian principles were left entire, was the same who stood firm and strong as a rock when any thing was demanded which trenched upon Christian principle. When some required as a matter of necessity for salvation, that these converts should be circumcised, the apostle says—" To whom we gave place by subjection, no, not for an hour!" It was not indifference—it was not cowardice—it was not the mere love of peace, purchased by the sacrifice of principle, that prompted this counsel—but it was Christian love—that delicate and Christian love which dreads to tamper with the sanctities of a brother's conscience.

2. The second thing we have to say is this—that this abridgement of their liberty is a duty more especially incumbent upon all who are possessed of influence. There are some men, happily for themselves we may say, who are so insignificant that they can take their course quietly in the valleys of life, and who can exercise the fullest Christian liberty without giving pain to others. But it is the price which all who are possessed of influence must pay—that their acts must be measured, not in themselves, but according to their influence on others. So, my Christian brethren, to bring this matter home to every-day experience and common life, if the landlord uses his authority and influence to induce his tenant to vote against his conscience, it may be he has secured one voice to the principle which is right, or at all events, to that which seemed to him to be right: but he has gained that single voice at the sacrifice and expense of a brother's soul. Or again—if for the sake of ensuring personal politeness and attention, the rich man puts a gratuity into the hand of a servant of some company which

has forbidden him to receive it, he gains the attention, he ensures the politeness, but he gains it at the sacrifice and expense of a man and a Christian brother.

3. The last remark which we have to make is this:— How possible it is to mix together the vigour of a masculine and manly intellect with the tenderness and charity which is taught by the gospel of Christ! No man ever breathed so freely when on earth the air and atmosphere of heaven as the Apostle Paul—no man ever soared so high above all prejudices, narrowness, littlenesses, scruples, as he: and yet no man ever bound himself as Paul bound himself to the ignorance, the scruples, the prejudices of his brethren. So that what in other cases was infirmity, imbecility, and superstition, gathered round it in his case the pure high spirit of Christian charity and Christian delicacy.

And now, out of the writings, and sayings, and deeds of those who loudly proclaim "the rights of man" and the "rights of liberty," match us if you can with one sentence so sublime, so noble, one that will so stand at the bar of God hereafter, as this single, glorious sentence of his, in which he asserts the rights of Christian conscience above the claims of Christian liberty—"Wherefore if meat make my brother to offend, I will eat no flesh while the world standeth, lest I make my brother to offend."

XVII.

Preached May 16, 1852.

VICTORY OVER DEATH.

"The sting of death is sin, and the strength of sin is the law. But thanks be to God which giveth us the victory through our Lord Jesus Christ."—1 Cor. xv. 56, 57.

ON Sunday last I endeavoured to bring before you the subject of that which Scripture calls the glorious liberty of the Sons of God. The two points on which we were trying to get clear notions were these: what is meant by being under the law, and what is meant by being free from the law? When the Bible says that a man led by the Spirit is not under the law, it does not mean that he is free because he may sin without being punished for it, but it means that he is free because being taught by God's Spirit to love what His law commands he is no longer conscious of acting from restraint. The law does not drive him, because the Spirit leads him.

There is a state brethren, when we recognize God, but do not love God in Christ. It is that state when we admire what is excellent, but are not able to perform it. It is a state when the love of good comes to nothing, dying away in a mere desire. That is the state of nature, when we are under the law, and not converted to the love of Christ. And then there is another state, when God writes His law upon our hearts by love instead of fear. The one state is this, "I cannot do the things that I would"—the other state is this, "I will walk at liberty; for I seek Thy commandments."

Just so far therefore, as a Christian is led by the Spirit, he is a conqueror. A Christian in full possession of his privileges is a man whose very step ought to have in it all the elasticity of triumph, and whose very look ought to have in it all the brightness of victory. And just so far as a Christian suffers sin to struggle in him and overcome his resolutions, just so far he is under the law. And that is the key to the whole doctrine of the New Testament. From first to last the great truth put forward is—The law can neither save you nor sanctify you. The gospel can do both; for it is rightly and emphatically called the perfect law of liberty.

We proceed to-day to a further illustration of this subject —of Christian victory. In the verses which I have read out, the Apostle has evidently the same subject in his mind: slavery through the law: victory through the gospel. "The strength of sin," he says, "is the law." God giveth us the victory through Christ. And when we are familiar with St. Paul's trains of thinking, we find this idea coming in perpetually. It runs like a coloured thread through embroidery, appearing on the upper surface every now and then in a different shape—a leaf, it may be, or a flower; but the same thread still, if you only trace it back with your finger. And this was the golden recurring thread in the mind of Paul. Restraint and law cannot check sin; they only gall it and make it struggle and rebel. The love of God in Christ, that, and only that can give man the victory.

But in this passage the idea of victory is brought to bear upon the most terrible of all a Christian's enemies. It is faith here conquering in death. And the apostle brings together all the believer's antagonists—the law's power, sin, and death the chief antagonist of all; and then, as it were on a conqueror's battle field, shouts over them the hymn of triumph—"Thanks be to God, which giveth us the victory, through our Lord Jesus Christ." We shall take up these two points to dwell upon.

I. The awfulness which hangs round the dying hour.
II. Faith conquering in death.

That which makes it peculiarly terrible to die is asserted in this passage to be, guilt. We lay a stress upon this expression—the sting. It is not said that sin is the only bitterness, but it is the sting which contains in it the venom of a most exquisite torture. And in truth brethren, it is no mark of courage to speak lightly of human dying. We may do it in bravado, or in wantonness; but no man who thinks can call it a trifling thing to die. True thoughtfulness must shrink from death without Christ. There is a world of untold sensations crowded into that moment, when a man puts his hand to his forehead and feels the damp upon it which tells him his hour is come. He has been waiting for death all his life, and now it is come. It is all over—his chance is past, and his eternity is settled. None of us know, except by guess, what that sensation is. Myriads of human beings have felt it to whom life was dear; but they never spoke out their feelings, for such things are untold. And to every individual man throughout all eternity that sensation in its fulness can come but once. It is mockery brethren, for a man to speak lightly of that which he cannot know till it comes.

Now the first cause which makes it a solemn thing to die, is the instinctive cleaving of every thing that lives to its own existence. That unutterable thing which we call our being —the idea of parting with it is agony. It is the first and the intensest desire of living things, to be. Enjoyment, blessedness, everything we long for, is wrapped up in being. Darkness and all that the spirit recoils from, is contained in this idea, not to be. It is in virtue of this unquenchable impulse that the world, in spite of all the misery that is in it, continues to struggle on. What are war, and trade, and labour, and professions? Are they all the result of struggling to be great? No, my brethren, they are the result of struggling *to be*. The first thing that men and nations labour for is existence. Reduce the nation or the man to their last resources, and only see what marvellous energy of contrivance the love of being arms them with. Read back the pauper's history at the end of seventy years —his strange sad history, in which scarcely a single day could ensure subsistence for the morrow—and yet learn what he has done these long years in the stern struggle with impossibility to hold his being where everything is against him, and to keep an existence, whose only conceivable charm is this, that it *is* existence.

Now it is with this intense passion for being, that the idea of death clashes. Let us search why it is we shrink from death. This reason brethren, we shall find, that it presents to us the idea of *not being*. Talk as we will of immortality, there is an obstinate feeling that we cannot master, that we end in death; and *that* may be felt together with the firmest belief of a resurrection. Brethren, our faith tells us one thing, and our sensations tell us another. When we die, we are surrendering in truth all that with which we have associated existence. All that we know of life is connected with a shape, a form, a body of materialism; and now that that is palpably melting away into nothingness, the boldest heart may be excused a shudder, when there is forced upon it, in spite of itself, the idea of ceasing for ever.

The second reason is not one of imagination at all, but most sober reality. It is a solemn thing to die, because it is the parting with all round which the heart's best affections have twined themselves. There are some men who have not the capacity for keen enjoyment. Their affections have nothing in them of intensity, and so they pass through life without ever so uniting themselves with what they meet, that there would be anything of pain in the severance. Of course, with them the bitterness of death does not attach so much to the idea of parting. But my brethren, how is it with human nature generally? Our feelings do not weaken as we go on in life; emotions are less shown, and we get a command over our features and our expressions; but the man's feelings are deeper than the boy's. It is length of time that makes attachment. We become wedded to the sights and sounds of this lovely world more closely as years go on.

Young men, with nothing rooted deep, are prodigal of life. It is an adventure to them, rather than a misfortune, to leave their country for ever. With the old man it is like tearing his own heart from him. And so it was that when Lot quitted Sodom, the younger members of his family went on gladly. It is a touching truth; it was the aged one who looked behind to the home which had so many recollections connected with it. And therefore it is, that when men approach that period of existence when they must go, there is an instinctive lingering over things which they shall never see again. Every time the sun sets, every time the old man sees his children gathering round him, there is a filling of the eye with an emotion that we can understand. There is upon his soul the thought of parting, that strange wrench from all we love which makes death (say what moralists will of it) a bitter thing.

Another pang which belongs to death, we find in the sensation of loneliness which attaches to it. Have we ever seen a ship preparing to sail with its load of pauper emigrants to a distant colony? If we have we know what that desolation is which comes from feeling unfriended on a new and untried excursion. All beyond the seas, to the ignorant poor man, is a strange land. They are going away from the helps and the friendships and the companionships of life, scarcely knowing what is before them. And it is in such a moment, when a man stands upon a deck, taking his last look of his fatherland, that there comes upon him a sensation new, strange, and inexpressibly miserable—the feeling of being alone in the world.

Brethren, with all the bitterness of such a moment, it is but a feeble image when placed by the side of the loneliness of death. We die alone. We go on our dark mysterious journey for the first time in all our existence, without one to accompany us. Friends are beside our bed, they must stay behind. Grant that a Christian has something like familiarity with the Most High, *that* breaks this solitary feeling; but what is it with the mass of men? It is a question full of loneliness to them. What is it they are to see? What are they to meet? Is it not true, that, to the larger number of this congregation, there is no one point in all eternity on which the eye can fix distinctly and rest gladly—nothing beyond the grave, except a dark space into which they must plunge alone?

And yet my brethren, with all these ideas no doubt vividly before his mind, it was none of them that the apostle selected as the crowning bitterness of dying. It was not the thought of surrendering existence. It was not the parting from all bright and lovely things. It was not the shudder of sinking into the sepulchre alone. " The sting of death is *sin*."

Now there are two ways in which this deep truth applies itself. There is something that appals in death when there are distinct separate acts of guilt resting on the memory; and there is something too in the possession of a guilty heart, which is quite another thing from acts of sin, that makes it an awful thing to die. There are some who carry about with them the dreadful secret of sin that has been done; guilt that has a name. A man has injured some one; he has made money, or got on by unfair means; he has been unchaste; he has done some of those thousand things of life which leave upon the heart the dark spot that will not come out. All these are sins which you can count up and number. And the recollection of things like these is that agony which we call remorse. Many of us have remembrances of this kind which are fatal to serenity. We shut them out, but it will not do. They bide their time, and then suddenly present themselves, together with the thought of a judgment-seat. When a guilty man begins to think of dying, it is like a vision of the Son of Man presenting itself and calling out the voices of all the unclean spirits in the man— " Art thou come to torment us before the time?"

But my brethren, it is a mistake if we suppose that is the common way in which sin stings at the thought of death. Men who have lived the career of passionate life have distinct and accumulated acts of guilt before their eyes. But with most men it is not guilty acts, but guiltiness of heart that weighs the heaviest. Only take yesterday as a specimen of life. What was it with most of us? A day of sin. Was it sin palpable and dark, such as we shall remember painfully this day year? Nay my brethren, unkindness, petulance, wasted time, opportunities lost, frivolous conversation, *that* was our chief guilt. And yet with all that trifling as it may be, when it comes to be the history of life, does it not leave behind a restless undefinable sense of fault, a vague idea of debt, but to what extent we know not, perhaps the more wretched just because it is uncertain?

My Christian brethren, this is the sting of sinfulness, the wretched consciousness of an unclean heart. It is just this feeling, "God is not my friend; I am going on to the grave, and no *man* can say aught against me, but my heart is not right; I want a river like that which the ancients fabled—the river of forgetfulness—that I might go down into it and bathe, and come up a new man. It is not so much what I have done; it is what I am. Who shall save me from myself?" Oh, it is a desolate thing to think of the coffin when that thought is in all its misery before the soul. It is the sting of death.

And now let us bear one thing in mind, the sting of sin is not a constant pressure. It may be that we live many years in the world before a death in our own family forces the thought personally home. Many years before all those sensations which are so often the precursors of the tomb—the quick short cough, lassitude, emaciation, pain—come in startling suddenness upon us in our young vigour, and make us feel what it is to be here with death inevitable to ourselves. And when those things become habitual, habit makes delicacy the same forgetful thing as health, so that neither in sickness, nor in health, is the thought of death a constant pressure. It is only now and then; but so often as death is a reality, the sting of death is sin.

Once more we remark, that all this power of sin to agonize, is traced by the Apostle to the law—"the strength of sin is the law;" by which he means to say that sin would not be so violent if it were not for the attempt of God's law to restrain it. It is the law which makes sin strong. And he does not mean particularly the law of Moses. He means any law, and all law. Law is what forbids and threatens; law bears gallingly on those who want to break it. And St. Paul declares this, that no law, not even God's law, can make men righteous in heart, unless the Spirit has taught men's hearts to acquiesce in the law. It can only force out into rebellion the sin that is in them.

It is so, brethren, with a nation's law. The voice of the nation must go along with it. It must be the expression of their own feeling, and then they will have it obeyed. But if it is only the law of a government, a law which is against the whole spirit of the people, there is first the murmur of a nation's disapprobation, and then there is transgression, and then, if the law be vindicated with a high hand, the next step is the bursting that law asunder in national revolution. And so it is with God's law. It will never control a man long who does not from his heart love it. First comes a sensation of restraint, and then comes a murmuring of the heart; and last, there comes the rising of passion in its giant might, made desperate by restraint. That is the law giving strength to sin.

And therefore brethren, if all we know of God be this, that He has made laws, and that it is terrible to break them ; if all our idea of religion be this, that it is a thing of commands and hindrances—Thou shalt, and thou shalt not ; we are under the law, and there is no help for it. We *must* shrink from the encounter with death.

We pass to our second subject—Faith conquering in death.

And, before we enter upon this topic, there are two general remarks that we have to make. The first is, The elevating power of faith. There is nothing in all this world that ever led man on to real victory but faith. Faith is that looking forward to a future with something like certainty, that raises man above the narrow feelings of the present. Even in this life he is a greater man, a man of more elevated character, who is steadily pursuing a plan that requires some years to accomplish, than he who is living by the day. Look forward but ten years, and plan for it, live for it ; there is something of manhood, something of courage required to conquer the thousand things that stand in your way. And therefore it is, that faith, and nothing but faith, gives victory in death. It is that elevation of character which we get from looking steadily and for ever forward, till eternity becomes a real home to us, that enables us to look down upon the last struggle, and the funeral, and the grave, not as the great end of all, but only as something that stands between us and the end. We are conquerors of death when we are able to look beyond it.

Our second remark is for the purpose of fixing special attention upon this, that ours is not merely to be victory, it is to be victory through Christ. "Thanks be to God which giveth us the victory through our Lord Jesus Christ." Victory brethren, mere victory over death is no unearthly thing. You may get it by infidelity. Only let a man sin long enough, and desperately enough to shut judgment altogether out of his creed, and then you have a man who can bid defiance to the grave. It was so that our country's greatest infidel historian met death. He quitted the world without parade and without display. If we want a specimen of victory apart from Christ, we have it on his death-bed. He left all this strange world of restlessness, calmly, like an unreal show that must go to pieces, and he himself an unreality departing from it. A sceptic can be a conqueror in death.

Or again, mere manhood may give us a victory. He who has only learned not to be afraid to die, has not learned much. We have steel and nerve enough in our hearts to dare anything. And after all, it is a triumph so common as scarcely to deserve the name. Felons die on the scaffold like men ; soldiers can be hired by tens of thousands, for a few pence a day, to front death in its worst form. Every minute that we live sixty of the human race are passing away, and the greater part with courage—the weak, and the timid, as well as the resolute. Courage is a very different thing from the Christian's victory.

Once more brethren, necessity can make man conqueror over death. We can make up our minds to anything when it once becomes inevitable. It is the agony of suspense that makes danger dreadful. History can tell us that men can look with desperate calmness upon hell itself when once it has become a certainty. And it is this after all, that commonly makes the dying hour so quiet a thing. It is more dreadful in the distance than in the reality. When a man feels that there is no help, and he must go, he lays him down to die, as quietly as a tired traveller wraps himself in his cloak to sleep. It is quite another thing from all this that Paul meant by victory.

In the first place, it is the prerogative of a Christian to be conqueror over Doubt. Brethren, do we all know what doubt means? Perchance not. There are some men who have never believed enough to doubt. There are some who have never thrown their hopes with such earnestness on the world to come, as to feel anxiety for fear it should not all be true. But every one who knows what Faith is, knows too, what is the desolation of Doubt. We pray till we begin to ask, Is there one who hears, or am I whispering to myself? —We hear the consolation administered to the bereaved, and we see the coffin lowered into the grave, and the thought comes, What if all this doctrine of a life to come be but the dream of man's imaginative mind, carried on from age to age, and so believed, because it is a venerable superstition? Now Christ gives us victory over that terrible suspicion in two ways—first, He does it by His own resurrection. We have got a fact there that all the metaphysics about impossibility cannot rob us of. In moments of perplexity we look back to this. The grave has once, and more than once, at the Redeemer's bidding, given up its dead. It is a world fact. It tells us what the Bible means by our resurrection—not a spiritual rising into new holiness merely—that, but also something more. It means that in our own proper identity, we shall live again. Make that thought real, and God has given you, so far, victory over the grave through Christ.

There is another way in which we get the victory over doubt, and that is by living in Christ. All doubt comes from living out of habits of affectionate obedience to God. By idleness, by neglected prayer, we lose our power of realizing things not seen. Let a man be religious and irreligious at intervals—irregular, inconsistent, without some distinct thing to live for—it is a matter of impossibility that he can be free from doubts. He must make up his mind for a dark life. Doubts can only be dispelled by that kind of active life that realizes Christ. And there is no faith that gives a victory so steadily triumphant as that. When such a man comes near the opening of the vault, it is no world of sorrows he is entering upon. He is only going to see things that he has felt, for he has been living in heaven. He has his grasp on things that other men are only groping after and touching now and then. Live above this world, Brethren, and then the powers of the world to come are so upon you that there is no room for doubt.

Besides all this, it is a Christian's privilege to have victory over the fear of death. And here it is exceedingly easy to paint what after all is only the image-picture of a dying hour. It is the easiest thing to represent the dying Christian as a man who always sinks into the grave full of hope, full of triumph, in the certain hope of a blessed resurrection. Brethren, we must paint things in the sober colours of truth; not as they might be supposed to be, but as they are. Often that is only a picture. Either very few death-beds are Christian ones, or else triumph is a very different thing from what the word generally implies. Solemn, subdued, full of awe and full of solemnity, is the dying hour generally of the holiest men: sometimes almost darkness.— Rapture is a rare thing, except in books and scenes.

Let us understand what really is the victory over fear. It may be rapture or it may not. All that depends very much on temperament; and after all, the broken words of a dying man are a very poor index of his real state before

God. Rapturous hope has been granted to martyrs in peculiar moments. It is on record of a minister of our own Church, that his expectation of seeing God in Christ became so intense as his last hour drew near, that his physician was compelled to bid him calm his transports, because in so excited a state he could not die. A strange unnatural energy was imparted to his muscular frame by his nerves overstrung with triumph. But brethren, it fosters a dangerous feeling to take cases like those as precedents. It leads to that most terrible of all unrealities—the acting of a death-bed scene. A Christian conqueror dies calmly. Brave men in battle do not boast that they are not afraid. Courage is so natural to them that they are not conscious they are doing anything out of the common way—Christian bravery is a deep, calm thing, unconscious of itself. There are more triumphant death-beds than we count, if we only remember this—true fearlessness makes no parade.

Oh, it is not only in those passionate effusions in which the ancient martyrs spoke sometimes of panting for the crushing of their limbs by the lions in the amphitheatre, or of holding out their arms to embrace the flames that were to curl round them—it is not then only that Christ has stood by His servants, and made them more than conquerors :— there may be something of earthly excitement in all that. Every day His servants are dying modestly and peacefully —not a word of victory on their lips; but Christ's deep triumph in their hearts—watching the slow progress of their own decay, and yet so far emancipated from personal anxiety that they are still able to think and to plan for others, not knowing that they are doing any great thing. They die, and the world hears nothing of them; and yet theirs was the completest victory. They came to the battle field, the field to which they had been looking forward all their lives, and the enemy was not to be found. There was no Foe to fight with.

The last form in which a Christian gets the victory over death is by means of his resurrection. It seems to have been this which was chiefly alluded to by the Apostle here ; for he says, "when this corruptible shall have put on incorruption . . . *then* shall come to pass the saying which is written, Death is swallowed up in victory." And to say the truth, brethren, it is a rhetorical expression rather than a sober truth when we call anything, except the resurrection, victory over death. We may conquer doubt and fear when we are dying, but that is not conquering death. It is like a warrior crushed to death by a superior antagonist refusing to yield a groan, and bearing the glance of defiance to the last. You feel that he is an unconquerable spirit, but he is not the conqueror. And when you see flesh melting away, and mental power becoming infantine in its feebleness, and lips scarcely able to articulate, is there left one moment a doubt upon the mind, as to *who* is the conqueror in spite of all the unshaken fortitude there may be? The victory is on the side of Death, not on the side of the dying.

And my brethren, if we would enter into the full feeling of triumph contained in this verse, we must just try to bear in mind what this world would be without the thought of a resurrection. If we could conceive an unselfish man looking upon this world of desolation with that infinite compassion which all the brave and good feel, what conception could he have but that of defeat, and failure, and sadness—the sons of man mounting into a bright existence, and one after another falling back into darkness and nothingness, like soldiers trying to mount an impracticable breach, and falling back crushed and mangled into the ditch before the bayonets and the rattling fire of their conquerors. Misery and guilt, look which way you will, till the heart gets sick with looking at it.

Brethren, until a man looks on evil till it seems to him almost like a real personal enemy rejoicing over the destruction that it has made, he can scarcely conceive the deep rapture which rushed into the mind of the Apostle Paul when he remembered that a day was coming when all this was to be reversed. A day was coming, and it was the day of reality for which he lived, ever present and ever certain, when this sad world was to put off *for ever* its changefulness and its misery, and the grave was to be robbed of its victory, and the bodies were to come forth purified by their long sleep. He called all this a victory, because he felt that it was a real battle that has to be fought and won before that can be secured. One battle has been fought by Christ, and another battle, most real and difficult, but yet a conquering one, is to be fought by us. He hath imparted to us the virtue of His wrestlings, and the strength of His victory. So that, when the body shall rise again, the power of the law to condemn is gone, because we have learned to love the law.

And now to conclude all this, there are but two things which remain to say. In the first place, brethren, if we would be conquerors, we must realize God's love in Christ. Take care not to be under the law. Constraint never yet made a conqueror: the utmost it can do is to make either a rebel or a slave. Believe that God loves you. He gave a triumphant demonstration of it in the Cross. Never shall we conquer self till we have learned *to love*. My Christian brethren, let us remember our high privilege. Christian life, so far as it deserves the name, is victory. We are not going forth to mere battle—we are going forth to conquer. To gain mastery over self, and sin, and doubt, and fear: till the last coldness, coming across the brow, tells us that all is over, and our warfare accomplished—that we are safe, the everlasting arms beneath us—*that* is our calling. Brethren beloved, do not be content with a slothful, dreamy, uncertain struggle. You are to conquer, and the banner under which we are to win is not Fear, but Love. "The strength of sin is the law;" the victory is by keeping before us God in Christ.

Lastly, there is need of encouragement for those of us whose faith is not of the conquering, but the timid kind. There are some whose hearts will reply to all this, Surely victory is not always a Christian's portion. Is there no cold dark watching in Christian life—no struggle when victory seems a mockery to speak of—no times when light and life seem feeble, and Christ is to us but a name, and death a reality? "Perfect love casteth out fear," but who has it? Victory is by faith, but, oh God, who will tell us what this faith *is* that men speak of as a thing so easy; and how we are to get it! You tell us to pray for faith, but how shall we pray in earnest unless we first have the very faith we pray for?

My Christian brethren, it is just to this deepest cry of the human heart that it is impossible to return a full answer. All that is true. To feel Faith is the grand difficulty of life. Faith is a deep impression of God and God's love, and personal trust in it. It is easy to say "Believe and thou shalt be saved," but well we know it is easier said than done. We cannot say how men are to *get* faith. It is God's gift, almost in the same way that genius is. You cannot work *for* faith; you must have it first, and then work *from* it.

But brethren beloved, we can say, Look up, though we know not how the mechanism of the will which directs the eye is to be put in motion; we can say, Look to God in Christ, though we know not how men are to obtain faith to do it. Let us be in earnest. Our polar star is the love of the Cross. Take the eye off that, and you are in darkness and bewilderment at once. Let us not mind what is past. Perhaps it is all failure, and useless struggle, and broken resolves. What then? Settle this first, brethren, Are you in earnest? If so, though your faith be weak and your struggles unsatisfactory, you may begin the hymn of triumph *now*, for victory is pledged. "Thanks be to God, which" not *shall* give, but "*giveth* us the victory through our Lord Jesus Christ."

XVIII.

Preached June 20, 1852.

MAN'S GREATNESS AND GOD'S GREATNESS.

"For thus saith the High and Lofty One that inhabiteth Eternity, whose Name is Holy. I dwell in the high and holy place—with him also that is of a contrite and humble spirit."—Isaiah lvii. 15.

THE origin of this announcement seems to have been the state of contempt in which religion found itself in the days of Isaiah. One of the most profligate monarchs that ever disgraced the page of sacred history, sat upon the throne of Judah. His court was filled with men who recommended themselves chiefly by their licentiousness. The altar was forsaken. Sacrilegious hands had placed the abominations of heathenism in the Holy Place; and Piety, banished from the State, the Church, and the Royal court, was once more as she had been before, and will be again, a wanderer on the face of the earth.

Now, however easy it may be to contemplate such a state of things at a distance, it never takes place in a man's own day and time, without suggesting painful perplexities of a twofold nature. In the first place suspicions respecting God's character; and, in the second place, misgivings as to his own duty. For a faithless heart whispers, Is it worth while to suffer for a sinking cause? Honour, preferment, grandeur, follow in the train of unscrupulous conduct. To be strict in goodness, is to be pointed at and shunned. To be no better than one's neighbours is the only way of being at peace. It seems to have been to such a state as this that Isaiah was commissioned to bring light. He vindicated God's character by saying that He is "the High and Lofty One that inhabiteth Eternity." He encouraged those who were trodden down, to perseverance, by reminding them that real dignity is something very different from present success. God dwells with him, "that is of a contrite and humble spirit." We consider

I. That in which the greatness of God consists.
II. That in which man's greatness consists.

The first measurement, so to speak, which is given us of God's greatness, is in respect of Time. He inhabiteth Eternity. There are some subjects on which it would be good to dwell, if it were only for the sake of that enlargement of mind which is produced by their contemplation. And eternity is one of these, so that you cannot steadily fix the thoughts upon it without being sensible of a peculiar kind of elevation, at the same time that you are humbled by a personal feeling of utter insignificance. You have come in contact with something so immeasurable—beyond the narrow range of our common speculations—that you are exalted by the very conception of it. Now the only way we have of forming any idea of eternity is by going, step by step, up to the largest measures of time we know of, and so ascending, on and on, till we are lost in wonder. We cannot grasp eternity, but we can learn something of it by perceiving, that, rise to what portion of time we will, eternity is vaster than the vastest.

We take up for instance, the history of our own country, and then, when we have spent months in mastering the mere outline of those great events which, in the slow course of revolving centuries, have made England what she is, her earlier ages seem so far removed from our own times that they appear to belong to a hoary and most remote antiquity. But then, when you compare those times with even the existing works of man, and when you remember that, when England was yet young in civilization, the pyramids of Egypt were already grey with 1500 years, you have got another step which impresses you with a doubled amount of vastness. Double that period, and you come to the far distant moment when the present aspect of this world was called, by creation, out of the formless void in which it was before.

Modern science has raised us to a pinnacle of thought beyond even this. It has commanded us to think of countless ages in which that formless void existed before it put on the aspect of its present creation. Millions of years before God called the light day, and the darkness night, there was, if science speaks true, creation after creation called into existence, and buried in its own ruins upon the surface of this earth. And then, there was a time beyond even this—there was a moment when this earth itself, with all its countless creations and innumerable ages, did not exist. And, again, in that far back distance it is more than conceivable, it seems by the analogy of God's dealings next to certain, that ten thousand worlds may have been called into existence, and lasted their unnumbered ages, and then perished in succession. Compared with these stupendous figures, 6,000 years of *our* planet sink into nothingness. The mind is lost in dwelling on such thoughts as these. When you have penetrated far, far back, by successive approximations, and still see the illimitable distance receding before you as distant as before, imagination absolutely gives way, and you feel dizzy and bewildered with new strange thoughts, that have not a name.

But this is only one aspect of the case. It looks only to time past. The same overpowering calculations wait us when we bend our eyes on that which is to come. Time stretches back immeasurably, but it also stretches on and on for ever. Now it is by such a conception as this that the inspired prophet attempts to measure the immeasurable of God. All that eternity, magnificent as it is, never was without an Inhabitant. Eternity means nothing by itself. It merely expresses the existence of the High and Lofty One that inhabiteth it. We make a fanciful distinction between eternity and time—there is no real distinction. We are in eternity at this moment. That has begun to be with us which never began with God. Our only measure of time is by the succession of ideas. If ideas flow fast, and many sights and many thoughts pass by us, time seems lengthened. If we have the simple routine of a few engagements, the same every day, with little variety, the years roll by us so fast that we cannot mark them. It is not so with God. There is no succession of ideas with Him. Every possible idea is present with Him now. It was present with Him ten thousand years ago. God's dwelling-place is that eternity which has neither past nor future, but one vast, immeasurable present.

There is a second measure given us of God in this verse. It is in respect of Space. He dwelleth in the High and Lofty place. He dwelleth moreover, in the most insignificant place—even the heart of man. And the idea by which the prophet would here exhibit to us the greatness of God is that of His eternal Omnipresence. It is difficult to say which conception carries with it the greatest exaltation —that of boundless space or that of unbounded time. When we pass from the tame and narrow scenery of our own country, and stand on those spots of earth in which nature puts on her wilder and more awful forms, we are conscious of something of the grandeur which belongs to the thought of space. Go where the strong foundations of the earth lie around you in their massive majesty, and mountain after mountain rears its snow to heaven in a giant chain, and then, when this bursts upon you for the first time in life, there is that peculiar feeling which we call, in common language, an enlargement of ideas. But when we are told that the sublimity of those dizzy heights is but a nameless speck in comparison with the globe of which they form the girdle; and when we pass on to think of that globe itself as a minute spot in the mighty system to which it belongs, so that our world might be annihilated, and its loss would not be felt; and when we are told that eighty millions of such systems roll in the world of space, to which our own system again is as nothing; and when we are again pressed with the recollection that beyond those furthest limits creative power is exerted immeasurably further than eye can reach, or thought can penetrate; then, brethren, the awe which comes upon the heart is only, after all, a tribute to a *portion* of God's greatness.

Yet we need not science to teach us this. It is the thought which oppresses very childhood—the overpowering thought of space. A child can put his head upon his hands, and think and think till it reaches in imagination some far distant barrier of the universe, and still the difficulty presents itself to his young mind, "And what is beyond that barrier?" and the only answer is "The high and lofty place." And this brethren, is the inward seal with which God has stamped Himself upon man's heart. If every other trace of Deity has been expunged by the fall, these two at least defy destruction—the thought of Eternal Time, and the thought of Immeasurable Space.

The third measure which is given us of God respects His character. His name is Holy. The chief idea which this would convey to us is separation from evil. Brethren, there is perhaps a time drawing near when those of us who shall stand at His right hand, purified from all evil taint, shall be able to comprehend absolutely what is meant by the Holiness of God. At present, with hearts cleaving down to earth, and tossed by a thousand gusts of unholy passion, we can only form a dim conception *relatively* of that which it implies. None but the pure can understand purity. The chief knowledge which we have of God's holiness comes from our acquaintance with unholiness. We know what impurity is—God is *not* that. We know what injustice is—God is *not* that. We know what restlessness, and guilt, and passion are, and deceitfulness, and pride, and waywardness—all these we know. God is none of these. And this is our chief acquaintance with His character. We know what God is *not*. We scarcely can be rightly said to know, that is to feel, what God *is*. And therefore, this is implied in the very name of holiness. Holiness in the Jewish sense means simply separateness. From all that is wrong, and mean, and base, our God is for ever separate.

There is another way in which God gives to us a conception of what this holiness implies. Tell us of His justice, His truth, His loving-kindness. All these are cold abstractions. They convey no distinct idea of themselves to our hearts. What we wanted was, that these should be exhibited to us in tangible reality. And it is just this which God has done. He has exhibited all these attributes, not in the light of *speculation*, but in the light of *facts*. He has given us His own character in all its delicacy of colouring in the history of Christ. Love, Mercy, Tenderness, Purity—these are no mere names when we see them brought out in the human actions of our Master. Holiness is only a shadow to our minds, till it receives shape and substance in the life of Christ. All this character of holiness is intelligible to us in Christ. "No man hath seen God at any time, the only begotten of the Father He hath declared Him."

There is a third light in which God's holiness is shown to us, and that is in the sternness with which He recoils from guilt. When Christ died for man, I know what God's love means; and when Jesus wept human tears over Jerusalem, I know what God's compassion means; and when the stern denunciations of Jesus rung in the Pharisees' ears, I can comprehend what God's indignation is; and when Jesus stood calm before His murderers, I have a conception of what serenity is. Brethren, revelation opens to us a scene beyond the grave, when this shall be exhibited in full operation. There will be an everlasting banishment from God's presence of that impurity on which the last efforts have been tried in vain. It will be a carrying out of this sentence by a law that cannot be reversed—"Depart from me, ye cursed." But it is quite a mistake to suppose that this is only a matter of revelation. Traces of it we have now on this side the sepulchre. Human life is full of God's recoil from sin. In the writhings of a heart which has been made to possess its own iniquities—in the dark spot which guilt leaves upon the conscience, rising up at times in a man's gayest moments, as if it will not come out—in the restlessness and the feverishness which follow the efforts of the man who has indulged habits of sin too long,—in all these there is a law repelling wickedness from the presence of the Most High,—which proclaims that God is holy.

Brethren, it is in these that the greatness of God consists —Eternal in Time—Unlimited in Space—Unchangeable— Pure in character—His serenity and His vastness arise from His own perfections.

We are to consider, in the second place, the greatness of man.
1. The nature of that greatness.
2. The persons who are great.

Now, this is brought before us in the text in this one fact, that man has been made a habitation of the Deity— "I dwell with him that is of a contrite and humble spirit." There is in the very outset this distinction between what is great in God and what is great in man. To be independent of everything in the universe is God's glory, and to be independent is man's shame. All that God has, He has from Himself—all that man has, He has from God. And the moment man cuts himself off from God, that moment he cuts himself off from all true grandeur.

There are two things implied in Scripture, when it is said that God dwells with man. The first is that peculiar presence which He has conferred upon the members of His church. Brethren, we presume not to define what that Presence is, and how it dwells within us—we are content to leave it as a mystery. But this we know, that something of a very peculiar and supernatural character takes place in the heart of every man upon whom the gospel has been brought to bear with power. "Know ye not," says the Apostle, "that your bodies are the temples of the Holy Ghost." And again in the Epistle to the Ephesians—"In Christ ye are builded for an habitation of God through the Spirit." There is something in these expressions which refuses to be explained away. They leave us but one conclusion, and that is—that in all those who have become Christ's by faith, God personally and locally has taken up His dwelling-place.

There is a second meaning attached in Scripture to the expression God dwells in man. According to the first meaning, we understand it in the most plain and literal sense the words are capable of conveying. According to the second, we understand His dwelling in a figurative sense, implying this—that He gives an acquaintance with Himself to man. So, for instance, when Judas asked, "Lord, how is it, that Thou wilt manifest Thyself to us and not to the world?" Our Redeemer's reply was this—"If a man love me, he will keep my words, and my Father will love him, and We will come unto him and make Our abode with him." In the question it was asked *how* God would manifest Himself to His servants. In the answer it was shown *how* He would make His abode with them. And if the answer be any reply to the question at all, what follows is this—that God making His abode or dwelling in the heart is the same thing exactly as God's manifesting himself to the heart.

Brethren, in these two things the greatness of man consists. One is to have God so dwelling in us as to impart His character to us; and the other is to have God so dwelling in us that we recognise His presence, and know that we are His and He is ours. They are two things perfectly distinct. To *have* God in us, this is salvation ; to *know* that God is in us, this is assurance.

Lastly, we inquire as to the persons who are truly great. And these the Holy Scripture has divided into two classes —those who are humble and those who are contrite in heart. Or rather, it will be observed that it is the same class of character under different circumstances. Humbleness is the frame of mind of those who are in a state of innocence, contrition of those who are in a state of repentant guilt. Brethren, let not the expression innocence be misunderstood. Innocence in its true and highest sense never existed but once upon this earth. Innocence cannot be the religion of man now. But yet there are those who have walked with God from youth, not quenching the spirit which He gave them, and who are therefore *comparatively* innocent beings. All they have to do is to go on, whereas the guilty man has to stop and turn back before he can go on. Repentance with them is the gentle work of every day, not the work of one distinct and miserable part of life. They are those whom the Lord calls just men which need no repentance, and of whom He says, " He that is clean needeth not save to wash his feet."

Now they are described here as the humble in heart. Two things are required for this state of mind. One is that a man should have a true estimate of God, and the other is that he should have a true estimate of himself.

Vain, blind man, places himself on a little corner of this planet, a speck upon a speck of the universe, and begins to form conclusions from the small fraction of God's government which he can see from thence. The astronomer looks at the laws of motion and forgets that there must have been a First Cause to commence that motion. The surgeon looks at the materialism of his own frame and forgets that matter cannot organise itself into exquisite beauty. The metaphysician buries himself in the laws of mind and forgets that there may be spiritual influences producing all those laws. And this brethren, is the unhumbled spirit of philosophy—intellectual pride. Men look at Nature, but they do not look through it up to Nature's God. There is awful ignorance of God, arising from indulged sin, which produces an unhumbled heart. God may be shut out from the soul by pride of intellect, or by pride of heart.

Pharaoh is placed before us in Scripture almost as a type of pride. His pride arose from ignorance of God. "Who is the Lord that I should obey His voice? I know not the Lord, neither will I let Israel go." And this was not intellectual pride; it was pride in a matter of duty. Pharaoh had been immersing his whole heart in the narrow politics of Egypt. The great problem of his day was to aggrandise his own people and prevent an insurrection of the Israelites; and that small kingdom of Egypt had been his universe. He shut his heart to the voice of justice and the voice of humanity; in other words, great in the pride of human majesty, small in the sight of the High and Lofty One, he shut himself out from the knowledge of God.

The next ingredient of humbleness is, that a man must have a right estimate of himself. There is a vast amount of self-deception on this point. We say of ourselves that which we could not bear others to say of us. A man truly humbled would take it only as his due when others treated him in the way that he says that he deserves. But my brethren, we kneel in our closets in shame for what we are, and we tell our God that the lowest place is too good for us;

and then we go into the world, and if we meet with slight or disrespect, or if our opinion be not attended to, or if another be preferred before us, there is all the anguish of a galled and jealous spirit, and half the bitterness of our lives comes from this, that we are smarting from what we call the wrongs and the neglect of men. My beloved brethren, if we saw ourselves as God sees us, we should be willing to be anywhere, to be silent when others speak, to be passed by in the world's crowd, and thrust aside to make way for others. We should be willing to put others in the way of doing that which we might have got reputation for by doing ourselves. This was the temper of our Master—this is the meek and the quiet spirit, and this is the temper of the humble with whom the High and Lofty One dwells.

The other class of those who are truly great are the contrite in spirit. At first sight it might be supposed that there must ever be a vast distinction between the innocent and the penitent. It was so that the elder son in the parable thought when he saw his brother restored to his father's favour. He was surprised and hurt. He had served his father these many years—his brother had wasted his substance in riotous living. But in this passage God makes no distinction. He places the humble consistent follower and the broken-hearted sinner on a level. He dwells with both, with Him that is contrite, *and* with him that is humble. He sheds around them both the grandeur of His own presence, and the annals of Church history are full of exemplifications of this marvel of God's grace. By the transforming grace of Christ men, who have done the very work of Satan, have become as conspicuous in the service of heaven, as they were once conspicuous in the career of guilt.

So indisputably has this been so, that men have drawn

from such instances the perverted conclusion, that if a man is ever to be a great saint, he must first be a great sinner. God forbid brethren, that we should ever make such an inference. But this we infer for our own encouragement, that past sin does not necessarily preclude from high attainments. We must "forget the things that are behind." We must not mourn over past years of folly as if they made saintliness impossible. Deep as we may have been once in earthliness, so deep we may also be in penitence, and so high we may become in spirituality.

We have so many years the fewer to do our work in. Well brethren, let us try to do it so much the faster. Christ can crowd the work of years into hours. He did it with the dying thief. If the man who has set out early may take his time, it certainly cannot be so with *us* who have lost our time. If we have lost God's bright and happy presence by our wilfulness, what then? Unrelieved sadness? Nay, brethren, calmness, purity, may have gone from our heart; but *all* is not gone yet. Just as sweetness comes from the bark of the cinnamon when it is bruised, so can the spirit of the Cross of Christ bring beauty and holiness and peace out of the bruised and broken heart. God dwells with the contrite as much as with the humble.

And now brethren, to conclude, the first inference we collect from this subject, is the danger of coming into collision with such a God as our God. Day by day we commit sins of thought and word of which the dull eye of man takes no cognisance. He whose name is Holy cannot pass them by. We may elude the vigilance of a human enemy and place ourselves beyond his reach. God fills all space—there is not a spot in which His piercing eye is not on us, and His uplifted hand cannot find us out. Man must strike soon if he would strike at all; for opportunities pass away from him, and his victim may escape his vengeance by death. There is no passing of opportunity with God, and it is this which makes His long suffering a solemn thing. God can wait, for He has a whole eternity before Him in which He may strike. "All things are open, and naked to Him with whom we have to do."

In the next place we are taught the heavenly character of condescension. It is not from the insignificance of man that God's dwelling with him is so strange. It is as much the glory of God to bend His attention on an atom as to uphold the universe. But the marvel is that the habitation which He has chosen for Himself is an impure one. And when He came down from His magnificence to make this world His home, still the same character of condescension was shown through all the life of Christ. Our God selected the society of the outcasts of earth, those whom none else would speak to.

Brethren, if we would be Godlike, we must follow in the same steps. Our temptation is to do exactly the reverse. We are for ever wishing to obtain the friendship and the intimacy of those above us in the world. To win over men of influence to truth—to associate with men of talent and station, and title. This is the world-chase, and this, brethren, is too much the religious man's chase. But if you look simply to the question of resemblance to God, then the man who makes it a habit to select that one in life to do good to, and that one in a room to speak with, whom others pass by because there is nothing either of intellect, or power, or name, to recommend him, but only humbleness, *that* man has stamped upon his heart more of heavenly similitude by condescension, than the man who has made it his business to win this world's great ones, even for the sake of truth.

Lastly, we learn the guilt of two things of which this world is full—vanity and pride. There is a distinction between these two. But the distinction consists in this, that the vain man looks for the admiration of others—the proud man requires nothing but his own. Now, it is this distinction which makes vanity despicable to us all. We can easily find out the vain man—we soon discover what it is he wants to be observed, whether it be a gift of person, or a gift of mind, or a gift of character. If he be vain of his person, his attitudes will tell the tale. If he be vain of his judgment, or his memory, or his honesty, he cannot help an unnecessary parade. The world finds him out, and this is why vanity is ever looked on with contempt. So soon as we let men see that we are suppliants for their admiration, we are at their mercy. We have given them the privilege of feeling that they are above us. We have invited them to spurn us. And therefore vanity is but a thing for scorn. But it is very different with pride. No man can look down on him that is proud, for he has asked no man for anything. They are forced to feel respect for pride, because it is thoroughly independent of them. It wraps itself up in the consequence of its own excellences, and scorns to care whether others take note of them or not.

It is just here that the danger lies. We have exalted a sin into a virtue. No man will acknowledge that he is vain, but almost any man will acknowledge that he is proud. But tried by the balance of the sanctuary, there is little to choose between the two. If a man look for greatness out of God, it matters little whether he seek it in his own applause, or in the applause of others. The *proud* Pharisee, who trusted in himself that he was righteous, was condemned by Christ as severely, and even more, than the *vain* Jews who "could not believe because they sought honour from one another, and not that honour which cometh from God only." It may be a more dazzling, and a more splendid sin to be proud. It is not less hateful in God's sight. Let us speak God's word to our own unquiet, swelling, burning hearts. Pride may disguise itself as it will in its own majesty, but in the presence of the High and Lofty One, it is but littleness after all.

XIX.

Preached June 27, 1852.

THE LAWFUL AND UNLAWFUL USE OF LAW.

(A FRAGMENT.)

"But we know that the law is good, if a man use it lawfully."
1 Tim. i. 8.

IT is scarcely ever possible to understand a passage without some acquaintance with the history of the circumstances under which it was written.

At Ephesus, over which Timothy was bishop, people had been bewildered by the teaching of converted Jews, who mixed the old leaven of Judaism with the new spirituality of Christianity. They maintained the perpetual obligation of the Jewish law.—v. 7. They desired to be teachers of the law. They required strict performance of a number of severe observances. They talked mysteriously of angels and powers intermediate between God and the human soul.—v. 4. The result was an interminable discussion at Ephesus. The Church was filled with disputations and controversies.

Now there is something always refreshing to see the Apostle Paul descending upon an arena of controversy, where minds have been bewildered; and so much is to be said on both sides, that people are uncertain which to take. You know at once that he will pour light upon the question, and illuminate all the dark corners. You know that he will not trim, and balance, and hang doubtful, or become a partisan; but that he will seize some great principle which lies at the root of the whole controversy, and make its true bearings clear at once.

This he always does, and this he does on the present occasion.—v. 5 and 6. He does not, like a vehement polemic, say Jewish ceremonies and rules are all worthless, nor some ceremonies are worthless, and others essential; but he says, the root of the whole matter is charity. If you turn aside from this, all is lost; here at once the controversy closes. So far as any rule fosters the spirit of love, that is, is used lawfully, it is wise, and has a use. So far as it does not, it is chaff. So far as it hinders it, it is poison.

Now observe how different this method is from that which is called the sober, moderate way—the *via media*. Some would have said, the great thing is to avoid extremes. If the question respects fasting—fast—only in *moderation*. If the observance of the Sabbath day, observe it on the Jewish principle, only *not so strictly*.

St. Paul, on the contrary, went down to the root; he said, the true question is not whether the law is good or bad, but on what principle; he said, you are both wrong—*you*, in saying that the observance of the law is essential, for the end of it is charity, and if *that* be got what matter *how*—*you*, in saying rules may be dispensed with entirely and always, "for we know that the law is good."

I. The unlawful use, and
II. The lawful use of law.

I. The unlawful use.

Define law.—By law, Paul almost always means not the Mosaic law, but law in its essence and principle, that is, constraint. This chiefly in two forms expresses itself— 1st, a custom; 2nd, a maxim. As examples of custom, we might give Circumcision, or the Sabbath, or Sacrifice, or Fasting.

Law said, thou shalt *do* these things; and law, as mere law, constrained them. Or again, law may express itself in maxims and rules.

In rules, as when law said, "Thou shalt not steal"—not saying a word about secret dishonesty of heart, but simply taking cognizance of *acts*.

In maxims, as when it admonished that man ought to give a tenth to God, leaving the principle of the matter untouched. Principle is one thing, and maxim is another. A principle requires liberality, a maxim says one-tenth. A principle says, "A merciful man is merciful to his beast," leaves mercy to the heart, and does not define how; a maxim says, thou shalt not muzzle the ox that treadeth out thy corn. A principle says, Forgive; a maxim defines " seven times;" and thus the whole law falls into two divisions.

The ceremonial law, which constrains life by customs.

The moral law, which guides life by rules and maxims.

Now it is an illegitimate use of law. First. To expect by obedience to it to make out a title to salvation.

By the deeds of the law, shall no man living be justified. Salvation is by faith: a state of heart right with God; faith is the spring of holiness—a well of life. Salvation is not the having committed a certain number of good acts. Destruction is not the having committed a certain number of crimes. Salvation is God's Spirit in us, leading to good. Destruction is the selfish spirit in us, leading to wrong.

For a plain reason then, obedience to law cannot save, because it is merely the performance of a certain number of acts which may be done by habit, from fear, from compulsion. Obedience remains still imperfect. A man may have obeyed the rule, and kept the maxim, and yet not be perfect. "All these commandments have I kept from my youth up." "Yet lackest thou one thing." The law he had kept. The spirit of obedience in its high form of sacrifice he had not.

Secondly. To use it superstitiously.

It is plain that this was the use made of it by the Ephesian teachers.—v. 4. It seemed to them that *law* was pleasing to God as restraint. Then unnatural restraints came to be imposed—on the appetites, fasting; on the affections, celibacy. This is what Paul condemns.—ch. iv., v. 8. "Bodily exercise profiteth little."

And again, this superstition showed itself in a false reverence—wondrous stories respecting angels—respecting the eternal genealogy of Christ — awful thoughts about spirits. The Apostle calls all these, very unceremoniously, "endless genealogies," v. 4, and "old wives' fables."—ch. iv., v. 7.

The question at issue is, wherein true reverence consists: according to them, in the multiplicity of the objects of reverence; according to St. Paul, in the character of the object revered. . . . . God and Right the true object.

But you are not a whit the better for solemn and reverential feelings about a mysterious, invisible world. To tremble before a consecrated wafer is spurious reverence. To bend before the Majesty of Right is Christian reverence.

Thirdly. To use it as if the letter of it were sacred.

The law commanded none to eat the shewbread except the priests. David ate it in hunger. If Abimelech had scrupled to give it, he would have used the law unlawfully.

The law commanded no manner of work. The apostles in hunger rubbed the ears of corn. The Pharisees used the law unlawfully, in forbidding that.

II. The lawful use of law.

1. As a restraint to keep outward evil in check .... "The law was made for sinners and profane." .... Illustrate this by reference to capital punishment. No sane man believes that punishment by death will make a nation's heart right, or that the sight of an execution can soften or ameliorate. Punishment does not work in that way. It is not meant for that purpose. It is meant to guard society.

The law commanding a blasphemer to be stoned, could not teach one Israelite love to God, but it could save the streets of Israel from scandalous ribaldry.

And therefore clearly understand, law is a mere check to bad men: it does not improve them; it often makes them worse; it cannot sanctify them. God never intended that it should. It saves society from the open transgression; it does not contemplate the amelioration of the offender.

Hence we see for what reason the apostle insisted on the use of the law for Christians. Law never can be abrogated. Strict rules are needed exactly in proportion as we want the power or the will to rule ourselves. It is not because the Gospel has come that we are free from the law, but because, and only so far, as we are in a Gospel state. "It is for a righteous man" that the law is not made, and thus we see the true nature of Christian liberty. The liberty to which we are called in Christ, is not the liberty of devils, the liberty of doing what we will, but the blessed liberty of being on the side of the law, and therefore unrestrained by it in doing right.

Illustrate from laws of coining, housebreaking, &c. We are not under them.—Because we may break them as we like? Nay—the moment we desire, the law is alive again to us.

2. As a primer is used by a child to acquire by degrees, principles and a spirit.

This is the use attributed to it in verse 5. "The end of the commandment is charity."

Compare with this, two other passages—" Christ is the end of the law for righteousness," and " love is the fulfilling of the law." " Perfect love casteth out fear."

In every law there is a spirit; in every maxim a principle; and the law and the maxim are laid down for the sake of conserving the spirit and the principle which they enshrine.

St. Paul compares God's dealing with man to a wise parent's instruction of his child.—See the Epistle to the Galatians. Boyhood is under law; you appeal not to the boy's reason, but his will, by rewards and punishments: Do this, and I will reward you; do it not, and you will be punished. So long as a man is under law, this is salutary and necessary, but only while under law. He is free when he discerns principles, and at the same time has got, by habit, the will to obey. So that rules have done for him a double work, taught him the principle and facilitated obedience to it.

Distinguish however.—In point of time, law is first—in point of importance, the Spirit.

In point of *time*, Charity is the "end" of the commandment—in point of *importance*, first and foremost.

The first thing a boy has to do, is to learn implicit obedience to rules. The first thing in importance for a man to learn is, to sever himself from maxims, rules, laws. Why? That he may become an Antinomian, or a Latitudinarian? No. He is severed from submission to the *maxim* because he has got allegiance to the *principle*. He is free from the rule and the law because he has got the Spirit written in his heart.

This is the Gospel. A man is redeemed by Christ so far as he is not under the law; he is free from the law so far as he is free from the evil which the law restrains; he progresses so far as there is no evil in him which it is an effort to keep down; and perfect salvation and liberty are —when we,—who though having the first fruits of the Spirit, yet groan within ourselves, waiting for the adoption, "to wit, the redemption of our body"—shall have been freed in body, soul, and spirit, from the last traces of the evil which can only be kept down by force. In other words, so far as Christ's statement is true of *us*, "The Prince of this world cometh, and hath nothing in me."

XX.

Preached February 21, 1853.

THE PRODIGAL AND HIS BROTHER.

"And he said unto him, Son, thou art ever with me, and all that I have is thine. It was meet that we should make merry, and be glad: for this thy brother was dead, and is alive again; was lost, and is found."—Luke xv. 31, 32.

THERE are two classes of sins. There are some sins by which man crushes, wounds, malevolently injures his brother man: those sins which speak of a bad, tyrannical, and selfish heart. Christ met those with denunciation. There are other sins by which a man injures himself. There is a life of reckless indulgence; there is a career of yielding to ungovernable propensities, which most surely conducts to wretchedness and ruin, but makes a man an object of compassion rather than of condemnation.

The reception which sinners of this class met from Christ was marked by strange and pitying mercy. There was no maudlin sentiment on his lips. He called sin sin, and guilt guilt. But yet there were sins which His lips scourged, and others over which, containing in themselves their own scourge, His heart bled. That which was melancholy, and marred, and miserable in this world, was more congenial to the heart of Christ than that which was proudly happy. It was in the midst of a triumph, and all the pride of a procession, that He paused to weep over ruined Jerusalem. And if we ask the reason why the character of Christ was marked by this melancholy condescension it is that he was in the midst of a world of ruins, and there was nothing there to gladden, but very much to touch with grief. He was here to restore that which was broken down and crumbling into decay. An enthusiastic antiquarian, standing amidst the fragments of an ancient temple surrounded by dust and moss, broken pillar, and defaced architrave, with magnificent projects in his mind of restoring all this to *former* majesty, to draw out to light from mere rubbish the ruined glories, and therefore stooping down amongst the dank ivy and the rank nettles; such was Christ amidst the wreck of human nature. He was striving to lift it out of its degradation. He was searching out in revolting places that which had fallen down, that He might build it up again in fair proportions a holy temple to the Lord.

Therefore He laboured among the guilty; therefore He was the companion of outcasts; therefore He spoke tenderly and lovingly to those whom society counted undone; therefore He loved to bind up the bruised and the brokenhearted; therefore His breath fanned the spark which seemed dying out in the wick of the expiring taper, when men thought that it was too late, and that the hour of *hopeless* profligacy was come. It was that feature in His character, that tender, hoping, encouraging spirit of His which the prophet Isaiah fixed upon as characteristic. "A bruised reed will He not break."

It was an illustration of this spirit which He gave in the parable which forms the subject of our consideration to-day. We find the occasion which drew it from Him in the commencement of this chapter, "Then drew near unto Him all the publicans and sinners for to hear Him. And the Pharisees and Scribes murmured, saying, This man receiveth sinners, and eateth with them." It was then that Christ condescended to offer an excuse or an explanation of His conduct. And His excuse was this: It is natural, humanly natural, to rejoice more over that which has been recovered than over that which has been never lost. He proved that by three illustrations taken from human life. The first illustration intended to show the feelings of Christ in winning back a sinner, was the joy which the shepherd feels in the recovery of a sheep from the mountain wilderness. The second was the satisfaction which a person feels for a recovered coin. The last was the gladness which attends the restoration of an erring son.

Now the three parables are alike in this, that they all describe more or less vividly the feelings of the Redeemer on the recovery of the lost. But the third parable differs from the other two in this, that besides the feelings of the Saviour, it gives us a multitude of particulars respecting the feelings, the steps, and the motives of the penitent who is reclaimed back to goodness. In the two first the thing lost is a coin or a sheep. It would not be possible to find any picture of remorse or gladness there. But in the third parable the thing lost is not a lifeless thing, nor a mute thing, but a being, the workings of whose human heart are all described. So that the subject opened out to us is a more extensive one—not merely the feelings of the finder, God in Christ, but besides that, the sensations of the wanderer himself.

In dealing with this parable, this is the line which we shall adopt. We shall look at the picture which it draws of—1. God's treatment of the penitent. 2. God's expostulation with the saint. God's treatment of the penitent divides itself in this parable into three distinct epochs. The period of alienation, the period of repentance, and the circumstances of a penitent reception. We shall consider all these in turn.

The first truth exhibited in this parable is the alienation of man's heart from God. Homelessness, distance from our Father—that is man's state by nature in this world. The youngest son gathered all together and took his journey into a *far* country. Brethren, this is the history of worldliness. It is a state far from God; in other words, it is a state of homelessness. And now let us ask what that means. To English hearts it is not necessary to expound elaborately the infinite meanings which cluster round that blessed expression "home." Home is the one place in all this world where hearts are sure of each other. It is the place of confidence. It is the place where we tear off that mask of guarded and suspicious coldness which the world forces us to wear in self-defence, and where we pour out the unreserved communications of full and confiding hearts. It is the spot where expressions of tenderness gush out without any sensation of awkwardness and without any dread of ridicule. Let a man travel where he will, home is the place to which "his heart untravelled fondly turns." He is to double all pleasure there. He is there to divide all pain. A *happy home* is the single spot of rest which a man has upon this earth for the cultivation of his noblest sensibilities.

And now my brethren, if that be the description of home, is God's place of rest your home? Walk abroad and alone by night. That awful other world in the stillness and the solemn deep of the eternities above, is it your home?

Those graves that lie beneath you, holding in them the infinite secret, and stamping upon all earthly loveliness the mark of frailty and change and fleetingness — are those graves the prospect to which in bright days and dark days you can turn without dismay? God in his splendours,— dare we feel with Him affectionate and familiar, so that trial comes softened by this feeling—it is my Father, and enjoyment can be taken with a frank feeling; my Father has given it me, without grudging, to make me happy? All that is having a home in God. Are we at home there? Why there is demonstration in our very childhood that we are not at home with that other world of God's. An infant fears to be alone, because he feels he is not alone. He trembles in the dark, because he is conscious of the presence of the world of spirits. Long before he has been told tales of terror, there is an instinctive dread of the supernatural in the infant mind. It is the instinct which we have from childhood that gives us the feeling of another world. And mark, brethren, if the child is not at home in the thought of that world of God's, the deep of darkness and eternity is around him—God's home, but not his home, for his flesh creeps. And that feeling grows through life; not the fear— when the child becomes a man he gets over fear—but the dislike. The man feels as much aversion as the child for the world of spirits.

Sunday comes. It breaks across the current of his worldliness. It suggests thoughts of death and judgment and everlasting existence. Is that home? Can the worldly man feel Sunday like a foretaste of his Father's mansion? If we could but know how many have come here to-day, not to have their souls lifted up heavenwards, but from curiosity, or idleness, or criticism, it would give us an appalling estimate of the number who are living in a far country "having no hope and without God in the world."

The second truth conveyed to us in this parable is the unsatisfying nature of worldly happiness. The outcast son tried to satiate his appetite with husks. A husk is an empty thing; it is a thing which looks extremely like food, and promises as much as food; but it is not food. It is a thing which when chewed will stay the appetite, but leaves the emaciated body without nourishment. Earthly happiness is a husk. We say not that there is no satisfaction in the pleasures of a worldly life. That would be an overstatement of the truth. Something there is, or else why should men persist in living for them? The cravings of man's appetite may be stayed by things which cannot satisfy him. Every new pursuit contains in it a new hope; and it is long before hope is bankrupt. But my brethren, it is strange if a man has not found out long before he has reached the age of thirty, that everything here is empty and disappointing. The nobler his heart and the more unquenchable his hunger for the high and the good, the sooner will he find that out. Bubble after bubble bursts, each bubble tinted with the celestial colours of the rainbow, and each leaving in the hand which crushes it a cold damp drop of disappointment. All that is described in Scripture by the emphatic metaphor of "sowing the wind and reaping the whirlwind," the whirlwind of blighted hopes and unreturned feelings and crushed expectations—that is the harvest which the world gives you to reap.

And now is the question asked, Why is this world unsatisfying? Brethren, it is the grandeur of the soul which God has given us, which makes it insatiable in its desires—with an infinite void which cannot be filled up. A soul which was made for God, how can the world fill it? If the ocean can be still with miles of unstable waters beneath it, then the soul of man, rocking itself upon its own deep longings, with the Infinite beneath it, may rest. We were created once in majesty, to find enjoyment in God, and if our hearts are empty now, there is nothing for it but to fill up the hollowness of the soul with God.

Let not that expression—filling the soul with God—pass away without a distinct meaning. God is Love and Goodness. Fill the soul with goodness, and fill the soul with love, *that* is the filling it with God. If we love one another, God dwelleth in us. There is nothing else that can satisfy. So that when we hear men of this world acknowledge, as they sometimes will do, when they are wearied with this phantom chase of life, sick of gaieties and tired of toil, that it is not in their pursuits that they can drink the fount of blessedness; and when we see them, instead of turning aside either broken-hearted or else made wise, still persisting to trust to expectations—at fifty, sixty, or seventy years still feverish about some new plan of ambition—what we see is this: we see a soul formed with a capacity for high and noble things, fit for the banquet table of God Himself, trying to fill its infinite hollowness with husks.

Once more, there is degradation in the life of irreligion. The things which the wanderer tried to live on were not husks only. They were husks which the swine did eat. Degradation means the application of a thing to purposes lower than that for which it was intended. It is degradation to a man to live on husks, because these are not his true food. We call it degradation when we see the members of an ancient family, decayed by extravagance, working for their bread. It is not degradation for a born labourer to work for an honest livelihood. It is degradation for them, for they are not what they might have been. And therefore, for a man to be degraded, it is not necessary that he should have given himself up to low and mean practices. It is quite enough that he is living for purposes lower than those for which God intended him. He may be a man of unblemished reputation, and yet debased in the truest meaning of the word. We were sent into this world to love God and to love man; to do good—to fill up life with deeds of generosity and usefulness. And he that refuses to work out that high destiny is a degraded man. He may turn away revolted from everything that is gross. His sensuous indulgences may be all marked by refinement and taste. His house may be filled with elegance. His library may be adorned with books. There may be the sounds in his mansion which can regale the ear, the delicacies which can stimulate the palate, and the forms of beauty which can please the eye. There may be nothing in his whole life to offend the most chastened and fastidious delicacy; and yet, if the history of all this be, powers which were meant for eternity frittered upon time, the man is degraded—if the spirit which was created to find its enjoyment in the love of God has settled down satisfied with the love of the world, then, just as surely as the sensualist of this parable, that man has turned aside from a celestial feast to prey on garbage.

We pass on to the second period of the history of God's treatment of a sinner. It is the period of his coming to himself, or what we call repentance. The first fact of religious experience which this parable suggests to us is that common truth—men desert the world when the world deserts them. The renegade came to himself when there were no more husks to eat. He would have remained away if he could have got them, but it is written, " no man gave unto him." And this, brethren, is the record of our shame. Invitation is not enough; we must be driven to God. And the famine comes not by chance. God sends the famine into the soul—the hunger, and thirst, and the disappointment—to bring back his erring child again.

Now the world fastens upon that truth, and gets out of it a triumphant sarcasm against religion. They tell us that just as the caterpillar passes into the chrysalis, and the chrysalis into the butterfly, so profligacy passes into disgust, and disgust passes into religion. To use their own phraseology, when people become disappointed with the world, it is the last resource they say, to turn saint. So the men of the world speak, and they think they are profoundly philosophical and concise in the account they give. The world is welcome to its very small sneer. It is the glory of our Master's gospel that it *is* the refuge of the broken-hearted. It is the strange mercy of our God that he does not reject the writhings of a jaded heart. Let the world curl its lip if it will, when it sees through the causes of the prodigal's return. And if the sinner does not come to God taught by this disappointment, what then? If affections crushed in early life have driven one man to God; if wrecked and ruined hopes have made another man religious; if want of success in a profession has broken the spirit; if the human life lived out too passionately, has left a surfeit and a craving behind which end in seriousness; if one is brought by the sadness of widowed life, and another by the forced desolation of involuntary single life; if when the mighty famine comes into the heart, and not a husk is left, not a pleasure untried, then, and not till then, the remorseful resolve is made, "I will arise and go to my Father:"—Well, brethren, what then? Why this, that the history of penitence, produced as it so often is by mere disappointment, sheds only a brighter lustre round the Love of Christ, who rejoices to receive such wanderers, worthless as they are, back into His bosom. Thank God the world's sneer is true. It *is* the last resource to turn saint. Thanks to our God that when this gaudy world has ceased to charm, when the heart begins to feel its hollowness, and the world has lost its satisfying power, still all is not yet lost if penitence and Christ remain, to still, to humble, and to soothe a heart which sin has fevered.

There is another truth contained in this section of the parable. After a life of wild sinfulness religion is servitude at first, not freedom. Observe, he went back to duty with the feelings of a slave: "I am no more worthy to be called thy son, make me as one of thy hired servants." Any one who has lived in the excitement of the world, and then tried to settle down at once to quiet duty, knows how true that is. To borrow a metaphor from Israel's desert life, it is a tasteless thing to live on manna after you have been feasting upon quails. It is a dull cold drudgery to find pleasure in simple occupation when life has been a succession of strong emotions. Sonship it is not; it is slavery. A son obeys in love, entering heartily into his father's meaning. A servant obeys mechanically, rising early because he must; doing it may be, his duty well, but feeling in all its force the irksomeness of the service. Sonship does not come all at once. The yoke of Christ is easy, the burden of Christ is light; but it is not light to everybody. It is light when you love it, and no man who has sinned much can love it all at once.

Therefore, if I speak to any one who is trying to be religious, and heavy in heart because his duty is done too formally,—my Christian brother, fear not. You are returning, like the prodigal, with the feelings of a servant. Still it is a real return. The spirit of adoption will come afterwards. You will often have to do duties which you cannot relish, and in which you see no meaning. So it was with Naaman at the prophet's command. He bathed, not knowing why he was bidden to bathe in Jordan. When you bend to prayer, often and often you will have to kneel with wandering thoughts, and constraining lips to repeat words into which your heart scarcely enters. You will have to perform duties when the heart is cold, and without a spark of enthusiasm to warm you. But my Christian brother, onwards still. Struggle to the Cross, even though it be struggling as in chains. Just as on a day of clouds, when you have watched the distant hills, dark and gray with mist, suddenly a gleam of sunshine passing over reveals to you, in that flat surface, valleys and dells and spots of sunny happiness, which slept before unsuspected in the fog, so in the gloom of penitential life there will be times when God's deep peace and love will be felt shining into the soul with supernatural refreshment. Let the penitent be content with the servant's lot at first. Liberty and peace, and the bounding sensations of a Father's arms around you, come afterwards.

The last circumstance in this division of our subject is the reception which a sinner meets with on his return to God. "Bring forth the best robe and put it on him, and put a ring on his hand, and shoes on his feet, and bring hither the fatted calf and kill it, and let us eat and be merry." This banquet represents to us two things. It tells of the father's gladness on his son's return. That represents God's joy on the reformation of a sinner. It tells of a banquet and a dance given to the long lost son. That represents the sinner's gladness when he first understood that God was reconciled to him in Christ. There is a strange, almost wild, rapture, a strong gush of love and happiness in those days which are called the days of first conversion. When a man who has sinned much—a profligate—turns to God, and it becomes first clear to his apprehension that there is love instead of spurning for him, there is a luxury of emotion—a banquet of tumultuous blessedness in the moment of first love to God, which stands alone in life, nothing before and nothing after like it. And brethren, let us observe:—This forgiveness is a thing granted while a man is yet afar off. We are not to wait for the right of being happy till we are good: we might wait for ever. Joy is not delayed till we deserve it. Just so soon as a sinful man trusts that the mercy of God in Christ has done away with his transgression, the ring, and the robe, and the shoes are his, the banquet and the light of a Father's countenance.

Lastly, we have to consider very briefly God's expostulation with a saint. There is another brother mentioned in this parable, who expressed something like indignation at the treatment which his brother met with. There are commentators who have imagined that this personage represents the Pharisees who complained that Jesus was receiving sinners. But this is manifestly impossible, because his father expostulates with him in this language, "Son, thou, art ever with me;" not for one moment could that be true of the Pharisees. The true interpretation seems to be that this elder brother represents a real Christian perplexed with God's mysterious dealings. We have before us the description of one of those happy persons who have been filled with the Holy Ghost from their mother's womb, and on the whole (with imperfections of course) remained God's servant all his life. For this is his own account of himself, which the father does not contradict. "Lo! these many years do I serve thee."

We observe then: The objection made to the reception of a notorious sinner: "Thou never gavest me a kid." Now, in this we have a fact true to Christian experience. Joy seems to be felt more vividly and more exuberantly by men who have sinned much, than by men who have grown up consistently from childhood with religious education. Rapture belongs to him whose sins, which are forgiven, are many. In the perplexity which this fact occasions, there is a feeling which is partly right and partly wrong. There is a surprise which is natural. There is a resentful jealousy which is to be rebuked.

There is first of all a natural surprise. It was natural that the elder brother should feel perplexed and hurt. When a sinner seems to be rewarded with more happiness than a saint, it appears as if good and evil were alike undistinguished in God's dealings. It seems like putting a reconciled enemy over the head of a tried servant. It looks as if it were a kind of encouragement held out to sin, and a man begins to feel, Well if this is to be the caprice of my father's dealing; if this rich feast of gladness be the reward of a licentious life, "Verily I have cleansed my heart in vain, and washed my hands in innocency." This is natural surprise.

But besides this there is a jealousy in these sensations of ours which God sees fit to rebuke. You have been trying to serve God all your life, and find it struggle, and heaviness, and dulness still. You see another who has outraged every obligation of life, and he is not tried by the deep prostration you think he ought to have, but bright with happiness at once. You have been making sacrifices all your life, and your worst trials come out of your most generous sacrifices. Your errors in judgment have been followed by sufferings sharper than those which crime itself could have brought. And you see men who never made a sacrifice unexposed to trial—men whose life has been rapture purchased by the ruin of others' innocence—tasting first the pleasures of sin, and then the banquet of religion. You have been a moral man from childhood, and yet with all your efforts you feel the crushing conviction that it has never once been granted you to win a soul to God. And you see another man marked by inconsistency and impetuosity, banqueting every day upon the blest success of impressing and saving souls. All that is startling. And then comes sadness and despondency; then come all those feelings which are so graphically depicted here: irritation — "he was angry;" swelling pride — "he would not go in;" jealousy, which required soothing—"his father went out and entreated him."

And now brethren, mark the father's answer. It does not account for this strange dealing by God's sovereignty. It does not cut the knot of the difficulty, instead of untying it, by saying, God has a *right* to do what He will. He does not urge, God has a right to act on favouritism if He please. But it assigns two reasons. The first reason is, "It was *meet*, right that we should make merry." It is meet that God should be glad on the reclamation of a sinner. It is meet that that sinner, looking down into the dreadful chasm over which he had been tottering, should feel a shudder of delight through all his frame on thinking of his escape. And it is meet that religious men should not feel jealous of one another, but freely and generously join in thanking God that others have got happiness, even if *they* have not. The spirit of religious exclusiveness, which looks down contemptuously instead of tenderly on worldly men, and banishes a man for ever from the circle of its joys because he has sinned notoriously, is a bad spirit.

Lastly the reason given for this dealing is, "Son, thou art always with Me, and all that I have is thine." By which Christ seems to tell us that the disproportion between man and man is much less than we suppose. The profligate had had one hour of ecstacy—the other had had a whole life of peace. A consistent Christian may not have rapture; but he has that which is much better than rapture: calmness—God's serene and perpetual presence. And after all brethren, that is the best. One to whom much is forgiven, has much joy. He must have it, if it were only to support him through those fearful trials which are to come — those haunting reminiscences of a polluted heart—those frailties—those inconsistencies to which the habit of past indulgence have made him liable. A terrible struggle is in store for him yet. Grudge him not one hour of unclouded exultation. But religion's best gift—rest, serenity—the quiet daily love of one who lives perpetually with his Father's family—uninterrupted usefulness — *that* belongs to him who has lived steadily, and walked with duty, neither grieving nor insulting the Holy Spirit of his God. The man who serves God early has the best of it; joy is well in its way, but a few flashes of joy are trifles in comparison with a life of peace. Which is best: the flash of joy lighting up the whole heart, and then darkness till the next flash comes—or the steady calm sunlight of day in which men work?

And now, one word to those who are living this young.

man's life—thinking to become religious as he did, when they have got tired of the world. I speak to those who are leading what, in the world's softened language of concealment, is called a gay life. Young brethren, let two motives be urged earnestly upon your attention. The first is the motive of mere honourable feeling. We will say nothing about the uncertainty of life. We will not dwell upon this fact, that impressions resisted now, may never come back again. We will not appeal to terror. That is not the weapon which a Christian minister loves to use. If our lips were clothed with thunder, it is not denunciation which makes men Christians; let the appeal be made to every high and generous feeling in a young man's bosom.

Deliberately and calmly you are going to do *this*: to spend the best and most vigorous portion of your days in idleness—in uselessness—in the gratification of self—in the contamination of others. And then weakness, the relics, and the miserable dregs of life;—you are going to give *that* sorry offering to God, because His mercy endureth for ever! Shame—shame upon the heart which can let such a plan rest in it one moment. If it be there, crush it like a man. It is a degrading thing to enjoy husks till there is no man to give them. It is a base thing to resolve to give to God as little as possible, and not to serve Him till you must.

Young brethren, I speak principally to you. You have health for God now. You have strength of mind and body. You have powers which may fit you for real usefulness. You have appetites for enjoyment which can be consecrated to God. You acknowledge the law of honour. Well then, by every feeling of manliness and generosity remember this: now, and not later, is your time to learn what religion means.

There is another motive, and a very solemn one, to be

urged upon those who are delaying. Every moment of delay adds bitterness to after struggles. The moment of a feeling of hired servitude must come. If a man will not obey God with a warm heart, he may hereafter have to do it with a cold one. To be holy is the work of a long life. The experience of ten thousand lessons teaches only a little of it; and all this, the work of becoming like God, the man who delays is crowding into the space of a few years, or a few months. When we have lived long a life of sin, do we think that repentance and forgiveness will obliterate all the traces of sin upon the character? Be sure that every sin pays its price: "Whatsoever a man soweth, that shall he also reap."

Oh! there are recollections of past sin which come crowding up to the brain, with temptation in them. There are old habits which refuse to be mastered by a few enthusiastic sensations. There is so much of the old man clinging to the penitent who has waited long—he is so much as a religious man, like what he was when he was a worldly man—that it is doubtful whether he ever reaches in this world the full stature of Christian manhood. Much warm earnestness, but strange inconsistencies, that is the character of one who is an old man and a young Christian. Brethren, do we wish to risk all this? Do we want to learn holiness with terrible struggles, and sore affliction, and the plague of much remaining evil? Then *wait* before you turn to God.

XXI.

Preached May 15, 1853.

JOHN'S REBUKE OF HEROD.

"But Herod the tetrarch, being reproved by him for Herodias, his brother Philip's wife, and for all the evils which Herod had done, added yet this above all, that he shut up John in prison."—Luke iii. 19, 20.

THE life of John the Baptist divides itself into three distinct periods. Of the first we are told almost nothing, but we may conjecture much. We are told that he was in the deserts till his showing unto Israel. It was a period probably, in which, saddened by the hollowness of all life in Israel, and perplexed with the controversies of Jerusalem, the controversies of Sadducee with Pharisee, of formalist with mystic, of the disciples of one infallible Rabbi with the disciples of another infallible Rabbi, he fled for refuge to the wilderness, to see whether God could not be found there by the heart that sought Him, without the aid of churches, rituals, creeds, and forms. This period lasted thirty years.

The second period is a shorter one. It comprises the few months of his public ministry. His difficulties were over; he had reached conviction enough to live and die on. He knew not all, but he knew something. He could not baptize with the Spirit, but he could at least baptize with water. It was not given to him to build up, but it was given to him to pull down all false foundations. He knew that the highest truth of spiritual life was to be given by One that should come after. What he had learned in the desert was contained in a few words—Reality lies at the root of religious life. Ye must be real, said John. "Bring forth fruits meet for repentance." Let each man do his own duty; let the rich impart to those who are not rich; let the publican accuse no man falsely; let the soldier be content with his wages. The coming kingdom is not a mere piece of machinery which will make you all good and happy without effort of your own. Change yourselves, or you will have no kingdom at all. Personal reformation, personal reality, *that* was John's message to the world.

It was an incomplete one; but he delivered it as his all, manfully; and his success was signal, astonishing even to himself. Successful it was, because it appealed to all the deepest wants of the human heart. It told of peace to those who had been agitated by tempestuous passion. It promised forgetfulness of past transgression to those whose consciences smarted with self-accusing recollections. It spoke of refuge from the wrath to come to those who had felt it a fearful expectation to fall into the hands of an angry God. And the result of that message, conveyed by the symbol of baptism, was that the desert swarmed with crowds who owned the attractive spell of the power of a new life made possible. Warriors, paupers, profligates—some admiring the nobleness of religious life, others needing it to fill up the empty hollow of an unsatisfied heart; the penitent, the heart-broken, the worldly, and the disappointed, all came. And with them there came two other classes of men, whose approach roused the Baptist to astonishment.

The formalist, not satisfied with his formality, and the

infidel, unable to rest on his infidelity—they came too—startled, for one hour at least, to the real significance of life, and shaken out of unreality. The Baptist's message wrung the confession from their souls. "Yes, our system will not do. We are not happy after all; we are miserable. Prophet, whose solitary life, far away there in the desert, has been making to itself a home in the mysterious and the invisible, what hast thou got to tell us from that awful other world? What are we to do?"

These things belong to a period of John's life anterior to the text. The prophet has been hitherto in a self-selected solitude, the free wild desert, opening his heart to the strange sights and sounds through which the grand voice of oriental nature speaks of God to the soul, in a way that books cannot speak.

We have arrived at the third period of his history. We are now to consider him as the tenant of a *compelled* solitude, in the dungeon of a capricious tyrant. Hitherto, by that rugged energy with which he battled with the temptations of this world, he has been shedding a glory round human life. We are now to look at him equally alone; equally majestic, shedding by martyrdom, almost a brighter glory round human death. He has hitherto been receiving the homage of almost unequalled popularity. We are now to observe him reft of every admirer, every soother, every friend. He has been hitherto overcoming the temptations of existence by entire seclusion from them all. We are now to ask how he will stem those seductions when he is brought into the very midst of them, and the whole outward aspect of his life has laid aside its distinctive and peculiar character; when he has ceased to be the anchorite, and has become the idol of a court.

Much instruction, brethren, there ought to be in all this, if we only knew rightly how to bring it out, or even to paint in anything like intelligible colours the picture which our own minds have formed. Instructive, because human life must ever be instructive. How a human spirit contrived to get its life accomplished in this confused world: what a man like us, and yet no common man, felt, did, suffered; how he fought, and how he conquered; if we could only get a clear possession and firm grasp of *that*, we should have got almost all that is worth having in truth, with the technicalities stripped off, for what is the use of truth except to teach man how to live? There is a vast value in genuine biography. It is good to have real views of what Life is, and what Christian Life may be. It is good to familiarize ourselves with the history of those whom God has pronounced the salt of the earth. We cannot help contracting good from such association.

And just one thing respecting this man whom we are to follow for some time to-day. Let us not be afraid of seeming to rise into a mere enthusiastic panegyric of a man. It is a rare man we have to deal with, one of God's heroic ones, a true conqueror; one whose life and motives it is hard to understand without feeling warmly and enthusiastically about them. One of the very highest characters, rightly understood, of all the Bible. Panegyric such as we can give, what is it after he has been stamped by his Master's eulogy, "A prophet? Yea, I say unto you, and more than a prophet. Among them that are born of women there hath not risen a greater than John the Baptist." In the verse which is to serve us for our guidance on this subject there are two branches which will afford us fruit of contemplation. It is written, "Herod being *reproved* by John for Herodias."

Here is our first subject of thought. The truthfulness of Christian character.

And then next, he "shut up John in prison."

Here is our second topic. The apparent failure of religious life.

The point which we have to look at in this section of the Baptist's life is the truthfulness of religious character. For the prophet was now in a sphere of life altogether new. He had got to the third act of his history. The first was performed right manfully in the desert — that is past. He has now become a known man, celebrated through the country, brought into the world, great men listening to him, and in the way, if he chooses it, to become familiar with the polished life of Herod's court. For this we read: Herod observed John, that is, cultivated his acquaintance, paid him marked attention, heard him, did many things at his bidding, and heard him gladly.

For thirty long years John had lived in that far-off desert, filling his soul with the grandeur of solitude, content to be unknown, not conscious, most likely, that there was anything supernatural in him—living with the mysterious God in silence. And then came the day when the qualities, so secretly nursed, became known in the great world: men felt that there was a greater than themselves before them, and then came the trial of admiration, when the crowds congregated round to listen. And all that trial John bore uninjured, for when those vast crowds dispersed at night, he was left alone with God and the universe once more. That prevented his being spoilt by flattery. But now comes the great trial. John is transplanted from the desert to the town: he has quitted simple life: he has come to artificial life. John has won a king's attention, and now the question is, Will the diamond of the mine bear polishing without breaking into shivers? Is the iron prophet melting into voluptuous softness? Is he getting the world's manners and the world's courtly insincerity? Is he becoming artificial through his change of life? My Christian brethren, we find nothing of the kind. There he stands in Herod's voluptuous court the prophet of the desert still, unseduced by blandishment from his high loyalty, and fronting his patron and his prince with the stern unpalatable truth of God.

It is refreshing to look on such a scene as this—the highest, the very highest moment, I think, in all John's history; higher than his ascetic life. For after all, ascetic life such as he had led before, when he fed on locusts and wild honey, is hard only in the first resolve. When you have once made up your mind to that, it becomes a habit to live alone. To lecture the poor about religion is not hard. To speak of unworldliness to men with whom we do not associate, and who do not see *our* daily inconsistencies, *that* is not hard. To speak contemptuously of the world when we have no power of commanding its admiration, *that* is not difficult. But when God has given a man accomplishments, or powers, which would enable him to shine in society, and he can still be firm, and steady, and uncompromisingly true; when he can be as undaunted before the rich as before the poor; when rank and fashion cannot subdue him into silence: when he hates moral evil as sternly in a great man as he would in a peasant, there is truth in that man. This was the test to which the Baptist was submitted.

And now contemplate him for a moment; forget that he is an historical personage, and remember that he was a man like us. Then comes the trial. All the habits and rules of polite life would be whispering such advice as this: " Only keep your remarks within the limits of politeness. If you cannot approve, be silent; you can do no good by finding fault with the great." We know how the whole spirit of a man like John would have revolted at that. Imprisonment? Yes. Death? Well, a man can die but once,—anything but not cowardice,—not meanness,—not pretending what I do not feel, and disguising what I do feel. Brethren, death is not the worst thing in this life; it is not difficult to die—five minutes and the sharpest agony is past. The worst thing in this life is cowardly untruthfulness. Let men be rough if they will, let them be unpolished, but let Christian men in all they say be sincere. No flattery, no speaking smoothly to a man before his face, while all the time there is a disapproval of his conduct in the heart. The thing we want in Christianity is not politeness, it is sincerity.

There are three things which we remark in this truthfulness of John. The first is its straightforwardness, the second is its unconsciousness, and the last its unselfishness. The straightforwardness is remarkable in this circumstance, that there is no indirect coming to the point. At once, without circumlocution, the true man speaks. "It is not lawful for thee to have her." There are some men whom God has gifted with a rare simplicity of heart, which make them utterly incapable of pursuing the subtle excuses which can be made for evil. There is in John no morbid sympathy for the offender: "It is not lawful." He does not say, "It is *best* to do otherwise; it is unprofitable for your own happiness to live in this way." He says plainly, "It is wrong for you to do this evil."

Earnest men in this world have no time for subtleties and casuistry. Sin is detestable, horrible, in God's sight, and when once it has been made clear that it is not lawful, a Christian has nothing to do with toleration of it. If we dare not tell our patron of his sin we must give up his patronage. In the next place there was unconsciousness in John's rebuke. We remark, brethren, that he was utterly ignorant that he was doing a fine thing. There was no sidelong glance, as in a mirror, of admiration for himself. He was not feeling, This is brave. He never stopped to feel that after-ages would stand by, and look at that deed of his, and say, "Well done." His reproof comes out as the natural impulse of an earnest heart. John was the last of all men to feel that he had done anything extraordinary. And this we hold to be an inseparable mark of truth. No true man is conscious that he is true; he is rather conscious of insincerity. No brave man is conscious of his courage; bravery is *natural* to him. The skin of Moses' face shone after he had been with God, but Moses wist not of it.

There are many of us who would have prefaced that rebuke with a long speech. We should have begun by observing how difficult it was to speak to a monarch, how delicate the subject, how much proof we were giving of our friendship. We should have asked the great man to accept it as a proof of our devotion. John does nothing of this. Prefaces betray anxiety about self; John was not thinking of himself. He was thinking of God's offended law, and the guilty king's soul. Brethren, it is a lovely and a graceful thing to see men natural. It is beautiful to see men sincere without being haunted with the consciousness of their sincerity. There is a sickly habit that men get of looking into themselves, and thinking how they are appearing. We are always unnatural when we do that. The very tread of one who is thinking how he appears to others, becomes dizzy with affectation. He is too conscious of what he is doing, and self-consciousness is affectation. Let us aim at being natural. And we can only become natural by thinking of God and duty, instead of the way in which we are serving God and duty.

There was lastly, something exceedingly unselfish in John's truthfulness. We do not build much on a man's being merely true. It costs some men nothing to be true, for they have none of those sensibilities which shrink from inflicting pain. There is a surly bitter way of speaking truth which says little for a man's heart. Some men have not delicacy enough to feel that it is an awkward and a painful thing to rebuke a brother: they are in their element when they can become censors of the great. John's truthfulness was not like that. It was the earnest loving nature of the man which made him say sharp things. Was it to gratify spleen that he reproved Herod for all the evils he had done? Was it to minister to a diseased and disappointed misanthropy? Little do we understand the depth of tenderness which there is in a rugged, true nature, if we think that. John's whole life was an iron determination to crush self in everything.

Take a single instance. John's ministry was gradually superseded by the ministry of Christ. It was the moon waning before the Sun. They came and told him that, "Rabbi, He to whom thou barest witness beyond Jordan baptizeth, and all men come unto Him." Two of his own personal friends, apparently some of the last he had left, deserted him, and went to the new teacher.

And now let us estimate the keenness of that trial. Remember John was a man: he had tasted the sweets of influence; that influence was dying away, and just in the prime of life he was to become *nothing*. Who cannot conceive the keenness of that trial? Bearing that in mind—what is the prophet's answer? One of the most touching sentences in all Scripture—calmly, meekly, the hero recognises his destiny—"He must increase, but I must decrease." He does more than recognise it—he rejoices in it, rejoices to be nothing, to be forgotten, despised, so as only Christ can be everything. "The friend of the bridegroom rejoiceth because he heareth the bridegroom's voice, this my joy is fulfilled." And it is *this* man, with self so thoroughly crushed—the outward self by bodily austerities, the inward self by Christian humbleness—it is this man who speaks so sternly to his sovereign. "It is not lawful." Was there any gratification of human feeling there? Or was not the rebuke unselfish? Meant for God's honour, dictated by the uncontrollable hatred of all evil, careless altogether of personal consequences?

Now it is this, my brethren, that *we* want. The world-spirit can rebuke as sharply as the Spirit which was in John; the world-spirit can be severe upon the great when it is jealous. The worldly man cannot bear to hear of another's success, he cannot endure to hear another praised for accomplishments, or another succeeding in a profession, and the world can fasten very bitterly upon a neighbour's faults, and say, "It is not lawful." We expect that in the world. But that this should creep among religious men, that *we* should be bitter—that we, *Christians*, should suffer jealousy to enthrone itself in our hearts—that we should find fault from spleen, and not from love—that we should not be able to be calm and gentle, and sweet-tempered, when we decrease, when our powers fail—*that* is the shame. The love of Christ is intended to make such men as John, such high and heavenly characters. What is our Christianity worth if it cannot teach us a truthfulness, an unselfishness, and a generosity beyond the world's?

We are to say something in the second place of the apparent failure of Christian life.

The concluding sentence of this verse informs us that John was shut up in prison. And the first thought which suggests itself is, that a magnificent career is cut short too soon. At the very outset of ripe and experienced manhood the whole thing ends in failure. John's day of active usefulness is over; at thirty years of age his work is done; and what permanent effect have all his labours left? The crowds that listened to his voice, awed into silence by Jordan's side, we hear of them no more. Herod heard John gladly, did much good by reason of his influence. What was all that worth? The prophet comes to himself in a dungeon, and wakes to the bitter conviction, that his influence had told much in the way of commanding attention, and even winning reverence, but very little in the way of gaining souls; the bitterest, the most crushing discovery in the whole circle of ministerial experience. All this was seeming failure.

And this, brethren, is the picture of almost all human life. To some moods, and under some aspects, it seems, as it seemed to the psalmist, "Man walketh in a vain shadow and disquieteth himself in vain." Go to any churchyard, and stand ten minutes among the grave-stones; read inscription after inscription recording the date of birth, and the date of death, of him who lies below, all the trace which myriads have left behind, of their having done their day's work on God's earth,—that is failure or—seems so. Cast the eye down the columns of any commander's despatch after a general action. The men fell by thousands; the officers by hundreds. Courage, high hope, self-devotion, ended in smoke—forgotten by the time of the next list of slain: that is the failure of life once more. Cast your eye over the shelves of a public library—there is the hard toil of years, the product of a life of thought; all that remains of it is there in a worm-eaten folio, taken down once in a century. Failure of human life again. Stand by the most enduring of all human labours, the pyramids of Egypt. One hundred thousand men, year by year, raised those enormous piles to protect the corpses of the buried from rude inspection. The spoiler's hand has been there, and the bodies have been rifled from their mausoleum, and three thousand years have written "failure" upon that. In all that, my Christian brethren, if we look no deeper than the surface, we read the grave of human hope, the apparent nothingness of human labour.

And then look at this history once more. In the isolation of John's dying hour, there appears failure again. When a great man dies we listen to hear what he has to say, we turn to the last page of his biography first, to see what he had to bequeath to the world as his experience of life. We expect that the wisdom, which he has been hiving up for years, will distil in honeyed sweetness then. It is generally not so. There is stupor and silence at the last. "How dieth the wise man?" asks Solomon: and he answers bitterly, "As the fool." The martyr of truth dies privately in Herod's dungeon. We have no record of his last words. There were no crowds to look on. We cannot describe how he received his sentence. Was he calm? Was he agitated? Did he bless his murderer? Did he give utterance to any deep reflections on human life? All that is shrouded in silence. He bowed his head, and the sharp stroke fell flashing down. We know that, we know no more—apparently a noble life abortive.

And now let us ask the question distinctly, Was all this indeed failure? No, my Christian brethren, it was sublimest victory. John's work was no failure; he left behind him no sect to which he had given his name, but his disciples passed into the service of Christ, and were absorbed in the Christian church. Words from John had made impressions, and men forgot in after years *where* the impressions first came from, but the day of judgment will not forget. John laid the foundations of a temple, and others built upon it. He laid it in struggle, in martyrdom. It was covered up like the rough masonry below ground, but when we look round on the vast Christian Church, we are looking at the superstructure of John's toil.

There is a lesson for us in all that, if we will learn it. Work, true work, done honestly and manfully for Christ, *never* can be a failure. Your own work, my brethren, which God has given you to do, whatever that is, let it be done truly. Leave eternity to show that it has not been in vain in the Lord. Let it but be work, it will tell. True Christian life is like the march of a conquering army into a fortress which has been breached; men fall by hundreds in the ditch. Was their fall a failure? Nay, for their bodies bridge over the hollow, and over them the rest pass on to victory. The quiet religious worship that we have this day—how comes it to be ours? It was purchased for us by the constancy of such men as John, who freely gave their lives. We are treading upon a bridge of martyrs. The suffering was theirs —the victory is ours. John's career was no failure.

Yet we have one more circumstance which *seems* to tell

of failure. In John's prison, solitude, misgiving, black doubt, seem for a time to have taken possession of the prophet's soul. All that we know of those feelings is this:— John while in confinement sent two of his disciples to Christ, to say to Him, "Art thou He that should come, or do we look for another?" Here is the language of painful uncertainty. We shall not marvel at this, if we look steadily at the circumstances. Let us conceive John's feelings. The enthusiastic child of Nature, who had roved in the desert, free as the air he breathed, is now suddenly arrested, and his strong restless heart limited to the four walls of a narrow dungeon. And there he lay startled. An eagle cleaving the air with motionless wing, and in the midst of his career brought from the black cloud by an arrow to the ground, and looking round with his wild, large eye, stunned, and startled there; just such was the free prophet of the wilderness, when Herod's guards had curbed his noble flight, and left him alone in his dungeon.

Now there is apparent failure here, brethren; it is not the thing which we should have expected. We should have expected that a man who had lived so close to God all his life, would have no misgivings in his last hours. But, my brethren, it is not so. It is the strange truth that some of the highest of God's servants are tried with darkness on the dying bed. Theory would say, when a religious man is laid up for his last struggles, now he is alone for deep communion with his God. Fact very often says, "No—now he is alone, as his Master was before him, in the wilderness to be tempted of the devil." Look at John in imagination, and you would say, "Now his rough pilgrimage is done. He is quiet, out of the world, with the rapt foretaste of heaven in his soul." Look at John in fact.

He is agitated, sending to Christ, not able to rest, grim doubt wrestling with his soul, misgiving for one last black hour whether all his hope has not been delusion.

There is one thing we remark here by the way. Doubt often comes from inactivity. We cannot give the philosophy of it, but this is the fact, Christians who have nothing to do but to sit thinking of themselves, meditating, sentimentalising, are almost sure to become the prey of dark, black misgivings. John struggling in the desert needs no proof that Jesus is the Christ. John shut up became morbid and doubtful immediately. Brethren all this is very marvellous. The history of a human soul *is* marvellous. We are mysteries, but here is the practical lesson of it all. For sadness, for suffering, for misgiving, there is no remedy but stirring and doing.

Now look once more at these doubts of John's. All his life long John had been wishing and expecting that the kingdom of God would come. The kingdom of God is Right triumphant over Wrong, moral evil crushed, goodness set up in its place, the true man recognised, the false man put down and forgotten. All his life long John had panted for that; his hope was to make men better. He tried to make the soldiers merciful, and the publicans honest, and the Pharisees sincere. His complaint was, Why is the world the thing it is? All his life long he had been appealing to the invisible justice of Heaven against the visible brute force which he saw around him. Christ had appeared, and his hopes were straining to the utmost. "Here is the Man!" And now behold, here is no Kingdom of Heaven at all, but one of darkness still, oppression and cruelty triumphant, Herod putting God's prophet in prison, and the Messiah quietly letting things take their course. Can that be indeed Messiah? All this was exceedingly startling. And it seems that then John began to feel the horrible doubt whether the whole thing were not a mistake, and whether all that which he had taken for inspiration were not, after all, only the excited hopes of an enthusiastic temperament. Brethren, the prophet was well nigh on the brink of failure.

But let us mark—that a man has doubts—*that* is not the evil; all earnest men must expect to be tried with doubts. All men who feel, with their whole souls, the value of the truth which is at stake, cannot be satisfied with a "perhaps." Why, when all that is true and excellent in this world, all that is worth living for, is in that question of questions, it is no marvel if we sometimes wish, like Thomas, to see the prints of the nails, to know whether Christ be indeed our Lord or not. Cold hearts are not anxious enough to doubt. Men who love will have their misgivings at times; that is not the evil. But the evil is, when men go on in that languid, doubting way, content to doubt, proud of their doubts, morbidly glad to talk about them, liking the romantic gloom of twilight, without the manliness to say—I must and will know the truth. That did not John. Brethren, John appealed to Christ. He did exactly what we do when we pray—and he got his answer. Our Master said to his disciples, Go to my suffering servant, and give him proof. Tell John the things ye see and hear—"The blind see, the deaf hear, the dead are raised, to the poor the Gospel is preached." There is a deep lesson wrapped up in this. We get a firm grasp of truth by prayer. Communion with Christ is the best proof of Christ's existence and Christ's love. It is so even in human life. Misgivings gather darkly round our heart about our friend in his absence; but we seek his frank smile, we feel his affectionate grasp: our suspicions go to sleep again. It is just so in religion. No man is in the habit of praying to God in Christ, and then doubts whether Christ is He "that should come." It is in the power of prayer to realize Christ, to bring him near, to make you feel His life stirring like a pulse within you. Jacob could not doubt whether he had been with God when his sinew shrunk. John could not doubt whether Jesus was the Christ when the things He had done were pictured out so vividly in answer to his prayer. Let but a man live with Christ anxious to have his own life destroyed, and Christ's life established in its place, losing himself in Christ, that man will have all his misgivings silenced. These are the two remedies for doubt—Activity and Prayer. He who works, and *feels* he works—he who prays, and *knows* he prays, has got the secret of transforming life-failure into life-victory.

In conclusion brethren, we make three remarks which could not be introduced into the body of this subject. The first is—Let young and ardent minds, under the first impressions of religion, beware how they pledge themselves by any open profession to more than they can perform. Herod warmly took up religion at first, courted the prophet of religion, and then when the hot fit of enthusiasm had passed away, he found that he had a clog round his life from which he could only disengage himself by a rough, rude effort. Brethren whom God has touched, it is good to count the cost before you begin. If you give up present pursuits *impetuously*, are you sure that present impulses will last? Are you quite certain that a day will not come when you will curse the hour in which you broke altogether with the world? Are you quite sure that the revulsion back again, will not be as impetuous as Herod's, and your hatred of the religion which has become a clog, as intense as it is now ardent?

Many things doubtless there are to be given up—amusements that are dangerous, society that is questionable. What we give up, let us give up, not from quick feeling, but from principle. Enthusiasm is a lovely thing, but let us be calm in what we do. In that solemn, grand thing—Christian life—one step backward is religious death.

Once more we get from this subject the doctrine of a resurrection. John's life was hardness, his end was agony. That is frequently Christian life. Therefore, says the apostle, if there be no resurrection the Christian's choice is wrong; "If in this life only we have hope in Christ, then are we of all men most miserable." Christian life is not visible success—very often it is the apparent opposite of success. It is the resurrection of Christ working itself out *in* us; but it is very often the Cross of Christ imprinting itself on us very sharply. The highest prize which God has to give here is martyrdom. The highest style of life is the Baptist's—heroic, enduring, manly love. The noblest coronet which any son of man can wear is a crown of thorns. Christian, *this* is not your rest. Be content to feel that this world is not your home. Homeless upon earth, try more and more to make your home in heaven, above with Christ.

Lastly we have to learn from this, that devotedness to Christ is our only blessedness. It is surely a strange thing to see the way in which men crowded round the austere prophet, all saying, "Guide us, we cannot guide ourselves." Publicans, Pharisees, Sadducees, Herod, whenever John appears, all bend before him, offering him homage and leadership. How do we account for this? The truth is, the spirit of man groans beneath the weight of its own freedom. When a man has no guide, no master but himself, he is miserable; we want guidance, and if we find a man nobler, wiser than ourselves, it is almost our instinct to prostrate our affections before that man, as the crowds did by Jordan, and say, "Be my example, my guide, my soul's sovereign." That passionate need of worship—hero-worship it has been called—is a primal, universal instinct of the heart. Christ is the answer to it. Men will not do; we try to find men to reverence thoroughly, and we cannot do it. We go through life, finding guides, rejecting them one after another, expecting nobleness and finding meanness; and we turn away with a recoil of disappointment.

There is no disappointment in Christ. Christ can be our souls' sovereign. Christ can be our guide. Christ can absorb all the admiration which our hearts long to give. We want to worship men. These Jews wanted to worship man. They were right—man is the rightful object of our worship; but in the roll of ages there has been but one man whom we can adore without idolatry,—the Man Christ Jesus.

THE END.

Spottiswoode & Co., Printers, New-street Square, London.

A SELECTION FROM THE NOTICES

OF

MR. ROBERTSON'S SERMONS,

AND OF THE

LIFE AND LETTERS OF F. W. ROBERTSON.

BY THE REV. STOPFORD A. BROOKE, M.A.

Chaplain in Ordinary to the Queen.

A SELECTION FROM THE NOTICES OF

MR. ROBERTSON'S SERMONS,

AND OF THE

LIFE AND LETTERS OF F. W. ROBERTSON,

BY THE REV. STOPFORD A. BROOKE, M.A.

Chaplain in Ordinary to the Queen.

[BLACKWOOD'S MAGAZINE, August, 1862.]

"For while hapless Englishmen complain in the papers, and in private, in many a varied wail, over the sermons they have to listen to, it is very apparent that the work of the preacher has not fallen in any respect out of estimation. Here is a book which has gone through as great a number of editions as the most popular novel. It bears Mudie's stamp upon its dingy boards, and has all those marks of arduous service which are only to be seen in books which belong to great public libraries. It is thumbed, dog's-eared, pencil-marked, worn by much perusal. Is it then a novel? On the contrary, it is a volume of sermons. A fine, tender, and lofty mind, full of thoughtfulness, full of devotion, has herein left his legacy to his country. It is not rhetoric or any vulgar excitement of eloquence that charms so many readers to the book, so many hearers to this preacher's feet. It is not with the action of a Demosthenes, with outstretched arms and countenance of flame, that he presses his gospel upon his audience. On the contrary, when we read those calm and lofty utterances, this preacher seems seated, like his Master, with the multitude palpitating round, but no agitation or passion in his own thoughtful, contemplative breast. The Sermons of Robertson, of Brighton, have few of the exciting qualities of oratory. Save for the charm of a singularly pure and lucid style, their almost sole attraction consists in their power of instruction, in their faculty of opening up the mysteries of life and truth. It is pure teaching, so far as that ever can be administered to a popular audience, which is offered to us in these volumes."

[EDINBURGH CHRISTIAN MAGAZINE.]

"They are Sermons of a bold, uncompromising thinker—of a man resolute for the truth of God, and determined in the strength of God's grace to make that truth clear, to brush away all the fine-spun sophistries and half-truths by which the cunning sins of men have hidden it. . . . There must be a great and true heart, where there is a great and true preacher. And in that, beyond everything else, lay the secret of Mr. Robertson's influence. His Sermons show evidence enough of acute logical power. His analysis is exquisite in its subtleness and delicacy. . . . With Mr. Robertson style is but the vehicle, not the substitute for thought. Eloquence, poetry, scholarship, originality—his Sermons show proof enough of these to put him on a level with the foremost men of his time. But, after all, their charm lies in the warm, loving, sympathetic heart, in the well-disciplined mind of the true Christian, in his noble scorn of all lies, of all things mean and crooked, in his brave battling for right, even when wrong seems crowned with success, in his honest simplicity and singleness of purpose, in the high and holy tone—as if, amid the discord of earth, he heard clear, though far off, the perfect harmony of heaven; in the fiery earnestness of his love for Christ, the devotion of his whole being to the goodness and truth revealed in him."

[CHURCH OF ENGLAND MONTHLY REVIEW.]

"It is hardly too much to say, that had the Church of England produced no other fruit in the present century, this work alone would be amply sufficient to acquit her of the charge of barrenness. . . . The reputation of Mr. Robertson's Sermons is now so wide-spread, that any commendation of ours may seem superfluous. We will therefore simply, in conclusion, recommend such of our readers as have not yet made their acquaintance, to read them carefully and thoughtfully, and they will find in them more deeply suggestive matter than in almost any book published in the present century."

[MORNING POST.]

"They are distinguished by masterly exposition of Scriptural truths and the true spirit of Christian charity."

[BRITISH QUARTERLY.]

"These Sermons are full of thought and beauty, and admirable illustrations of the ease with which a gifted and disciplined mind can make the obscure transparent, the difficult plain. There is not a Sermon that does not furnish evidence of originality without extravagance, of discrimination without tediousness, and of piety without cant or conventionalism."

[ECLECTIC REVIEW.]

"We hail with unaffected delight the appearance of these volumes. The Sermons are altogether out of the common style. They are strong, free, and beautiful utterances of a gifted and cultivated mind. Occasionally, the expression of theological sentiment fails fully to represent our own thought, and we sometimes detect tendencies with which we cannot sympathize: but, taken as a whole, the discourses are fine specimens of a high order of preaching."

[GUARDIAN.]

"Very beautiful in feeling, and occasionally striking and forcible in conception to a remarkable degree. . . . . Even in the imperfect shape in which their deceased author left them, they are very remarkable compositions."

[CHRISTIAN REMEMBRANCER.]

"We should be glad if all preachers more united with ourselves, preached such Sermons as these."

[WESTMINSTER REVIEW.]

"To those who affectionately remember the author, they will recall, though imperfectly, his living eloquence and his living truthfulness."

[GLOBE.]

"Mr. Robertson, of Brighton, is a name familiar to most of us, and honoured by all to whom it is familiar. A true servant of Christ, a bold and heart-stirring preacher of the Gospel, his teaching was unlike the teaching of most clergymen, for it was beautified and intensified by genius. New truth, new light, streamed from each well-worn text when he handled it."

[BLACKWOOD'S MAGAZINE.]

"When teaching of this description keeps the popular ear and secures the general attention, it is unquestionable proof that the office of the preacher has, in no way, lost its hold on the mind of the people. The acceptance of a voice so unimpassioned and thoughtful, so independent of all vulgar auxiliaries, so intent upon bringing every theme it touches to the illustration and sanctifying of the living life of the hour, that which alone can be mended, and purified, and sanctified, is a better tribute to the undying office of the preacher than the success of a hundred Spurgeons. Attention and interest are as eager as ever where there is in reality any instruction to bestow."

[LITERARY GAZETTE.]

"In earnestness of practical appeal, and in eloquent and graceful diction, Mr. Robertson has few rivals, and these characteristics are sufficient to account for his unusual popularity."

[NATIONAL REVIEW.]

"A volume of very fine Sermons, quite equal to the previous series."

[BRIGHTON EXAMINER.]

"There is in the Sermons in this volume the same freshness, vigour of thought and felicity of expression, as characterised whatever Mr. Robertson said.

[ECONOMIST.]

"Mr. Robertson's Sermons have the great and rare merit of neutralising by a more charitable and affectionate spirit, and by a wider intelligence, all that may appear rigid and *doctrinaire* in the Church of England. The result seems to have been his special mission: it most fully explains the mind of the man. . . . . We recommend the Sermons to the perusal of our readers. They will find in them thought of so rare and beautiful a description, an earnestness of mind so steadfast in the search of truth, and a charity so pure and all-embracing, that we cannot venture to offer praise, which would be, in this case, almost as presumptuous as criticism."

[SATURDAY REVIEW.]

"When Mr. Robertson died, his name was scarcely known beyond the circle of his own private friends, and of those among whom he had laboured in his calling. Now, every word he wrote is eagerly sought for and affectionately treasured up, and meets with the most reverent and admiring welcome from men of all parties and all shades of opinion. . . . . To those that find in his writings what they themselves want, he is a teacher quite beyond comparison—his words having a meaning, his thoughts a truth and depth, which they cannot find elsewhere. And they never look to him in vain. . . . . He fixes himself upon the recollection as a most original and profound thinker, and as a man in whom excellence puts on a new form. . . . There are many persons, and the number increases every year, to whom Robertson's writings are the most stable, satisfactory, and exhaustless form of religious teaching which the nineteenth century has given—the most wise, suggestive, and practical."

[BRIGHTON HERALD.]

"To our thinking, no compositions of the same class, at least since the days of Jeremy Taylor, can be compared with these Sermons delivered to the congregation of Trinity Chapel, Brighton, by their late minister. They have that power over the mind which belongs only to the highest works of genius: they stir the soul to its inmost depths: they move the affections, raise the imagination, bring out the higher and spiritual part of our nature by the continual appeal that is made to it, and tend to make us, at the same time, humble and aspiring—merciful to others and doubtful of ourselves."

[From a SERMON preached at the CONSECRATION of the BISHOP of NORWICH, by the REV. J. H. GURNEY, late of MARYLEBONE.]

"I do not commit myself to all his theology; I may differ from the preacher in some things, and listen doubtfully to others. But I know of no modern sermons at once so suggestive and so inspiriting, with reference to the whole range of Christian duty. He is fresh and original without being recondite: plain-spoken without severity; and discusses some of the exciting topics of the day without provoking strife or lowering his tone as a Christian teacher. He delivers his message, in fact, like one who is commissioned to call men off from trifles and squabbles, and conventional sins and follies, to something higher and nobler than their common life: like a man in earnest, too, avoiding technicalities, speaking his honest mind in phrases that are his own, and with a directness from which there is no escape. O that a hundred like him were given us by God, and placed in prominent stations throughout our land!"

[GUARDIAN.]

"Without anything of that artificial symmetry which the traditional division into heads was apt to display, they present each reflection in a distinct method of statement, clearly and briefly worked out; the sentences are short and terse, as in all popular addresses they should be; the thoughts are often very striking, and entirely out of the track of ordinary sermonising. In matters of doctrine such novelty is sometimes unsafe; but the language is that of one who tries earnestly to penetrate into the very centre of the truth he has to expound, and differs as widely as possible from the sceptic's doubt or the controversialist's mistake. More frequently Mr. Robertson deals with questions of practical life, of public opinion, and of what we may call social casuistry—turning the light of Christian ethics upon this unnoticed though familiar ground. The use of a carriage on Sunday, the morality of feeing a railway porter against his employers' rules, are topics not too small for illustration or application of his lessons in divine truth."

[BRIGHTON GAZETTE.]

"As an author, Mr. Robertson was, in his lifetime, unknown; for with the exception of one or two addresses, he never published, having a singular disinclination to bring his thoughts before the public in the form of published sermons. As a minister, he was beloved and esteemed for his unswerving fidelity to his principles and his fearless propagation of his religious views. As a townsman, he was held in the highest estimation; his hand and voice being ever ready to do all in his power to advance the moral and social position of the working man. It was not till after his decease, which event created a sensation and demonstration such as Brighton never before or since witnessed, that his works were subjected to public criticism. It was then found that in the comparatively retired minister of Trinity Chapel there had existed a man possessed of consummate ability and intellect of the highest order; that the sermons laid before his congregation were replete with the subtleties of intellect, and bore evidence of the keenest perception and most exalted catholicity. His teaching was of an extremely liberal character, and if fair to assign a man possessed of such a universality of sympathy to any party, we should say that he belonged to what is denominated the 'Broad Church.' We, with many others, cannot agree in the fullest extent of his teaching, but, at the same time, feel bound to accord the tribute due to his genius."

[MORNING CHRONICLE.]

"A volume of very excellent Sermons, by the late lamented Incumbent of Trinity Chapel, Brighton."

[TITAN.]

"But the Sermons now under notice are, we venture to say, taking all the circumstances into consideration, the most remarkable discourses of the age. . . . They are throughout vital with the rarest force, burning with an earnestness perhaps never surpassed, and luminous with the light of genius. . . . We suspect that even Brighton little knew what a man Providence had placed in its midst."

On the "*Analysis of Mr. Tennyson's In Memoriam :*"—

[GUARDIAN.]

"An endeavour to give, in a few weighty words, the key-note (so to speak) of each poem in the series. Those will best appreciate the amount of success attained by Mr. Robertson who try to do the same work better."

From a few of the Notices on Mr. Robertson's "*Lectures on the Epistles to the Corinthians:*"—

[MORNING POST.]

"It was Mr. Robertson's custom every Sunday afternoon, instead of preaching from one text, to expound an entire chapter of some book in the Scriptures. The present volume is made up from notes of fifty-six discourses of this kind. 'Some people were startled by the introduction of what they called secular subjects into the pulpit. But the lecturer in all his ministrations refused to recognize the distinction so drawn. He said that the whole life of a Christian was sacred—that common every-day doings, whether of a trade, or of a profession, or the minuter details of a woman's household life, were the arenas in which trial and temptation arose ; and that therefore it became the Christian minister's duty to enter into this family working life with his people, and help them to understand its meaning, its trials, and its compensations.' It is enough to add that the lectures now given to the public are written in this spirit."

[CRITIC.]

"Such discourses as these before us, so different from the shallow rhapsodies or tedious hair-splitting which are now so much in vogue, may well make us regret that Mr. Robertson can never be heard again in the pulpit. This single volume would in itself establish a reputation for its writer."

[BRIGHTON HERALD.]

". . . . Were there no name on the title-page, the spirit which shines forth in these lectures could but be recognized as that of the earnest, true-hearted man, the deep thinker, the sympathizer with all kinds of human trouble, the aspirant for all things holy, and one who joined to these rare gifts, the faculty of speaking to his fellow-men in such a manner as to fix their attention and win their love. . . . . In whatever spirit the volume is read—of doubt, of criticism, or of full belief in the truths it teaches—it can but do good ; it can but leave behind the conviction that here was a genuine, true-hearted man, gifted with the highest intellect, inspired by the most disinterested motives and the purest love for his fellow-men, and that the fountain at which he warmed his heart and kindled his eloquence was that which flows from Christ."

[BRITISH QUARTERLY REVIEW.]

"This volume will be a welcome gift to many an intelligent and devout mind. There are few of our modern questions, theological or ecclesiastical, that do not come up for discussion in the course of these Epistles to the Christians at Corinth."

[MORNING HERALD.]

"No one can read these lectures without being charmed by their singular freshness and originality of thought, their earnest, simple eloquence, and their manly piety. There is no mawkish sentiment, no lukewarm, semi-religious twaddle, smacking of the *Record;* no proclamation of party views or party opinions, but a broad, healthy, living, and fervent exposition of one of the most difficult books in the Bible. Every page is full of personal earnestness and depth of feeling; but every page is also free from the slightest trace of vanity and egotism. The words come home to the reader's heart as the utterance of a sincere man who felt every sentence which flowed from his lips."

[PRESS.]

"One of the most marked features of these lectures is the deep feeling which the preacher had of the emptiness and hollowness of the conventional religionism of the day. The clap-trap of popular ministers, the pride and uncharitableness of exclusive Evangelicalism, the pomp and pretension of ritualism and priestly affectation — the miserable Pharisaism which is lurking underneath them all—form the subject of many strikingly true and often cutting remarks. He has no patience with the unrealities of sectarian purism and pedantic orthodoxy. His constant cry, the constant struggle of his soul is for reality. Hence while his views of objective truth are at times deficient, or, at least, very imperfectly stated, he leaves a deep impress of subjective religion upon the mind, by a style of teaching which, far from uninstructive, is yet more eminently suggestive."

A SELECTION FROM THE
NOTICES BY THE PRESS OF
"THE LIFE AND LETTERS OF THE LATE REV. F. W. ROBERTSON."

[THE SPECTATOR.]

"No book published since the 'Life of Dr. Arnold' has produced so strong an impression on the moral imagination and spiritual theology of England as we may expect from these volumes. Even for those who knew Mr. Robertson well, and for many who knew *him*, as they thought, better than his Sermons, the free and full discussion of the highest subjects in the familiar letters so admirably selected by the Editor of Mr. Robertson's *Life*, will give a far clearer insight into his remarkable character and inspire a deeper respect for his clear and manly intellect. Mr. Brooke has done his work as Dr. Stanley did his in writing the 'Life of Arnold,' and it is not possible to give higher praise. . . . . Everyone will talk of Mr. Robertson, and no one of Mr. Brooke, because Mr. Brooke has thought much of his subject, nothing of himself, and hence the figure which he wished to present comes out quite clear and keen, without any interposing haze of literary vapour."

[THE CHRISTIAN WORLD.]

"The Life of Robertson of Brighton supplies a very unique illustration of the way in which a man may attain his highest fame after he has passed away from earth. There are few who make any pretension to an acquaintance with modern literature who do not know something of Mr. Robertson's works. His sermons are indisputably ranked with the highest sacred classics. . . . . The publication of his 'Life and Letters' helps us to some information which is very precious, and explains much mystery that hangs around the name of the great Brighton preacher. It will be generally admitted that these two volumes will furnish means for estimating the character of Mr. Robertson which are not supplied in any or all of his published works. . . . . There was no artificiality or show about the pulpit production, no half-utterances or whispers of solemn belief; but there was the natural restraint which would be imposed by a true gentleman upon his words when speaking to mixed congregations. Many of us wanted to know how he talked and wrote when the restraint was removed. This privilege is granted to us in these volumes. . . . . There was no romance of scene and circumstance in the life of Frederick Robertson; but there was more than romance about the real life of the man. In some respects it was like the life of a new Elijah. . . . . A more thoughtful, suggestive, and beautiful preacher never entered a pulpit; a simpler and braver man never lived; a truer Christian never adorned any religious community. His life and death were *vicarious*, as he himself might have put it. He lived and died for others, for us all. The sorrows and agonies of his heart pressed rare music out of it, and the experience of a terribly bitter life leaves a wealth of thought and reflection never more than equalled in the history of men."

[THE GUARDIAN.]

"With all drawbacks of what seem to us imperfect taste, an imperfect standard of character, and an imperfect appreciation of what there is in the world beyond a given circle of interest, the book does what a biography ought to do—it shows us a remarkable man, and it gives us the means of forming our own judgment about him. It is not a tame panegyric or a fancy picture. The main portion of the book consists of Mr. Robertson's own letters, and his own account of himself, and we are allowed to see him, in a great degree at least, as he really was. . . . . It is the record of a genuine spontaneous character, seeking its way, its duty, its perfection, with much sincerity and elevation of purpose, many anxieties and sorrows, and not, we doubt not, without much of the fruits that come with real self-devotion; a record disclosing a man with great faults and conspicuous blanks in his nature.

[THE MORNING POST.]

"Mr. Brooke has done good service in giving to the world so faithful a sketch of so worthy a man. It would have been a reproach to the Church if this enduring and appropriate memorial had not been erected to one who was so entirely devoted to its service; and the labour of love, for such it evidently was, was committed to no unskilful hands. . . Mr. Robertson's epistolary writings—gathered in these valuable volumes —often unstudied, always necessarily from their nature free and unrestrained, but evidencing depth and vigour of thought, clear perception, varied knowledge, sound judgment, earnest piety, are doubtless destined to become as widely known and as largely beneficial as his published Sermons. It is impossible to peruse them without receiving impressions for good, and being persuaded that they are the offspring of no ordinary mind."

[THE MORNING HERALD.]

"Mr. Brooke has done his own work as a biographer with good sense, feeling, and taste. . . . . These volumes are of real value to all thoughtful readers. For many a year we have had no such picture of a pure and noble and well spent life."

[THE ATHENÆUM.]

"There is something here for all kinds of readers, but the higher a man's mind and the more general his sympathies, the keener will be his interest in the 'Life of Robertson.'"

[THE NONCONFORMIST.]

"As no English sermons of the century have been so widely read, and as few leaders of religious thought have exerted (especially by works in so much of an unperfected and fragmentary character) so penetrating and powerful an influence on the spiritual tendencies of the times, we can well believe that no biography since Arnold's will presently be possible to be compared with this, for the interest excited by it in the minds of readers who consciously live in the presence of the invisible and eternal, who feel the pressure of difficult questions and painful experiences, and who seek reality and depth, and freedom in the life and activity of the Church of Christ. . . . . Mr. Brooke has produced a 'Life of Robertson' which will not unworthily compare with Dean Stanley's 'Life of Arnold,' and which, with that, and Ryland's 'Life of Foster,' and the 'Life of Channing,' is likely to be prized as one of the most precious records of genuine manly and godly excellence."

[THE MORNING STAR.]

"The beautiful work which Mr. Brooke has written contains few, if any, romantic episodes. It is the life of a man who worked hard and died early. . . . . Mr. Brooke has acted wisely in allowing Mr. Robertson to speak so fully for himself, and in blending his letters with his narrative, and arranging them in chronological order. These letters are in themselves a mine of intellectual wealth. They contain little of table-talk or parlour gossip; but they abound with many of his best and most ripened thoughts on multitudes of subjects, political, literary, and scientific, as well as theological. We wish we could present our readers with extracts from them; but even if we had space, it would be unfair to the writer to quote disjointed fragments from a correspondence which now belongs to the literature of the country. . . . . Mr. Brooke has performed his responsible task as a biographer and an editor in a spirit of just and discriminating appreciation, and with admirable ability."

www.ingramcontent.com/pod-product-compliance
Lightning Source LLC
Chambersburg PA
CBHW022025240426
43667CB00042B/1151